More Praise for
MORE FROM LESS

"I've always believed that technological progress and entrepreneurship make our lives better. Here, Andrew McAfee shows how these powerful forces are helping us make our planet better, too, instead of degrading it. For anyone who wants to help create a future that is both sustainable and abundant, this book is essential reading."

—Reid Hoffman, cofounder of LinkedIn
and coauthor of *Blitzscaling*

"Andrew McAfee's optimistic and humane book documents a profoundly important and under-appreciated megatrend—the dematerialization of our economy. In a world where there is much to worry about, his analytical optimism is very welcome. Anyone who worries about the future will have their fears allayed and hopes raised by reading this important book."

—Lawrence H. Summers, former
Secretary of the Treasury and director
of the National Economic Council

"In *More from Less* Andrew McAfee conclusively demonstrates how environmentalism requires *more* technology and capitalism, not less. Our modern technologies actually dematerialize our consumption, giving us higher human welfare with lower material inputs. This is an urgently needed and clear-eyed view of how to have our technological cake and eat it too."

—Marc Andreessen, cofounder of Netscape
and Andreessen Horowitz

"In *More from Less* Andrew McAfee lays out a compelling blue-print showing how we can support human life using fewer natural resources, improve the state of the world, and replenish the planet for centuries to come."

—Marc Benioff, chairman and co-CEO of Salesforce

"A must-read—timely and refreshing! Amid the din of voices insisting that the ravages of climate change are unstoppable, McAffee offers a desperately needed nuanced perspective on what governments and society have got right, and he compellingly argues that commendable progress has already been made. His book is not a call for complacency; rather, it's a welcome and thoughtful recognition of where we've succeeded and a practical path for what more can be achieved in the efficient use of natural resources. A gem of a book!"

—Dambisa Moyo, author of *Dead Aid*, *How the West Was Lost*, *Winner Take All*, and *Edge of Chaos*

"Andrew McAfee's new book addresses an urgent need in our world today: defining a framework for addressing big global challenges. His proposals are based on a thorough analysis of the state of the world, combined with a refreshing can-do attitude."

—Klaus Schwab, founder and executive chairman of the World Economic Forum

"Yet another magnificent contribution from Andrew McAfee. Along with his prior works, *More from Less* will help us navigate society's future in profound ways."

—Clayton M. Christensen, Kim B. Clark Professor of Business Administration at Harvard Business School

MORE
FROM
LESS

MORE
FROM
LESS

THE SURPRISING STORY OF HOW WE LEARNED
TO PROSPER USING FEWER RESOURCES—
AND WHAT HAPPENS NEXT

ANDREW McAFEE

SIMON &
SCHUSTER

London · New York · Sydney · Toronto · New Delhi

A CBS COMPANY

First published in the United States by Scribner,
an imprint of Simon & Schuster, Inc., 2019
First published in Great Britain by Simon & Schuster UK Ltd, 2019
A CBS COMPANY

1 3 5 7 9 10 8 6 4 2

Simon & Schuster UK Ltd
1st Floor
222 Gray's Inn Road
London WC1X 8HB

www.simonandschuster.co.uk
www.simonandschuster.com.au
www.simonandschuster.co.in

Simon & Schuster Australia, Sydney
Simon & Schuster India, New Delhi

A CIP catalogue record for this book is available from the British Library.

Hardback ISBN: 978-1-4711-8033-0
Trade Paperback ISBN: 978-1-4711-8034-7
eBook ISBN: 978-1-4711-8035-4

Interior design by Kyle Kabel
Printed in the UK by CPI Group (UK) Ltd, Croydon, CR0 4YY

To my mother, Nancy,
who showed her children the world
and taught them to love it

We are as gods and might as well get good at it.

—Stewart Brand,
Whole Earth Catalog, 1968

Contents

MORE
FROM
LESS

README

Listen! I will be honest with you,
I do not offer the old smooth prizes, but offer rough new prizes

—Walt Whitman,
"Song of the Open Road," 1856

We have finally learned how to tread more lightly on our planet. It's about time.

For just about all of human history our prosperity has been tightly coupled to our ability to take resources from the earth. So as we became more numerous and prosperous, we inevitably took more: more minerals, more fossil fuels, more land for crops, more trees, more water, and so on.

But not anymore. In recent years we've seen a different pattern emerge: the pattern of more from less. In America—a large, rich country that accounts for about 25 percent of the global economy— we're now generally using less of most resources year after year, even as our economy and population continue to grow. What's more, we're also polluting the air and water less, emitting fewer greenhouse gases, and seeing population increases in many animals that had almost vanished. America, in short, is post-peak in its exploitation of the earth. The situation is similar in many other rich countries, and even developing countries such as China are now taking better care of the planet in important ways.

This book is about how we turned the corner and started getting more from less, and what happens from here forward.

I want to make one thing clear at the start: my argument is *not* that things are good enough now, or that there's nothing to be concerned about. Those claims would be absurd. Human-caused global warming is both real and bad, and we urgently need to take action to deal with it. We also need to reduce pollution levels around the world and bring back the species we've pushed to the brink of extinction. And we have to keep fighting poverty, disease, malnutrition, fraying communities, and other roadblocks to human flourishing.

So we have plenty of work ahead. The broad point I want to make is that we know how to succeed with this work. In large parts of the world we've already turned the corner and are now improving both the human condition *and* the state of nature. The trade-off between the two has ended, and I'm confident it's never going to reappear if we play our cards right. In these pages I'll explain where this confidence comes from and try to get you to share it.

The Thread of the Argument

This book shows that we've started getting more from less and tells how we reached this critical milestone. The strangest aspect of the story is that we didn't make many radical course changes to eliminate the trade-off between human prosperity and planetary health. Instead, we just got a lot better at doing the things we'd already been doing.

In particular, we got better at combining technological progress with capitalism to satisfy human wants and needs. That conclusion will strike many people as bizarre, and for good reason. After all, it's exactly this combination that caused us to massively increase our resource use and environmental harms starting with the Industrial

Revolution in the late eighteenth century. The Industrial Era was a time of startlingly large and fast improvements in human prosperity, but these improvements came at the expense of our planet. We dug out resources, chopped down forests, killed animals, fouled the air and water with pollution, and committed countless other offenses against the earth. We committed more and more of them year after year, apparently without end.

The twin forces of tech progress and capitalism unleashed during the Industrial Era seemed to be impelling us in one direction: that of increasing human population and consumption while degrading our planet. By the time of the first Earth Day festival in 1970, it was obvious to many that these two forces would push us to our doom, since we couldn't continue to abuse our planet indefinitely.

And what actually happened? Something completely different, which is the subject of this book. As I'll show, capitalism continued and spread (just look around you), but tech progress changed. We invented the computer, the Internet, and a suite of other digital technologies that let us *dematerialize* our consumption: over time they allowed us to consume more and more while taking less and less from the planet. This happened because digital technologies offered the cost savings that come from substituting bits for atoms, and the intense cost pressures of capitalism caused companies to accept this offer over and over. Think, for example, how many devices have been replaced by your smartphone.

In addition to capitalism and tech progress, two other forces have also been essential for allowing us to get more from less. These are *public awareness* of the harms we're doing our planet (such as pollution and species loss) and *responsive governments*, which act on the desires of their people and put in place sound measures to counteract these harms. Both public awareness and responsive government were greatly accelerated by Earth Day and the environmental movement in the United States and around the world.

I call tech progress, capitalism, public awareness, and responsive government the "four horsemen of the optimist."* When all four are in place, countries can improve both the human condition and the state of nature. When the four horsemen don't all ride together, people and the environment suffer.

The good news is that all four are at present advancing around the world. So we don't need to make radical changes; instead, we need to do more of the good things that we're already doing. Let me switch, metaphorically, from horses to cars: we don't need to yank the steering wheel of our economies and societies in a different direction; we just need to step on the accelerator.

Something for Everyone to Dislike

As you read this book, it'll be important to keep an open mind because you're likely to come across at least a few ideas and conclusions that won't seem right at first. I've found that the book's fundamental concept—that capitalism and tech progress are now allowing us to tread more lightly on the earth instead of stripping it bare—is hard for many people to accept.

It was hard for *me* to accept when I came across it for the first time—in Jesse Ausubel's amazing essay "The Return of Nature: How Technology Liberates the Environment," published in 2015 in the *Breakthrough Journal*. When I encountered that headline, I had to click on it, which led me to one of the most interesting things I'd ever read.

Ausubel documented the dematerialization of the American economy. Even though he did it carefully and thoroughly, I found

---

* They stand in sharp contrast to the Four Horsemen of the Apocalypse portrayed in the New Testament's book of Revelation, which are commonly interpreted as war, famine, pestilence, and death.

myself thinking, "Well, that *can't* be right." It was hard to let go of the notion that as economies grow they must consume more resources. Ausubel's work started me down a path of questioning that notion, and eventually rejecting it.

An important part of traveling that research path was coming up with an explanation of *how* we started getting more from less. What caused economic growth to become decoupled from resource consumption? What caused dematerialization to take over? As I've already mentioned and as you'll see in the chapters ahead, capitalism is a big part of my explanation.

This is not a universally popular conclusion. Ever since Marx, capitalism has been passionately opposed by many—and viewed with much skepticism by many more. So my cheerleading for it is going to strike many as ignorant, or worse. If you're one of these people, I'm glad you're reading this book. I hope that you'll listen to what I mean when I talk about capitalism and evaluate my arguments based on the evidence and logic I present.

And if you're a fan of capitalism, you might not like that I argue here in favor of new taxes (on carbon) and strict regulation (on pollution and trade in products from endangered animals). Many ardent capitalists will dislike these ideas. I also propose more nuclear power and genetically modified organisms, both of which are adamantly opposed by many people.

So just about any reader will probably initially feel that something in this book is wrong. Again, I just ask that you approach the book's ideas with an open mind. I hope you'll believe that I'm arguing in good faith. My intention here is not to write a polemic or start a flame war. I'm not trying to troll or dunk on anyone (in other words, I'm not trying to provoke anyone into losing their temper or to demonstrate my superiority). I'm just trying to highlight a phenomenon that I find fascinating and deeply encouraging, explain how it came about, and discuss its implications. I hope you'll come along for the journey.

CHAPTER 1

All the Malthusian Millennia

[A state of war is similar] to the time wherein men live without other security than what their own strength, and their own invention, shall furnish them withal. In such condition, there is no place for Industry . . . and consequently no Culture of the Earth . . . and which is worst of all, continual fear, and danger of violent death; and the life of man, solitary, poor, nasty, brutish, and short.

—Thomas Hobbes, *Leviathan*, 1651

A lot of people would like to have their names echo down the centuries. But probably not as shorthand for "laughably wrong." Unfortunately for him (and his descendants), this is the role that the Reverend Thomas Robert Malthus plays for many in their discussions about humanity's relationship with our planet. *Malthusian* has become one of those words that function simultaneously as a label for an argument, a dismissal of it, and an insult toward the person advancing it.* This adjective has come to signify unwarranted and underinformed pessimism about the future.

In one sense, this is entirely fair. As we'll see, the gloomy predictions that Malthus made right at the end of the eighteenth century

---

* The natural sciences have a pretty good consensus about such words. Every biologist, for example, hears *creationist* the same way. The social sciences are more fractious. *Socialist* and *capitalist*—two terms we'll revisit later—are widely used both as insults and proud self-descriptions.

have proved to be so wrong that they deserve a special designation. But in another sense we're being too hard on the good reverend. Most discussions of his work overlook that while Malthus was badly wrong about the future, he was broadly correct about the past.

Bad Vibrations

Malthus is best known for *An Essay on the Principle of Population*, published in 1798. It's tough going for a modern reader. This is not only because prose styles have changed a lot over more than two centuries but also because his writing reveals casual racism and a loose command of the fact that combine to jarring effect. He maintains, for example, that "the passion between the sexes is less ardent among the North American Indians than among any other race of men."

Reading passages such as this, one can easily conclude that his *Essay* consists of nothing but smug Eurocentric generalizations. But later research revealed that Malthus was right. Not about the sex lives of North American indigenous people, but instead about an aspect of human history that is strikingly consistent across groups and over long periods. It's what Malthus called "oscillation" or "vibration" in population, by which he meant periods of growth followed by periods of decline in the number of people. As he wrote, "That in all old states some such vibration does exist . . . no reflecting man who considers the subject deeply can well doubt."

A main goal of his *Essay* was to show mathematically why such vibrations had to happen to every group of people. Malthus pointed out, correctly, that human populations grow rapidly if no force acts to reduce them. If a couple has two children, each of whom has two children, and this process keeps repeating, then the original couple's total number of descendants will double with each generation from two to four, then eight, then sixteen, and so on. People can do only two things to retard this exponential (or "geometric") growth in numbers: not have children, or die.

Malthus said that both of these checks on population were bound to occur, and to occur frequently enough to slow down or even reverse the total size of every human group. This would happen for a simple reason: the land can't keep feeding exponentially increasing numbers of people. Malthus held that while population increased geometrically (2, 4, 8, 16 . . .) the amount of food that could be obtained increased only arithmetically (or linearly: 2, 3, 4, 5 . . .). Much of his *Essay* is devoted to fleshing out the dire consequences of this mismatch: "Population, when unchecked, increases in a geometrical ratio. Subsistence increases only in an arithmetical ratio. A slight acquaintance with numbers will shew the immensity of the first power in comparison of the second. . . . This implies a strong and constantly operating check on population from the difficulty of subsistence. This difficulty must fall somewhere and must necessarily be severely felt by a large portion of mankind."*

Limits to Growth

Is this what actually happened? Thanks to a large body of fascinating research, we now know the answer to this question. Over the past forty years economic historians, led by the pioneering work of Angus Maddison, have pieced together lines of evidence spanning many centuries about peoples' standards of living—their ability to acquire the things they wanted and needed.

---

* Malthus didn't explain in detail *why* sustenance couldn't grow exponentially, as human population could. He just posited, "The most enthusiastic speculator cannot suppose a greater increase than [arithmetic]" for producing food.

Living standards are often expressed in terms of real wages or incomes.* Even though the currencies used within countries have changed over time, and even though medieval peasants often weren't paid with money in anything like the modern sense of these words, the notions of wages and incomes are valuable because they let us examine affluence and poverty in a consistent way. Another stream of research has given us a clear picture of historical demographics— how big populations were, and how they fluctuated.

The economic historian Gregory Clark put these two types of evidence together and provided my favorite view of what life was like in England over six centuries prior to the publication of Malthus's *Essay*. It's not a pretty picture.

Clark's graph, reproduced on the next page, puts England's population on the horizontal axis and a measure of personal prosperity on the vertical axis.† It has one data point for each decade between 1200 and 1800 and connects these data points with a line (I've alternated the shading and marked the start of each century to make it easier to follow the line).

If this line moved steadily up and to the right, it would mean that as the centuries passed England's population became both larger and more prosperous. But this is not at all what happened. Instead, for hundreds of years after 1200 the line moved back and forth in an arc between the upper left and lower right of the graph—between, in other words, a state of low population and relatively high prosperity and the opposite: a state of large population but low affluence. (Data sources for all of this book's graphs are given in the endnotes, and the data themselves are available at morefromlessbook.com/data.)

---

* In this context, *real* means "after taking inflation into account."

† Clark used as his measure of prosperity English craftsmen's wages because they're a good indicator of the overall health of the economy, and because high-quality data about them are available going back centuries.

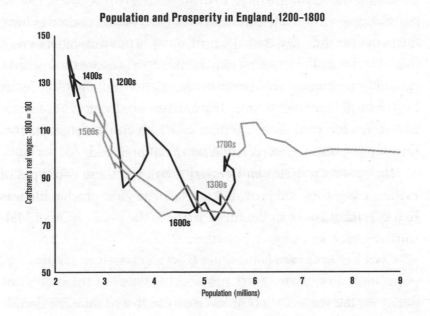

Population and Prosperity in England, 1200–1800

For hundreds of years after 1200 England's population oscillated just as described by Malthus. The country's population shrank and expanded by a factor of three until about 1700, mainly ranging between 2 million and 6 million people. They were relatively prosperous only when there were relatively few of them. There was essentially an upper limit on the amount of resources, primarily food, that humans could extract from the land. When population bumped up against this limit, the cruel correcting mechanisms of privation brought it back down.

The trade-off between population and prosperity eased a bit in the eighteenth century, most likely due to improved agricultural practices, but didn't change the grim overall picture. The average Briton, for example, was worse off throughout the 1700s than in 1200. Clark summarized, "As we go over 600 years from 1200 to 1800 we see confirmation of one of the basic tenets of the Malthusian model of pre-industrial society."

Researchers have also found Malthusian vibrations in the populations of Sweden, Italy, and other European countries over the same period. The transition of most human societies away from hunter-gatherer or nomadic lifestyles and toward settled agriculture—the so-called Neolithic revolution—did not free them from famines and starvation.* The basic math of "mouths to feed" versus "resources available" remained harsh and unforgiving and caused populations to oscillate. When they got too big for the land, resource scarcity drove them back down.

Us Against the World

Between the time we *Homo sapiens* left our African cradle over one hundred thousand years ago and the dawn of the Industrial Era in the late eighteenth century, we lived in a Malthusian world. We covered the planet, yet didn't conquer it.

Humans spread to every continent except permanently frozen Antarctica and adapted to virtually all of our planet's terrains and climates. We were ceaselessly busy and clever. We domesticated animals and plants, altering their genes via breeding programs so that they suited us better. We built great cities; the sixteenth-century Aztec city of Tenochtitlán (located at the site of modern Mexico City) spread out over five square miles, and London's population exceeded half a million by the end of the seventeenth century. We also invented a huge range of technologies that let us shape our environment, from irrigation and the plow to cement and gunpowder.

---

* Skeletons reveal that the first generations of farmers were noticeably shorter and less well nourished than their hunter-gatherer ancestors. It took a surprisingly long time for settled agriculture to yield healthier people than older lifestyles did.

But there were never very many of us. Ten thousand years ago, about 5 million people were on the planet. As we moved into new regions and improved our technologies, that number increased along a steady but shallow exponential curve, reaching almost 190 million people by the time of Christ. Agriculture allowed higher population densities, so as farming spread, human population growth accelerated in the Common Era.

By the year 1800, just about a billion of us were on the planet. That sounds like a big number, but when compared to the inhabitable area* of the earth, it starts to look small. If all the world's people were spread out evenly around the planet's inhabitable land in 1800, everyone would have had almost sixteen acres—an area about as large as nine World Cup soccer fields—to himself or herself. We would not have been able to hear each other, even by shouting.

Part of the reason population grew so slowly throughout all this time was that we didn't live long. According to demographer James Riley, "Global life expectancy at birth was about 28.5 years in 1800," and no region of the world at that time had a life expectancy as high as thirty-five years. In addition to not growing old, we also didn't grow rich. Angus Maddison notes, "The advance in per-capita income was a slow crawl—the world average increased only by half over a period of eight centuries [beginning in 1000]" and usually even more slowly before that.

In short, we lived in Malthus's world during just about all of our history as modern humans. The most basic task for any group of people is to get enough food and other resources from the environment to permit survival. But nature is stingy and does not give up its bounty easily. Over thousands of years it is remarkable how

---

* The human-inhabitable areas of the earth exclude mountains, deserts, and Antarctica.

little progress we made at taking more from the planet—enough more to make a meaningful difference in how big or prosperous human groups could be. We are tenacious creatures and we strove mightily, but it would be far too big a stretch to say we conquered nature prior to the end of the eighteenth century. Instead, it held us in check.

CHAPTER 2

Power over the Earth: The Industrial Era

If we are to bring the broad masses of the people in every land to the table of abundance, it can only be by the tireless improvement of all our means of technical production.

—Winston Churchill,
MIT Mid-Century Convocation, 1949

If Malthus was right about population oscillations and all the other ways that nature had limited the size of human communities throughout most of our time on this planet, then why is his name now widely used as a pejorative? Because the Industrial Revolution changed everything. In particular, a machine unveiled twenty-two years before Malthus published his *Essay* assured that the widespread famine he predicted would rank among the worst predictions anyone has ever made.

The Most Powerful Idea in the World

In March of the earthshaking year 1776* the inventor and investor team of James Watt and Matthew Boulton demonstrated their new

---

* Also in 1776 the American Declaration of Independence was signed and the Scottish economist Adam Smith published his landmark *The Wealth of Nations* (a book we'll come back to later).

steam engine at the Bloomfield coal mine outside Birmingham, England.

The idea of using steam-powered machines to pump out flooded English coal mines was not new; an engine developed by Englishman Thomas Newcomen had been used for that purpose for decades. In fact, it was used for little else because the Newcomen engine was so coal hungry that it was economical to use only where its fuel was most cheap and abundant, which was right at the mouths of mines. The engine Watt debuted at Bloomfield, which combined his eureka insights with years of dogged work, provided more than twice as much useful energy per bushel of coal as Newcomen's. Watt, Boulton, and others soon realized that the new engine's greater efficiency and power made it suitable for many, many other uses.

For all of human history to that point, the only power sources we could draw on were muscles (ours and those of the animals we domesticated), wind, and falling water. The Watt steam engine and its descendants added to that list a set of machines that drew on fossil fuels such as coal and profoundly changed our relationship with our planet. The new power-generating machines didn't create the Industrial Revolution entirely on their own— this also required many other kinds of innovations including joint-stock companies, patents and other types of intellectual property, and the diffusion throughout society of scientific and technical knowledge that had previously largely been reserved for elites—but without them there would have been nothing that merited the term *revolution*. The title of William Rosen's book about the history of steam power is apt; it was *The Most Powerful Idea in the World*.

From Steam to Soil

How exactly was steam powerful enough to end Malthusian oscillations? How does an engine that can extract large amounts of
chemical energy from coal and convert it to mechanical energy
(to, for example, turn a wheel or lift a weight) end the cycles of
population growth and decline that had plagued us throughout
history? A first guess might be that steam-powered tractors made
farms much more productive, but this is not what happened. A
few such tractors were produced in the latter half of the nineteenth
century, but they were too unreliable and too heavy to be practical.
They got bogged down in mud, and farms are muddy places. Steam
changed the course of humanity not by helping to plow farms, but
instead by helping to fertilize them.

Farmers have known for millennia that many minerals are
effective fertilizers. The discovery early in the nineteenth century
of huge deposits of sodium nitrate in Chile's Atacama Desert was
exciting news for English agriculturalists and the entrepreneurs
who wanted to supply them, since that salt is a key ingredient for
many fertilizers. Exciting, too, were the huge quantities of bird
droppings, called guano, found on islands off the South American
coast where seabirds had been congregating for centuries.

In 1838 William Wheelwright founded a company that sent cargo
ships back and forth between England and the west coast of South
America. Instead of using wind-powered sailing ships, however, he
used steamships. These were a relatively recent development—the
first transatlantic trip completed largely under steam power had
taken place only fifteen years earlier—but were already transforming
how people and goods moved over the world's waters. The first two
ships of Wheelwright's Pacific Steam Navigation Company, dubbed
the *Chile* and the *Peru*, entered service in 1840. Soon many more
Industrial Era ships were carrying English coal to South America,

and coming back full of minerals that would make English farms more productive.

The bones of slaughtered animals also yielded good fertilizer, as did coprolite, fossilized animal dung, discovered in huge deposits in Southeast England in the 1840s. For all of these materials, steam was essential at every stage of the transformation into fertilizer. The materials all had to be transported; over time, this was increasingly done by steamships and trains. The large-scale chemical reactions that converted minerals into fertilizers required a great deal of energy. Coal supplied this energy, and the mines that supplied this coal were kept free of water and ventilated by steam-driven equipment. The furnaces in chemical factories benefitted from a forced stream of combustion-supporting air, and the bellows supplying this stream were powered by steam. Steam trains then carried fertilizer from the factories to agricultural regions. Via fertilizer, in short, soil and steam became inextricably linked during the nineteenth century.

Farms that made use of Industrial Era fertilizers produced more food and so could feed more people. This phenomenon was not confined to England. Britain was the birthplace of the Industrial Revolution, but not its sole beneficiary. Steamships, trains, mass-produced fertilizer, and many other industrial novelties spread quickly because they were so much better than what was available before.

The rapid spread of powerful technologies heightened a long-standing tension caused by the fact that some regions of the European mainland were able to produce crops more cheaply than England. This did not sit well with the country's land-owning nobility, who were politically powerful enough to do something about it. Starting in 1815, they enacted a set of measures known as the Corn Laws, which restricted the sale of imported grain.

Most other groups in the country hated the Corn Laws since they made food more expensive. After extensive battles in Parliament, the Corn Laws were repealed in 1846.* Free trade exposed the weaknesses in English agriculture. By 1870 the total amount of cropland in the country had begun to shrink as uncompetitive farms went fallow.

Gains, Germs, and Meals

Luckily for the British, free trade also exposed the superiority of their manufacturing and mining industries. England became a powerhouse in global trade, and its economy grew and diversified rapidly.† By 1750 the country was producing about 8 percent of Europe's iron; a little more than a century later it was making almost 60 percent. In the middle of the nineteenth century, Britain, with less than 2 percent of the world's population, was responsible for half of all global cotton textile production and more than 65 percent of all coal mining. The country had no steam locomotives in commercial operation before 1825, but by 1850 steam railways covered six thousand miles. The number of patents issued rose twentyfold in the century leading up to 1850.

---

* The battles over the Corn Laws led the politician James Wilson, who was in favor of free trade, to found *The Economist*. It's still published today and is one of my favorite magazines (even though it calls itself a newspaper).

† It would have made sense for England to concentrate on manufacturing even if it were more productive than mainland Europe at both farming and manufacturing. "Comparative advantage" is the counterintuitive idea that even if country A is more efficient at producing both of two products than country B, the best thing is for it to produce only one of those products—the one where its comparative advantage in efficiency is bigger—and trade for the other one with country B. This arrangement is in the self-interest of *both* countries and leaves them both better off. Comparative advantage was first described by the English political economist David Ricardo in 1817. The Nobel Prize–winning economist Paul Samuelson tells the story that he was once asked by the mathematician Stanislaw Ulam to "name me one proposition in all of the social sciences which is both true and non-trivial." Samuelson's answer, which he only thought of years later, was comparative advantage. As he wrote, "That it is logically true need not be argued before a mathematician; that it is not trivial is attested by the thousands of important and intelligent men who have never been able to grasp the doctrine for themselves or to believe it after it was explained to them."

The new class of English inventors and entrepreneurs—people such as Watt and Boulton—did fantastically well for themselves as the Industrial Era progressed. But what about the rest of the British people? How did they fare? One way to answer this question is to extend Gregory Clark's graph of total population versus real wages. As we saw in the previous chapter, this graph showed clear evidence over centuries up to 1800 of the privation-caused oscillations in total population described by Malthus. So what happened after 1800?

Something completely different. So different that we have to greatly expand the graph along both axes—total population and average wage—to see all the data, which takes off along a trajectory never before seen. The line connecting population and average prosperity (wages, in other words) zooms off upward and to the right at the start of the nineteenth century and rarely again changes course. England's Malthusian oscillations and vibrations fade into a small corner of the past.

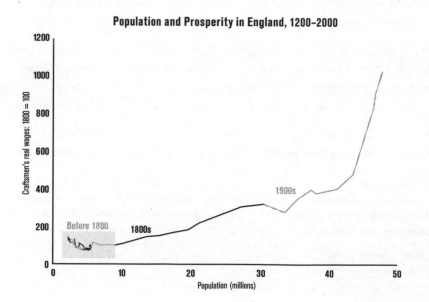

Population and Prosperity in England, 1200–2000

Among economic historians who study the effects of the Industrial Revolution a debate exists about exactly when the average English worker's real wages started to increase. Some, such as Clark, conclude from their research that this happened right at the start of the nineteenth century. Others believe that it happened decades later, only after workers' bargaining power over their employers increased. These decades have been called the Engels Pause, after Friedrich Engels, a German philosopher (and son of a Manchester textile-mill owner) who believed that English laborers were suffering greatly under Industrial Era capitalism. Engels wrote *The Condition of the Working Class in England* in 1845 and coauthored *The Communist Manifesto* with Karl Marx in 1848.

However real and long the Engels Pause was, it was ending by the time *The Communist Manifesto* was published. And when Marx wrote in 1867's *Das Kapital* that "as capital accumulates, the situation of the worker, be his payment high or low, must grow worse," events were showing just how durably wrong that statement was.* Capital was accumulating and economies were growing as never before in human history, but instead of growing worse, workers' situations were also improving as never before.†

Self-Healing Cities

But incomes don't tell the whole story. The quality of a person's life is determined by much more than his or her purchasing power, as

---

* I had a vague memory that Marx also wrote about "the machinery of capitalism being oiled with the blood of the workers." When I tracked down that quote, though, I learned that it comes from Homer Simpson.

† Marx thought workers' situations would be bad even if they had high wages because the prices they would have to pay for things would be even higher. He thought, in other words, that their *real* wages would not increase. As Clark's graph shows, this was not at all what happened.

important as that is. We all care about our health, and the common view is that the early decades of the Industrial Revolution were bad for it. The narrative most of us have heard is that industrialization turned England's towns and cities into densely populated cesspools of disease and misery.

That narrative is pretty accurate about the situation, but not about its causes. Urban environments were much less healthy than rural ones well before the Industrial Revolution started. England's cities and towns had dense populations, poor sanitation, and many unhealthy practices long before they were dotted with steam-powered factories. Available evidence suggests that cities in many ways became more healthy, not less, as the Industrial Era advanced. This is because while cities lend themselves to the spread of many diseases, they also lend themselves to epidemiology—the study of disease—and to effective interventions.

My favorite illustration of this is London's fight against cholera, a terrible bacterial disease that spreads when the diarrhea of its victims contaminates drinking water. After this illness reached London in 1832 from its home in the Ganges River delta two major outbreaks killed more than fifteen thousand people. "King Cholera" caused great fear in part because its roots were unknown. The idea that many diseases were caused by microorganisms was not yet widely accepted; most scientists, like the public, believed that illnesses were spread instead by miasmas, or "bad airs," from rotting vegetables and corpses.

A third cholera outbreak, in 1854, killed more than five hundred people in the Soho neighborhood within two weeks and threatened to sow panic throughout the city. It was stopped only when the physician John Snow plotted all London cholera cases on a map; they were tightly clustered around the public water pump on Broad Street, the water of which had become contaminated.

Snow persuaded the authorities to close this pump, stopping the outbreak. Citywide plumbing that brought clean water and took away sewage, combined with Louis Pasteur's convincing demonstrations that germs caused diseases such as cholera, ensured that this was London's last brush with King Cholera.

Cholera outbreaks hint at an important fact: something like an Engels Pause occurred in aspects of health at the start of the Industrial Era. Improvements were not immediate. Urban infant mortality, for example, increased for several decades after 1800 before beginning to fall late in the nineteenth century.* As we'll see in the next chapter, this was due in part to pollution. The air in cities was foul enough to end young lives and stunt growth. But things got much better. By 1970 the English were among the world's tallest people.

Yes! We Have Some Bananas

Some of the most striking changes brought to the lives of non-elite people by the Industrial Era were improvements to their nutrition and diets. Again, these improvements were widely felt only after a pause after the start of the Industrial Revolution. *A Plain Cookery Book for the Working Classes*, published in 1852 by Charles Elmé Francatelli (Queen Victoria's former chief cook), contains recipes that combine bland ingredients and remorseless thrift. Breakfast was boiled milk with a spoonful of flour and a dash of salt added, perhaps combined with bread or a potato. After boiling greens or beans, the leftover "pot liquor" was to be combined with oatmeal.

---

* In the nineteenth century, both the cities and the countryside in England were shockingly unhealthy. Infant mortality, for example, ranged from around 100 to 200 deaths per 1,000 births. In 2016, the United Kingdom had 3.8 infant deaths per 1,000 births.

Francatelli wished good fortune upon his readers: "I hope that at some odd times you may afford yourself an old hen or cock."

Eventually, they could afford them. In 1935, the English social reformer B. Seebohm Rowntree found the working classes in York were eating much the same diets as their employers, a huge change from what he had found during a similar 1899 survey. Even during the depths of the Depression, Rowntree observed that poor families could afford roast beef and fish each once a week, and sausages or other animal protein two more times.

By that time these families were probably also eating bananas, a previously unimaginable luxury. Because bananas grow far from England and spoil relatively quickly after being picked, they were close to unknown in the country well into the Industrial Era. Charles Dickens's *A Christmas Carol*, published in 1843, mentions apples, pears, oranges, and lemons as seasonal treats, but not bananas. Refrigerated steamships eventually shrank the time and distance between tropical plantations and northern Europe. In 1898 more than 650,000 bunches of bananas, each bearing as many as a hundred pieces of fruit, were exported from the Canary Islands.

So how big, overall, were the changes brought by the Industrial Revolution? An evidence-based answer comes from historian Ian Morris, who has constructed a numeric index that quantifies the level of social development in a civilization. Morris's index is calculated from four traits: per-person energy capture, information technology, war-making capacity, and organization.

It shows a startling change. As Morris puts it, "In 1776, Western* social development had clawed its way up just forty-five points

---

* Morris defines East and West as the societies that developed out of the easternmost and westernmost cores of domestication in Eurasia near the end of the last Ice Age.

since Ice Age hunter-gatherers had prowled the tundra in search of a meal; within the next hundred years it soared another hundred points. The transformation beggared belief. It turned the world inside out."

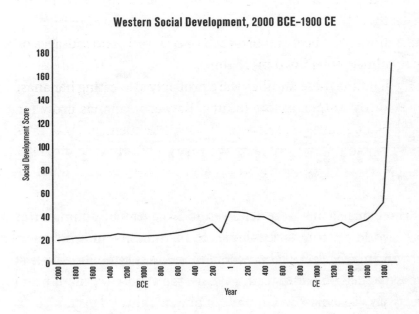

since Ice Age hunter-gatherers had prowled the tundra in search

The Electrifying, Combustible Second Century

Yet the transformations of the next hundred years were even bigger. In the West, after climbing 120 points in the century preceding 1900 to reach a level of 170 points, Morris's social development index then climbed *another* 736 points by 2000.*

---

* The East, starting from a lower level, gained over 2,300 percent over the same period.

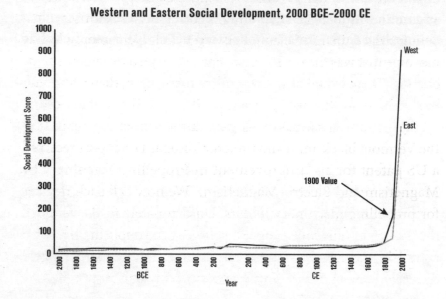

Western and Eastern Social Development, 2000 BCE–2000 CE

These huge gains were achieved in large part by adding three more world-altering technologies to the mix: the internal combustion engine, electrical power, and indoor plumbing. The first two expanded on what steam gave us: the ability to generate and effectively wield massive amounts of power. The third expanded on London's triumph over cholera and let us live longer and healthier lives, especially in the densely populated cities that became ever more common around the world.

More Power to the People: Internal Combustion and Electricity

Steamships bore the great weight of their engines and coal fuel by floating on water, and locomotives by traveling on railroads designed to support heavy loads. Outside of these uses, though, steam power wasn't mobile. The German gunsmith Gottlieb Daimler worked on early internal combustion engines and saw that these novelties might be well suited for transportation. Not only were the engines relatively light but they also burned energy-rich fuels such as gasoline. In 1885, Daimler and his colleague Wilhelm Maybach demonstrated their Petroleum Reitwagen, a clunky motorcycle-like machine that was the world's first vehicle powered by internal combustion. There would be many more of them, more than a few built by the company that became Daimler-Benz, the home of Mercedes.

Electric power started small, got big, then shrank again. In 1837 the Vermont blacksmith and tinkerer Thomas Davenport received a US patent for an "Improvement in Propelling Machinery by Magnetism and Electro-Magnetism." We now call such devices for propelling machinery *motors*. Unfortunately for Davenport, the batteries of his time were too primitive to supply the electrical energy his device needed, and power lines, utilities, and the grid did not yet exist. Davenport was apparently bankrupt when he died in 1851.

About half a century after Davenport's patent was granted, Thomas Edison, Nikola Tesla, and others made use of an electric motor running in reverse—it could be used to convert mechanical energy (from falling water or expanding steam) into electrical energy. When used in this way, a motor becomes a *generator*. The electricity could then be conducted over wires to one or more distant motors.

This sounds inefficient, but it wasn't. An 1891 comparison of steam and electric power for factories concluded, "We must look upon electricity as an enormously powerful and convenient means of transferring power from one point to another with the greatest simplicity and very small losses." From that point on the electrification of industry was unstoppable.

At first, factories electrified by simply replacing their single big steam engine with a single big electric motor. The new power source, just like the old one, was connected to all the machines in the plant by an elaborate and failure-prone (and often unsafe) system of shafts, pulleys, and belts. The belts were often made of leather, and factories needed so many of them that in 1850 leather manufacturing was America's fifth-largest industry.

People who were able to think differently about factories realized that electricity could cut through this rat's nest of twisting and turning equipment. They started using smaller motors to power smaller groups of machines, instead of an entire factory full of them. As the twentieth century progressed, they eventually went all the way and put motors on every individual piece of gear that needed power, an idea that had seemed ludicrous to most industry insiders in 1900.

Electricity affected more than just manufacturing. It lit homes, sidewalks, and streets; saved labor by powering vacuum cleaners, washing machines, dishwashers, and dryers; kept food fresh via refrigeration; allowed cities to grow vertically by powering skyscrapers' elevators; and enabled countless other transformations. And internal combustion's impact certainly didn't stop at motorcycles. Engines that converted petroleum products into mechanical energy were quickly deployed in everything from cars to airplanes to ships to tractors to chain saws.

Growing with the Flow: Indoor Plumbing

To some, indoor plumbing might not seem a profound enough innovation to stand alongside electricity and internal combustion. A flush toilet and water on demand out of a tap are certainly convenient, but are they fundamentally important to the story of twentieth-century growth? They absolutely are. Health researchers David Cutler and Grant Miller estimate that the availability of clean water explains fully half of the total decline in the overall US mortality rate between 1900 and 1936, and 75 percent of the decline in infant mortality. Historian Harvey Green calls the technologies of widespread clean water "likely the most important public health intervention of the twentieth century."

Plumbing was critical in the countryside as well as in the city. Before it came along, domestic work on farms could literally be close to backbreaking. Bringing enough water to run a household from a remote well each day was a staggering amount of work that often fell to women and children, since men typically worked outside the home all day. For example, in Texas's Hill Country the typical well was located so far from the house that bringing water required more than five hundred hours of labor and 1,750 miles of walking each year.*

Electricity and indoor plumbing eliminated this constant toil. In the 1930s a Tennessee farmer summarized the immense value of the technologies of the second century of the Industrial Era: "The greatest thing on earth is to have the love of God in your heart, and the next greatest thing is to have electricity in your house."

The transformations experienced during the first century of the Industrial Era—from the 1770s to 1870s—turned the world inside out. Lines on a graph of humanity's progress, whether measured by economic growth, population, or social development, were close to horizontal† over the millennia prior to the late eighteenth century. After that, they took off like a rocket leaving the launchpad.

The stunning fact about the second century of the Industrial Era is that the rocket kept right on ascending. It seems incredible that

---

* President Lyndon Johnson's programs brought electrified plumbing to the Hill Country, where he had grown up. His biographer Robert Caro traveled there for his research. He wrote, "An interviewer from the city is struck by the fact that Hill Country women of the older generation are noticeably stooped, much more so than city women of the same age. . . . More than once, and more than twice, a stooped and bent Hill Country farm wife says, 'You see how round-shouldered I am? Well, that's from hauling the water. . . . My back got bent from hauling the water, and it got bent when I was still young.'"

† Except for some Malthusian oscillations.

the progress kicked off by the Promethean steam engine and its kin could have been sustained, but electricity, internal combustion, and plumbing were more than up to the task.

Feed the World

In particular, they were up to the task of continuing to feed exponentially increasing numbers of people. Once again, innovations in fertilizer were critical in accomplishing this. In the first century of the Industrial Era the fertilizers essential for feeding more and more people came from the land. But in 1898 the chemist William Crookes, who was then the head of the British Association for the Advancement of Science, warned that the "bread eaters of the world," in their ever-increasing numbers, would soon exhaust South American supplies of guano and nitrates. Crookes predicted a global "general scarcity" of wheat unless science and technology came to the rescue.

They did, thanks to a pair of German chemists who allowed us to "win bread from air," as the physicist Max von Laue put it. They did this by fixing nitrogen, thereby fixing a huge problem.

We humans focus our attention on oxygen because going without it for even a short time is so unpleasant for us, but nitrogen is the most important element for life on Earth. It's necessary for fundamental things such as proteins, DNA, and chlorophyll. It's also abundant in the atmosphere, making up almost 80 percent of each breath we take. However, atmospheric nitrogen isn't much use to most life on the planet because it's chemically inert; it doesn't want to bond with other atoms. So it must be "fixed" to elements such as hydrogen before it can become fertilizer to help plants grow.

By the early twentieth century chemists had demonstrated that they could fix atmospheric nitrogen and create ammonia (which is one atom of nitrogen and three of hydrogen; it's poisonous to us, yet makes great fertilizer for plants). But these laboratory demos were far too small and expensive to be of practical use. Fritz Haber applied himself to the challenge of scaling them up.

Haber's work got a big boost when he started working with BASF, then the world's largest chemical company. In 1909, an experimental model less than three feet tall turned out liquid ammonia for five hours straight. Another boost came when BASF assigned Carl Bosch to help accelerate Haber's work.

Less than five years after the demonstration, a BASF factory was producing fertilizer at scale. Haber won a Nobel Prize in chemistry in 1918 for synthesizing ammonia. Bosch and his colleague Friedrich Bergius won theirs in 1931 for "chemical high pressure methods." Today, the Haber-Bosch process for producing fertilizer is so fundamental to human enterprise that, according to the energy analyst and author Ramez Naam, it uses about 1 percent of the world's industrial energy.

Is that energy well spent? Absolutely. Vaclav Smil, a prodigious scholar of humanity's relationship with our planet, estimates that "the prevailing diets of 45 percent of the world's population" depend on the Haber-Bosch process. Author Charles Mann writes, "More than three billion men, women, and children—an incomprehensively vast cloud of dreams, fears, and explorations—owe their existence to two early-twentieth-century German chemists."

Abundant energy gave us modern fertilizers, and these fertilizers gave us freedom from the severe, deprivation-induced Malthusian population oscillations that plagued societies before the Industrial Era. To maintain this freedom we also needed other breakthroughs, such as the Green Revolution, kicked off by the American agronomist Norman Borlaug. Borlaug's methods combined back-bending toil in fields with painstaking work at the laboratory bench to develop new varieties of crops. His work with wheat in Mexico showed what was possible and inspired similar breakthroughs, most notably at the International Rice Research Institute in the Philippines. He was awarded the Nobel Peace Prize in 1970.

Masters of Our Domain

The breakthroughs of the Industrial Era—technological, scientific, institutional, and intellectual—created a virtuous cycle of increasing human population and prosperity. It took over two hundred thousand years for the global population of *Homo sapiens* to hit 1 billion. It only took 125 years to add the next billion, a milestone that was reached in 1928. And the timescales kept getting shorter. Subsequent billions were added in thirty-one, fifteen, twelve, and eleven years.

Thanks to better nutrition and health, all these people kept living longer; global life expectancy more than doubled from less than twenty-nine years in 1770 to sixty years two centuries later. Around the world humans also became wealthier and enjoyed a higher standard of living. In the century leading up to 1970, for example, real GDP per capita increased by 500 percent or more in Western Europe and in Latin America, 400 percent in the Middle East and North Africa, and 250 percent in East Asia.

It's not correct to say that the advances of the Industrial Era have allowed us humans to entirely master our planet. We still can't direct the weather or control lightning, hurricanes, volcanoes, earthquakes, or tidal waves. Our planet's crust weighs 4.7 trillion times more than all of us put together and is composed of tectonic plates that are going to shift no matter what we do about it. So we are not its boss. But we are no longer at the Malthusian mercy of the environment as we try to scratch a living from the ground.

In fact, we have reversed the situation. We are now imposing ourselves on nature, instead of the other way around. Perhaps the clearest way to see this reversal is to look at changes in the biomass—the total worldwide weight—of mammals. As recently as the time of Christ all of us humans together probably weighed only about two-thirds as much as all the bison in North America, and less than one-eighth as much as all the elephants in Africa.

But in the Industrial Era our population exploded and, as we'll see, we killed bison and elephants at industrial scale and in nightmarish numbers. The balance shifted greatly as a result. At present, we humans weigh more than 350 times as much as all bison and elephants put together. We weigh over ten times more than all the earth's wild mammals combined. And if we add in all the mammals we've domesticated—cattle, sheep, pigs, horses, and so on—the comparison becomes truly ridiculous: we and our tamed animals now represent 97 percent of the earth's mammalian biomass.

This comparison illustrates a fundamental point: instead of being limited by the environment, we learned to shape it to our own ends during the Industrial Era. And did we do this wisely as well? In many ways and many places we did not.

CHAPTER 3

Industrial Errors

Perhaps you think the Creator sent you here to dispose of us as you see fit. If I thought you were sent by the Creator, I might be induced to think you had a right to dispose of me. Do not misunderstand me, but understand fully with reference to my affection for the land. I never said the land was mine to do with as I choose. The one who has a right to dispose of it is the one who has created it.

—Hinmaton-Yalaktit (known as Chief Joseph),
in a speech to US government representatives, 1876

Not all of the Industrial Era's transformations were for the better. Everyone who has spent time studying the period has probably compiled at least an informal list of its missteps, crimes, and moral failures. Prominent on many of these lists are slavery, child labor, colonialism, pollution, and the devastation of several species of animal.

Spending some time on these issues is important for two reasons. First, honesty demands that we do. It's simply wrong to portray the Industrial Era as great for everyone, or for the environment. The previous chapter was accurate about the huge gains that took place, but it was also incomplete. We need to also discuss the dark side of this unprecedented chapter in human history.

Second, the mistakes and failures of the Industrial Era led to a set of ideas that are still very much with us today. The heart of these ideas is the notion that we humans don't take adequate care of one another, or of the planet we live on. We use extraordinarily powerful tools such as the steam engine and electricity to dominate other peoples, and to plunder and befoul the earth.

As we'll see in this chapter, the history of the Industrial Era provides plenty of justification for this point of view. The interesting question is whether that viewpoint is still justified. We'll get to that question soon. First, let's look here at the events and actions that caused so many to think that industrialization—that combination of capitalism and technological progress that defined an era—was a terribly negative force.

As we've seen, the Industrial Era was such a sharp break from what had come before because we humans became so much better at producing things—at converting inputs into outputs. One way to look at the moral failures of this era is to see that they're perversions of the desire to produce more. The great mistakes we made were to force people to become part of the machinery of production (slavery and child labor), to take their land and resources and use them as inputs (colonialism), to use animals as inputs so wantonly that we wiped them out or nearly did, and to pay too little attention to the terrible pollution generated as a side effect of industrial production.

When we look at this era's great mistakes this way, an interesting pattern emerges. As industrialized countries advanced and became more prosperous, they first started treating humans better. They stopped enslaving people or making children work and eventually gave up claims to foreigners' lands. Better treatment of animals was slower to come and in some cases arrived too late to save a species. And better treatment of our planet came last of all. We kept heedlessly plundering and polluting it for almost two centuries after the Industrial Revolution started.

Let's look more closely at how this pattern of mistakes and corrections unfolded.

People as Property

It has been acceptable in many societies throughout history for people to own other people, especially if they come from a different ethnic group, religion, or tribe. The cognitive scientist Steven Pinker writes that sentiment toward slavery began to change in the late 1700s with the rise of humanism, or the belief that "the universal capacity of a person to suffer and flourish . . . call[s] on our moral concern." As Pinker writes in his book *Enlightenment Now*, "The Enlightenment is sometimes called the Humanitarian Revolution, because it led to the abolition of barbaric practices [such as slavery] that had been commonplace across civilizations for millennia." This humanitarian revolution has been hugely successful; around the world most people now believe that "if slavery is not wrong, nothing is wrong," as Abraham Lincoln put it in an 1864 letter.

Revulsion at slavery was so strong and so widespread that the movement to abolish it gained momentum even as the Industrial Era did. This era brought with it a great demand for labor (which was, as we'll see, sometimes satisfied by children), but many people and governments concluded that to buy, sell, and own humans to meet this demand was unacceptable.

The abolitionist movement in England began in 1787 with a meeting of twelve people in a London bookstore and printing shop. The speed with which it accomplished its goals is, in retrospect, astonishing. In 1807 the Abolition of the Slave Trade Act made it illegal to trade slaves throughout the British Empire. On August 1, 1838, it also became illegal to own them, and approximately eight hundred thousand people throughout the world gained their freedom. In Jamaica, the end of slavery was commemorated by the burial of a casket containing a whip and chains.

Most other European and Latin American countries abolished slavery around the same time as Great Britain. The United States took longer. The huge cotton industry of the American South was built on the back of slave labor, and plantation owners and their elected representatives were in no hurry to change the situation. It took the American Civil War—still by far the bloodiest in the country's history—to end slavery. President Lincoln issued the Emancipation Proclamation in 1863 while the war was still raging, and the Thirteenth Amendment to the US Constitution, which stated that "neither slavery nor involuntary servitude . . . shall exist within the United States," was passed in December 1865.

Suffer the Children

Children have long done useful work in human communities, but the dawn of the Industrial Era brought something new and grotesque: large-scale, grueling child labor in the factories, mills, and mines of rapidly growing economies. Poor families, especially those that had lost an adult breadwinner, were the most likely to send their children to work, and in Britain "parish apprentice" children, usually orphans who were wards of the state, were given no choice.

Many industrialists had no compunction about putting this labor force to work. A 1788 survey in England and Scotland, for example, found that approximately two-thirds of all employees in nearly 150 cotton mills were children. In 1815, a parliamentary commission heard testimony from women who had been working thirteen-hour days from the age of six at jobs strenuous enough to deform their bodies.

Outrage at such practices grew, and a succession of laws in the first half of the nineteenth century raised the ages at which children could be used as industrial laborers. The Factory Act of 1833 forbade employment of children younger than nine and limited the length of the workday for those younger than fourteen; the Mines Act of 1842 kept children younger than ten aboveground. To the modern eye these limits seem entirely inadequate, but they helped change things. By Queen Victoria's death in 1901, compulsory-schooling laws, public sentiment, and increasing levels of automation and standardization in factories and mills had combined to greatly reduce the importance of child labor in industry.

This Land Is Now My Land

The post-Enlightenment moral outrage that blossomed at the idea of taking people to serve as property apparently didn't extend to taking their land and its bounty. The Industrial Era's great appetite for resources was part of the reason that many European countries spread out around the world and claimed ownership, or at least control, over territories that already had inhabitants, societies, and governments.

The United States and most Central and South American countries had gained their independence by the mid-1800s, but other nations lost theirs over the nineteenth century. Much of South and Southeast Asia became colonized, as did many islands in the South Pacific. Europeans also engaged in a "Scramble for Africa": by the early twentieth century more than 90 percent of the continent had been claimed by France, Britain, Spain, Portugal, Germany, and Italy. King Leopold II of Belgium didn't even go through the motions of using his country's government as the instrument of colonization. He instead established himself as the "proprietor" of the Congo Free State, a huge amount of land in the middle of the continent corresponding roughly to the modern Democratic Republic of the Congo.

In 1542 the Spaniard Bartolomé de las Casas, a Dominican friar who was one of the first European settlers in the Americas, wrote an elegant and sad history of colonialism to that point, and an indictment of much future behavior. As he put it in his *Short Account of the Destruction of the Indies*, "The pretext upon which the Spanish invaded each of these provinces and proceeded to massacre the people and destroy their lands . . . was purely and simply that they were making good the claim of the Spanish Crown to the territories in question. . . . Whenever the natives did not drop everything and rush to recognize publicly the truth of the irrational and illogical claims that were made . . . they were dubbed outlaws and held to be in rebellion against His Majesty. . . . Everybody involved in the administration of the New World was blind to the simple truth enshrined in the first principles of law and government that nobody who is not a subject of a civil power in the first place can be deemed in law to be in rebellion against that power."

Some four hundred years later, the Austrian economist Ludwig von Mises elaborated on the colonizers' worldview. He wrote in 1944, "The most modern pretense for colonial conquest is condensed in the slogan 'raw materials.' Hitler and Mussolini tried to justify their plans by pointing out that the natural resources of the earth weren't fairly distributed. As have-nots they were eager to get their fair share from those nations which had more than they should have had."

The sun finally set on the colonial era after World War II. The postwar decades saw most countries around the world gain their independence. By 2018 the United Nations recognized only sixteen remaining "non-self-governing territories": a disputed African region called Western Sahara and fifteen island groups.

Nothing but Gray Skies

The combustion of coal produces smoke, soot, sulfur dioxide, and plenty of other forms of pollution. During the Industrial Era steam-powered factories and mills joined the households that were already burning coal, resulting in bad air and bad health. The author and artist William Blake described "dark Satanic Mills" in an 1804 poem. The image stuck because mills really did contribute to darkened skies.

Because English air-pollution levels weren't monitored before the twentieth century, it's hard to directly measure the effects of pollution earlier in the Industrial Era. Modern researchers, however, have developed clever ways to estimate these effects. And they are large. Economists Brian Beach and W. Walker Hanlon used the amount of industrial activity throughout the country as a proxy for the amount of coal burned and found that a 1 percent increase in the amount of coal used was associated with the death of one additional infant per one hundred births. As they write, "Industrial coal use explains roughly one-third of the urban mortality penalty observed during [the] period [1851–60]." Among British men born in the 1890s, those from most coal-intensive parts of the country were, on average, nearly an inch shorter as adults than those who grew up with the cleanest air. This gap was twice as large as that between children of white-collar and working-class families.

We kept on polluting in the twentieth century, to the point that the harms it caused became immediate and unignorable. In 1948 the fourteen-thousand-person town of Donora, Pennsylvania, was home to steel and zinc plants, both of which burned local coal that was full of pollutants. In late October of that year a layer of dense air settled over Donora and didn't move for several days. This "atmospheric inversion" acted as a lid; underneath it, locally generated pollution stayed close to the ground and kept accumulating.

The resulting haze became so thick that car headlights couldn't cut through it even in daylight, and driving was dangerous. Breathing was far more unsafe. Twenty people died before the weather changed and eliminated the pollution, and thousands more suffered acute symptoms. The lives of many survivors were certainly shortened and made more miserable by the pollution they inhaled during the episode.

The episode was extreme, but not isolated. As the Industrial Era progressed, people noticed that industrial towns and car-filled cities were experiencing a new kind of weather: periods of reduced visibility, itchy eyes, and sore throats. Some originally called it London fog. This term was replaced in the early 1900s by *smog*, a portmanteau of *smoke* and *fog*, which entered our vocabulary as it was entering our bodies.

Unhappy Hunting Grounds

As we increased our use of steam, electricity, and internal combustion, we relied less on the muscle power of animals. But we still ate them and turned their bodies into products. During the Industrial Era a clear distinction emerged: the animals we domesticated increased greatly in number and range, while many of the ones we hunted withered.

If the goal of a species is to become more numerous and propagate its genes across successive generations, then sheep, pigs, cattle, goats, chickens, and the other animals we've domesticated have been hugely successful. As we saw in chapter 2, 97 percent of the total mass of the earth's mammals now consists of us and the animals we raise.*

For many wild animals, on the other hand, the numerical and technological success of *Homo sapiens* during the Industrial Era posed a grave risk, and sometimes a terminal one. The most famous of all animal extinctions caused by humans is probably that of the passenger pigeon. It shocked Americans early in the twentieth century because it showed that huge numbers were no guarantee of survival.

---

* Success of a species is emphatically not the same as quality of life for its individual members. As the historian Yuval Harari writes, "A rare wild rhinoceros on the brink of extinction is probably more satisfied than a calf who spends its short life inside a tiny box, fattened to produce juicy steaks. . . . The numerical success of the calf's species is little consolation for the suffering the individual endures."

The passenger pigeon once flew over the United States in enormous numbers—in 1813 the naturalist John James Audubon witnessed a flock, dense enough to blot out the noonday sun, that took three days to pass overhead—but the pigeons were wiped out by deforestation and large-scale hunting beginning in the second half of the nineteenth century.

America's rapidly growing population was hungry for cheap protein, and electricity and steam helped supply passenger pigeons to meet this demand. The country's telegraph system communicated where huge flocks of the birds had landed, and trains full of hunters headed to these destinations. They killed as many pigeons as they could not only to feed their own families but also to send back by rail to urban markets.

The hunts ended the endless flocks. By 1900, only a single wild passenger pigeon was spotted in Ohio. The last one of all, a female named Martha, died in a Cincinnati zoo in 1914.

We relentlessly pursued animals not only for food but also for adornment. The sea otters of North America's west coast had been hunted for their luxurious pelts* since the late eighteenth century, primarily by Russian and American boats. By 1885 otter populations had been reduced so much that the total number of pelts available for sale on the London fur market was in steep decline. In 1911 only thirteen groups of the animals were estimated to remain from Mexico to Asia's Kamchatka Peninsula.

Many other animals with desirable fur or flesh were also hunted to the brink. As the journalist Jim Sterba recounts in his book *Nature Wars*, "By 1894, New York's Adirondack Mountains, the largest wild forested landscape in the eastern United States, was down to a single colony of five beavers." Sterba documents that much the

---

* A sea otter has many more hairs per square inch on its body than the typical human has on his or her entire head.

same happened with wild turkey, geese, white-tailed deer, and black bear. All these animals had large North American populations at the start of the Industrial Era. All were nearly wiped out.

The Massacre on the Plains

No animals better represent the voracious, nearly all-consuming appetite of the Industrial Era better than the North American bison and the whale. In 1800, an estimated 30 million bison* populated the Great Plains, coming together in huge herds to mate during the summer, then breaking into small bands to forage throughout the winter. Within a century, the total population had been reduced to something like a thousand animals.

Their near destruction occurred in two chapters, and steam power was important in both. At first, the biggest bison killers were Native Americans. By the start of the nineteenth century many Plains tribes were nomads, following the herds throughout the year on horseback. Their men were excellent hunters who became even more deadly once they began using repeating rifles instead of bows and arrows.

Starting in the 1830s these hunters found a new market for their skill at felling bison when fur companies' steamships began showing up along the Missouri and other rivers. Bison robes had become popular in the East, and Native American hunters and Euro-American traders came together to satisfy this demand. Historian Andrew Isenberg writes, "By the 1840s, the western plains nomads were annually bringing to the steamboats over 100,000 bison robes." This additional hunting came on top of the approximately half a million animals the Native Americans took each year for their own

---

* Although these animals are often called buffalo, that term is properly used only for Asian and African members of the same family of large grazing mammals.

purposes. It put great pressure on the overall population, especially because the robe hunt concentrated on young females in their reproductive prime. They had the softest hides.

The market for bison hides extended beyond robes and expanded greatly during the second half of the nineteenth century as America's steam-powered manufacturing sector grew. Recall that since the factories of that time needed so many belts, leather making was the country's fifth-largest industry by 1850. Bison leather, being so durable, was preferred for all this factory infrastructure. So as American manufacturing expanded, so too did the bison hunts. They came to be dominated not by Native American nomads, but by Euro-American profit seekers.

These men arrived in the Plains equipped with new .50-caliber rifles that could reliably kill their huge targets from distances of hundreds of yards. The bison were skinned where they dropped, their hides sent back East on the railroads that extended deep into the Great Plains by the early 1870s.

The leather hunts quickly achieved huge scale and had devastating impact. Isenberg recounts, "In 1872, Colonel [Irving] Dodge wrote that the area near Dodge City was thick with bison. By the fall of 1873, however, 'where there were myriads of buffalo the year before, there were now myriads of carcasses. The air was foul with sickening stench, and the vast plain which only a short twelve months before teemed with animal life, was a dead, solitary putrid desert.'" Dodge estimated that almost 1.4 million hides were sent east on three railroads between 1872 and 1874, and that because of losses to wolves and incompetent skinning, each hide actually represented five dead bison.*

---

* The final industrial product made from bison was fertilizer. In the 1880s millions of bison skeletons covering the Great Plains were picked up and shipped east to be rendered into "bone ash." In 1886, a pile of bones near the railroad station in Dodge City, Kansas, was a quarter of a mile long and at least one story high.

The population of the North American bison herd completely collapsed in the second half of the nineteenth century. Yellowstone National Park, established in 1872, served on paper as the only refuge from the remorseless hunting. However, poaching inside the park was rampant. By 1894, the Yellowstone herd numbered only twenty-five animals.

"Thou Brakest the Heads of Leviathan in Pieces"

Before humans with harpoons appeared, whales had faced few predators for 50 million years. Since these cetaceans had little to fear, many of them evolved to become massive, slow swimmers.* They also became abundant throughout the world's oceans.

The Vikings and Basques were the first people to pursue whales and throw harpoons at them. The English, Dutch, Americans, and many others followed. They refined the technologies and practices of whaling, but up to the late nineteenth century the hunts remained preindustrial. They relied on wind and muscle, and on a high tolerance for risk; most American whale crews, for example, experienced at least one fatality per voyage.

These hunts may have used Paleolithic technologies, but their cumulative impact was huge. They severely depleted the world's populations of sperm, bowhead, and right whales. Far worse was in store. Most whales faced the greatest threat not during the age of sail, but rather during the Industrial Era.

Two Norwegian inventions were critical in industrializing the whale hunt. The first was the harpoon cannon, which Svend Foyn refined and mounted on the bow of powered ships and chase boats. It used gunpowder instead of muscle power to fire an explosive

---

* The title of this section, from the Old Testament's book of Psalms, shows that people held whales in awe. Only God was mighty enough to kill them.

grenade that killed more quickly and reliably. The second innovation was the factory ship, designed by the whale gunner Petter Sørlle, which acted as a giant carving board for the animals' carcasses. These two technologies made it much easier and more profitable to hunt rorquals such as the blue, fin, and humpback whales.

Rorquals were difficult to hunt using preindustrial methods because they swim quickly and tend to sink when dead. Harpoon cannons, fast chase boats (first powered by steam, then by internal combustion diesel engines), and shipboard disassembly lines overcame these obstacles and opened up most of the world's whale populations to large-scale hunting by many nations. The results were as predictable as they were devastating. In 1900, as many as a quarter of a million blue whales may have lived in the Southern Ocean. By 1989, about five hundred remained. Fin whale populations were reduced by about 90 percent over the same time. These animals were used mainly to make margarine, soap, lubricants, and explosives (the glycerin in whale blubber can be used to make nitroglycerin)—all products that could easily have been made with other ingredients.

The Brothers Grim: Jevons and Marshall

As we'll see in the next chapter, we became aware of one other serious potential problem associated with the Industrial Era after it had been chugging along for almost two centuries. Quite simply, we might run out of the natural resources required to sustain our standards of living (and, indeed, our lives). This concern burst into public view around the time of the first Earth Day in 1970. But it had been around for more than a century and was born out of the work of two nineteenth-century English economists, William Jevons and Alfred Marshall. Their insights, when put together, seemed to predict an unavoidably grim future.

In 1865 Jevons published *The Coal Question*, a Malthusian book. Its arguments were supported not only by pure math, as was Malthus's *Essay*, but also by more than a century's worth of historical evidence.

Jevons saw clearly that his country's great increases in material prosperity were due to its abundant coal reserves and mastery of steam power. He saw also that the applications of this power were close to limitless. As he wrote, "[Coal] is the material energy of the country—the universal aid—the factor in everything we do. . . . No chemical or mechanical operation, perhaps, is quite impossible to us."

Britain faced no coal shortage in 1865. As *The Coal Question* put it, "We are growing rich and numerous upon a source of wealth of which the fertility does not yet apparently decrease with our demands upon it." But in yet another demonstration of why economics is called "the dismal science," Jevons warned that this happy situation would not last: "I must point out the painful fact that such a rate of growth will before long render our consumption of coal comparable with the total supply."

He was simply pointing out that coal is not an infinite resource, or a renewable one. Working with data about how rapidly coal consumption had been growing, and with estimates about how much total coal was still available to be mined under British soil, Jevons concluded that the country would run out of coal within a hundred years.

This was bad news since coal powered the entire economy. What was worse was that the problem had no solution. In particular, developing steam engines that used less coal would not help. Jevons's most lasting contribution to the debates around people, technology, and the environment was to argue that more efficient use of natural resources would *not* lead to lower overall use of them.

According to Jevons, this was because we'd use the greater efficiency not to get the same amount of the desired output (steam power) while using less of the resource (coal), but instead to get more and more of the output, thereby using more of the resource in total. As steam engines became more efficient—as they were able to supply the same amount of power while using less coal—more uses would be found for them. Steam engines would be not just at coal mines and huge manufacturers, but also in ships, locomotives, and small factories.

All these additional uses would drive up overall coal consumption. Jevons held, "It is wholly a confusion of ideas to suppose that the economical use of fuel is equivalent to a diminished consumption. The very contrary is the truth. . . . Whatever . . . conduces to increase the efficiency of coal, and to diminish the cost of its use, directly tends to augment the value of the steam-engine, and to enlarge the field of its operations."

A modern economist would say that Jevons was discussing the *price elasticity of demand* for energy (in this case, the energy stored inside lumps of coal). This intimidating term just refers to the fact that total demand for a product such as energy responds to a change in its price. For most products, demand goes up if price goes down. Jevons was saying that this was true for coal energy, but he was also saying something more: that the percentage increase in total demand would be greater than the percentage decrease in price. He was saying that in Britain in 1865 and for the foreseeable future, the price elasticity of energy from coal was greater than 1.*

At the heart of *The Coal Question* was a simple chain of argument: Britain had a finite amount of coal, total demand for it would use it up within a century, and more efficient steam engines would not prevent this exhaustion. But what if *total* demand slowed down, not just for coal, but for all goods and services put together? What if the people of England became so prosperous that they became

---

* To be precise, this elasticity is actually less than -1: demand goes up when price goes *down.*

sated and didn't feel the need to keep consuming more and more, year after year? After all, they could only eat so many meals (even ones containing new foods such as bananas), wear so many clothes, live in so many houses, and take so many trips. Might it not be possible that total consumption would taper off?

The Battle of Ever More

No, said Alfred Marshall, that's not how it works. Because fundamentally it's not how *we* work. Marshall is a giant in the field of economics. His 1890 book, *Principles of Economics*, expanded the discipline, made it more analytical and rigorous, and brought great clarity to many important concepts. His *Principles* took up Jevons's concept of elasticity of demand and solidified it, but that's not why we're bringing Marshall into this conversation. Instead, it's because of assertions he made in the book about the nature of demand.

In a famous passage, he wrote, "Human wants and desires are countless in number and very various in kind. . . . The uncivilized man indeed has not many more than the brute animal; but every step in his progress upwards increases the variety of his needs together with the variety in his methods of satisfying them. He desires not merely larger quantities of the things he has been accustomed to consume, but better qualities of those things; he desires a greater choice of things, and things that will satisfy new wants growing up in him."

Rather than making a dry point about economic growth rates, Marshall was making a deep statement about human nature: *we want more.* We do not get satisfied at any level of affluence or consumption. Instead, even as we grow comparatively rich, we continue to want more. We might not even know exactly what we desire next—these are the "wants growing up in" us—but some clever innovator or entrepreneur is going to help us realize what those wants are and offer them to satisfy them, for a price. In doing so, it's reasonable to assume that some of the planet's finite natural resources are going to be used up.

The arguments of Jevons and Marshall, taken together, are bleak. We humans can be relied upon to want more and more, without end. But our planet's resources are finite. So we're going to run out of them. Making more efficient the technologies that help us convert resources into goods and services won't help us conserve resources; we'll just use that greater efficiency to create ever more goods and services—so many more that total resource consumption will increase.

Is there any way out of this jam? Or are we, with all of the extraordinarily powerful technologies of the Industrial Era, just setting ourselves up for the greatest Malthusian crash of all time?

CHAPTER 4

Earth Day and Its Debates

Here and there awareness is growing that man, far from being the overlord of all creation, is himself part of nature, subject to the same cosmic forces that control all other life. Man's future welfare and probably even his survival depend upon his learning to live in harmony, rather than in combat, with these forces.

—Rachel Carson,
"Essay on the Biological Sciences," 1958

On April 22, 1970, America celebrated its first Earth Day. Thousands of events were held across the country, many on college campuses, with large-scale marches in several cities. It was the lead story in the *New York Times*, and the sole subject of an entire episode of *The CBS Evening News with Walter Cronkite*. Its impact was so strong that it's been called "the birth of the modern environmental movement."

Over the years, many ideas, events, and media have been cited as inspirations for Earth Day. Of these, the most beautiful is *Earthrise*, the name given to a stunning photo of the blue planet Earth, half in shadow and wrapped in clouds, rising above the surface of the Moon. *Earthrise* was taken by astronaut Bill Anders on December 24, 1968, during the Apollo 8 mission.

It immediately became a global sensation. The contrast in the photo between Earth's obvious vitality and the lifeless lunar terrain was stark and powerful. It caused many people to pay more attention to the world they lived on. As the author Robert Poole put it, "*Earthrise* marked the tipping point, the moment when the sense of the space age flipped from what it meant for space to what it means for Earth."

The day after the Apollo 8 crew sent its first images of the rising earth back to the planet, the poet Archibald MacLeish wrote, "To see the earth as it truly is, small and blue and beautiful in that eternal silence where it floats, is to see ourselves as riders on the earth together, brothers on that bright loveliness in the eternal cold." *Earthrise* helped us see that the human condition is inseparable from the state of the planet that we all live on.

Maybe Pollution Is a Problem?

A pair of events the next year drove home the point that we weren't being good caretakers of our "bright loveliness." In January of 1969 an explosion at a Union Oil rig off the coast of Santa Barbara, California, caused 3 million gallons of crude oil to spill into the ocean and onto the coast in a month. In June, a section of the Cuyahoga River in downtown Cleveland, Ohio, caught on fire. The Cuyahoga had long served as a dumping ground for used oil and other industrial by-products, to the point that its water served as a home for flames instead of an extinguisher of them.*

These events were loud notes in a crescendo of environmental problems. From the start of the twentieth century up to Earth Day, air pollution got steadily worse in the industrialized world. For example, levels of atmospheric sulfur dioxide (a pollutant that

---

* The picture of the fire that appeared a month later in *Time* magazine was actually a file photo from a fire on the same river that took place in 1952. By 1969, apparently, flames on the Cuyahoga were no longer newsworthy enough to merit a photo.

comes from the combustion of fuels that contain sulfur) more than doubled between 1900 and 1970 in the United States.

As amazing as it seems to us today, the idea that air pollution could be anything more than a minor annoyance was not widely accepted in the middle of the twentieth century. The acute smog that descended on Donora, Pennsylvania, and clearly killed many people started to change the situation. It led the director of the US Public Health Service to say, "We have to get over the idea that smog is just a nuisance," and to a commission to study the links between airborne pollution and human health. In 1949 the commission trumpeted that its work had established "for the first time that air contamination in an industrial community can actually cause acute disabling diseases."

Bad Breeding

The years leading up to Earth Day also surfaced the alarming thought that although pollution was bad and getting worse, it might not be the greatest of our environmental problems. Pollution is a side effect of human activity. By the 1960s, a number of observers had concluded that the most fundamental threat facing the planet was simply that there were too many of us humans, and that we were engaging in too much activity.

The biologist Paul Ehrlich became the most popular exponent of this view. In his bestselling 1968 book, *The Population Bomb*, Ehrlich laid out a scenario that made Malthus look like a sunny optimist. Early editions of the book began, "The battle to feed all of humanity is over. In the 1970s hundreds of millions of people will starve to death in spite of any crash programs embarked upon now. At this late date nothing can prevent a substantial increase in the world death rate."

The brothers William and Paul Paddock, who were respectively an agronomist and a foreign service professional, agreed that it was too late to prevent mass starvation. In their 1967 book, *Famine 1975! America's Decision: Who Will Survive?*,* they maintained that food-rich countries such as the United States couldn't feed all the hungry mouths in the world and so had to make life-and-death decisions. The Paddocks divided developing countries into three categories: "can't-be-saved nations," which is self-explanatory; the "walking wounded," which would probably survive without our help; and those that could and should be saved with our aid.

The idea that the world might be headed for a large-scale Malthusian disaster was not limited to ecologists and environmentalists. The American government also took it seriously. A classified 1974 National Security Council report titled "Implications of Worldwide Population Growth for U.S. Security and Overseas Interests" (informally known as "The Kissinger Report") stated, "The most serious consequence for the short and middle term is the possibility of massive famines in certain parts of the world, especially the poorest regions."

Nothing in Reserve

Other voices stressed that just as we were going to use up all of the planet's food-production capacity—all of the land and water—so, too, we'd exhaust all of its other bounty. Our Industrial Era habits of using technologies to yank resources from the earth to grow our population and prosperity ensured this.

As the graph on the following page shows, our consumption of resources such as fertilizer and metals was exponentially increasing in the years leading up to Earth Day (just as Jevons found was the case for coal about a hundred years earlier). In many cases,

* I'm not sure that title needs an exclamation point.

resource consumption was growing even more quickly than the overall economy. It seemed logical and inevitable that the planet's finite stock of these resources would someday be exhausted. The only question was when.

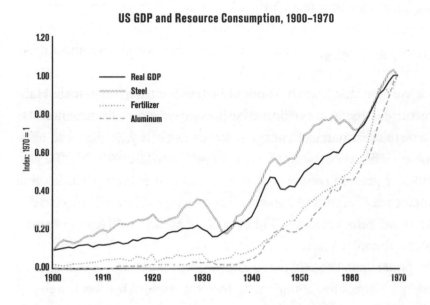

Around the time of Earth Day a team of computer modelers at MIT led by the biophysicist Donella Meadows tried to answer that question. They built a computer simulation of the entire world's economy that was centered on five key variables: "population, food production, industrialization, pollution, and consumption of nonrenewable natural resources." All of these interacted with one another and increased exponentially in the simulation, just as they had been doing in the real world.

The MIT team discussed the results of their work in the best-selling 1972 book *The Limits to Growth*. They found that even under their most optimistic scenarios about resource abundance, the known global reserves of aluminum, copper, natural gas, petroleum, and gold would all be exhausted within fifty-five years if population and the economy were both allowed to grow without constraint. Absent constraints, their model showed that the world's population would suffer a sudden and sharp collapse well before the end of the twenty-first century as resources vanished and economies around the planet ground to a halt.

Running out of Energy

As we've seen, energy sources are one of the most important resources for any economy. Some observers felt that *Limits to Growth*'s estimates of energy reserves were, if anything, too optimistic. The ecologist Kenneth Watt predicted in 1970, "By the year 2000, if present trends continue, we will be using up crude oil at such a rate . . . that there won't be any more crude oil. You'll drive up to the pump and say, 'Fill 'er up, buddy,' and he'll say, 'I am very sorry, there isn't any.'"

Others felt, though, that we humans were actually fortunate that energy was not too abundant. If it were, this thinking went, we'd just use it to grow our populations and exhaust the planet's resources even more quickly. In 1953 US president Dwight Eisenhower gave a speech at United Nations headquarters in New York titled "Atoms for Peace." Instead of using nuclear technologies only for weapons, Eisenhower proposed that they be used "to serve the peaceful pursuits of mankind. Experts would be mobilized to apply atomic energy to the needs of agriculture, medicine, and other peaceful activities. A special purpose would be to provide abundant electrical energy in the power-starved areas of the world."

The speech was received with rapturous applause at the United Nations, but some felt that "atoms for peace" would be a terrible idea. "It'd be little short of disastrous for us to discover a source of clean, cheap, abundant energy," physicist Amory Lovins said in

1977, "because of what we would do with it." Paul Ehrlich agreed, writing in 1975, "Giving society cheap, abundant energy at this point would be the moral equivalent of giving an idiot child a machine gun. With cheap, abundant energy, the attempt clearly would be made to pave, develop, industrialize, and exploit every last bit of the planet."

The debates about energy highlight how fundamental it is for growth. A graph of US GDP and energy consumption from 1800 to 1970—almost the entire period between the start of the Industrial Revolution and Earth Day—shows that the two went up essentially in lockstep for well over 150 years:

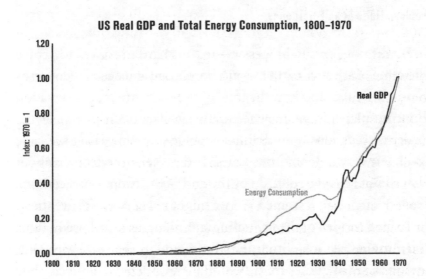

The extraordinarily tight relationship between the size of the economy and the amount of energy used led many researchers to think that the two were essentially equivalent—that if you could measure the amount of energy a society used, you'd have an excellent idea of how large, prosperous, and advanced it was. This line of study was kicked off with a series of articles in *Scientific American* in 1971, including geologist Earl Cook's "Flow of Energy in an Industrial Society."*

Like Jevons over a century earlier, Cook documented the ongoing exponential increases in both energy consumption and the size of the economy. And like Jevons, he warned that they couldn't continue indefinitely; his article concluded, "Indefinite growth in energy consumption, as in human population, is simply not possible." But Cook was not optimistic that we could arrest this growth. "Making the changes will call for hard political decisions . . . ," he wrote, but "democratic societies are not noted for their ability to take the long view in making decisions."

Proclamations in an Emergency

Cook was not alone in his pessimism. It is hard to convey to people who came of age after Earth Day just how broad and deep the concerns were at the time, and how the tone of the mainstream conversation about our planet was somewhere between alarmist and apocalyptic. Modern discussions around climate change sometimes have the same flavor, but very different timescales. Today, we are concerned about what climate change could do by the end of the twenty-first century. Around Earth Day, it seemed as if we might not survive the twentieth.

To give an idea of the prevailing mood, beliefs, and predictions of the mainstream environmental movement around Earth Day, here are a set of quotes from 1970 that I find representative.† They read to me like dispatches from a society in a panic attack.

---

* Ian Morris's social development index, which we saw in chapter 2, uses energy capture as one of its four measures of how advanced a society is.

† These quotes were collected by the science correspondent Ronald Bailey in a 2000 article for *Reason* magazine, and by economist Mark Perry in a 2018 blog for the American Enterprise Institute. Both of these sources are conservative, but this does not mean that they are misrepresenting the mood of Earth Day.

Senator Gaylord Nelson wrote in *Look* magazine, "Dr. S. Dillon Ripley, secretary of the Smithsonian Institution, believes that in 25 years, somewhere between 75 and 80 percent of all the species of living animals will be extinct."

Pete Gunter, a North Texas State University professor, wrote, "Demographers agree almost unanimously on the following grim timetable: by 1975 widespread famines will begin in India; these will spread by 1990 to include all of India, Pakistan, China and the Near East, Africa. By the year 2000, or conceivably sooner, South and Central America will exist under famine conditions. . . . By the year 2000, thirty years from now, the entire world, with the exception of Western Europe, North America, and Australia, will be in famine."

Life magazine reported, "Scientists have solid experimental and theoretical evidence to support . . . the following predictions: In a decade, urban dwellers will have to wear gas masks to survive air pollution. . . . By 1985 air pollution will have reduced the amount of sunlight reaching earth by one half."

Biologist and Nobel Prize winner George Wald estimated that "civilization will end within 15 or 30 years unless immediate action is taken against problems facing mankind."

"We are prospecting for the very last of our resources and using up the nonrenewable things many times faster than we are finding new ones," warned Sierra Club director Martin Litton in *Time*'s special "environmental report."

The day after the first Earth Day, the *New York Times* editorial page warned, "Man must stop pollution and conserve his resources, not

merely to enhance existence but to save the race from intolerable
deterioration and possible extinction."

In 1971 Ehrlich and the physicist John Holdren proposed in
Science the equation $I = P \times F$, where I represented a society's
total negative impact on the environment, P stood for population size, and F was a per-person factor. In later work F was
replaced by the product of affluence (in other words, per capita
GDP) and technology (measured in various ways). The resulting
equation was $I = P \times A \times T$, which became known as the IPAT
Model. It held that population and affluence were always bad news
for the environment. Technology could be either good (such as
solar power) or bad (more coal plants), but when it was good, it
"tend[ed] to be slow, costly, and insufficient in scale," as Ehrlich
and Holdren put it.

IPAT put an equation to the gloomy views dominant around
Earth Day about the state of the world, and about its future. Though
criticized as "mathematical propaganda," it endured as a model for
estimating environmental impact and a guide to what, if anything,
could be done.

CRIB or Graves

Famines. Deadly pollution. Resource exhaustion. Population and
societal collapse. The obvious enormity of these problems led to a
consensus within the nascent environmental movement about the
need for action. And also about what these actions should be. As
I read the dominant proposals and recommendations appearing
around the time of the first Earth Day, the acronym *CRIB* occurred
to me: the solutions to our planetary problems, we were told, were
to Consume less, to Recycle, to Impose limits, and to go Back to
the land.

The first two of these solutions were aimed at countering the problem of relentless increases in consumption that Marshall identified—the *A* in *IPAT*. The last was meant to deal with the perils highlighted by Jevons of living in an ever-more-technologically sophisticated society. Imposing limits, it was hoped, could address both Marshall and Jevons, in part by keeping population—the *P* in *IPAT*—low.

Consume Less

The most obvious answer to the challenges of resource depletion and pollution is simply to make and buy fewer things. A country's economy is largely created out of the spending decisions of its people, so perhaps if they became aware of the ecological problems associated with relentless economic growth, they'd buy less to tread more lightly on the earth. Maybe concern for the environment would prove Marshall wrong. Maybe we'd come to the collective conclusion that because our planet isn't infinite, our desires can't be, either.

To do this, though, we'd probably have to walk away from many of the basic assumptions and practices of the Industrial Era and discard the market-based economic thinking that Marshall helped define.

The Austrian-French philosopher André Gorz is credited with introducing the term *degrowth* in 1972, asking, "Is the earth's balance, for which no-growth—or even degrowth—of material production is a necessary condition, compatible with the survival of the capitalist system?" As you can probably guess, Gorz's answer was no.

In his 1975 book, *Ecology as Politics*, Gorz made clear his belief that slowing down growth in consumption wasn't enough—we had to actively reduce it: "Even at zero growth, the continued consumption of scarce resources will inevitably result in exhausting them completely. The point is not to refrain from consuming more and more, but to consume less and less—there is no other way of conserving the available reserves for future generations."

The "degrowth" movement that Gorz helped launch faced no shortage of obstacles in achieving its goals, but it had on its side a simple, pure, and obvious logic. If we all consumed less, we would in fact consume fewer resources.

And maybe we only needed to consume less of *some* things. In his 1971 bestseller, *The Closing Circle*, biologist Barry Commoner agreed, "The present system of production is self-destructive [and] the present course of human civilization is suicidal." But, he maintained, we didn't need to turn away from affluence altogether; we just needed to stop making chemical-laden products in big, polluting factories. The *T* in the *IPAT* was the real problem. If our means of production became smaller scale, closer to nature, and more organic, they would become sustainable (a concept Commoner helped popularize). As he wrote, "The needed productive reforms can be carried out without seriously reducing the present level of *useful* goods available."

Recycle

In addition to consuming less, recycling the materials we use is another obvious solution to resource depletion. Instead of throwing away newspapers, cardboard boxes, plastic and glass bottles, aluminum cans, and so on once we're done with them, we could use them as inputs to the same manufacturing processes that created them in the first place. That way we can get more of all these things without using additional raw materials.

Economist Kenneth Boulding boosted the recycling movement in 1966 with the vivid image of "Spaceship Earth," a vessel of finite resources on a long journey through the cosmos. To make this road trip successful, he wrote, "man must find his place in a cyclical ecological system which is capable of continuous reproduction of material form." People had long been reusing tools, clothes, and many other items because doing so saved them money. Spaceship Earth–style recycling was different. It was motivated not by self-interest but instead by a desire to take good care of the planet.

The mantra "Reduce, Reuse, Recycle" entered the lexicon in America by the mid-1970s. In 1980, the Philadelphia suburb of Woodbury, New Jersey, became the first community in the country with a curbside recycling program when the town's garbage truck started towing behind it a trailer dedicated to reusable household waste. The idea spread quickly. By 1995, approximately 25 percent of all municipal solid waste in the United States was being recycled.

Impose Limits

The environmental movement's most controversial recommendations concerned imposing limits. The most controversial of these were limits on the number of children that people could have. But Ehrlich, among others, saw no alternative. The Malthusian math was too clear. As he wrote in *The Population Bomb*, "We must rapidly bring the world population under control, reducing the growth rate to zero and eventually making it go negative. Conscious regulation of human numbers must be achieved."

In *Limits to Growth* the MIT team of computer modelers discussed constraints not only on population but also on industry. If profit-seeking businesses were using up the world's resources as they went about creating and satisfying customer demand, the argument went, then they needed to be stopped, or at least redirected. Companies could be forced by laws or nudged by taxes and subsidies to stop digging new mines, building more factories, or offering resource-heavy products such as the 1972 Cadillac 75 sedan, a land yacht that weighed over fifty-six hundred pounds.

The authors of *Limits to Growth* knew that such suggestions would be unpopular in America and other countries that prided themselves on *not* having centrally planned economies, but they saw little choice. As they wrote, "Such policies as reducing the birth rate and diverting capital from production of material goods, by whatever means they might be implemented, seem unnatural and unimaginable. . . . Indeed there would be little point even in discussing such fundamental changes in the functioning of modern society if we felt that the present pattern of unrestricted growth were sustainable into the future." But their simulations clearly showed that it was not. The computer models at the heart of the book presented a stark choice between free-market economics and the long-term health of planet Earth and its human societies. It didn't seem like much of a choice at all.

Another version of the push to impose constraints sought limits not on the markets companies could enter, but instead on a bad side effect of their activities: pollution. Evidence from Donora, Pennsylvania, and other excessively dirty places convinced many that pollution was much worse than "just a nuisance"; it was instead a danger to human life.

President Richard Nixon created the US Environmental Protection Agency in 1970, and a series of laws gave it and other federal agencies broad powers to set and enforce limits on many kinds of pollution. The Clean Air Act was substantially amended and strengthened in 1970 (and again in 1977 and 1990), and 1972 saw the Clean Water Act; 1974 the Safe Drinking Water Act; 1976 the Toxic Substances Control Act; and so on.

Some felt that attempts to reduce pollution would slow down economic progress. As former representative Paul Rogers recalled in 1990, "During the House floor debate on the amendments [to the

Clean Air Act], one of my colleagues quoted a small-town mayor, who [in expressing the previous conventional wisdom that environmental protection and economic growth were not compatible] is reported to have said, 'If you want this town to grow, it has got to stink.' " The public quickly grew intolerant of foul places, though, and in 1980 Congress created a "superfund" to clean up America's most polluted sites.

Back to the Land

The last of the four main strategies for avoiding environmental and societal devastation—the *B* in *CRIB*—was for individuals, families, and communities to turn away from the Industrial Era, and to go back to the land. Advocates of this approach appeared to be taking Jevons's arguments seriously: if technological progress leads to greater overall resource use, then ignoring this progress and instead using traditional technologies and methods could mean using fewer resources and treading more lightly on the planet.

Most members of the back-to-the-land movement, which gained momentum in the 1960s and '70s, were comparatively affluent and well educated. They came from urban or suburban backgrounds. Before they went back to the land they had little experience in getting food from it, or in other forms of rural self-sufficiency. If this population was going to have any chance at success with homesteading they needed both knowledge and tools.

The iconic writer, entrepreneur, and organizer Stewart Brand set out to provide both. In 1968 he christened a Dodge truck the Whole Earth Truck Store and took it on a "commune road trip" to educate back-to-the-landers about the best tools and techniques for sowing a field, drilling a well, and other important tasks. He also began producing a catalog, an early issue of which had *Earthrise* on its cover. The *Whole Earth Catalog* quickly became a huge hit. Some issues were more than an inch thick, and in 1971 it won a National Book Award in the Contemporary Affairs category.

The Foxfire books were a similar sensation. They began as a project in a Georgia high school in which students interviewed their older neighbors and relatives about rural Appalachian traditions and crafts. The interviews turned into magazine articles and eventually a 1972 book.* The first Foxfire book sold more than 9 million copies. Clearly, a lot of people were drawn to what they saw as a simpler and superior life—one more in harmony with nature than exploitative of it.

Is It Really So Bad?

Even as the mainstream conversation about the environment grew more panicked and urgent, a group of voices started making the case that things—at least some of them—might not be so dire. These comparative optimists, many of whom were economists, made two sets of observations based on evidence, and one broad statement of faith.

Their first evidence-based claim was that many of the bad things confidently predicted by the environmental movement—chronic food shortages and famines; irreversible ecosystem collapses; mass species die-offs; crippling shortages of natural resources; and so on—kept on not happening. Instead, some of the things that were supposed to get much worse kept getting better.

Around the world more people had access to more food year after year. There was still hunger—too much hunger for any compassionate person—but undernourishment was generally going down. And as the economist Amartya Sen pointed out in his 1981

---

* *Foxfire* is a term for bioluminescence caused by fungi that live in decaying wood.

book, *Poverty and Famines*, the famines that did occur as the Industrial Era progressed were not caused mainly by declines in food production. Instead, they were due to sharp political and societal shifts that took away people's "entitlements," or the normal means by which they got access to food. The years around Earth Day also did not witness massive die-offs of fish due to pollution, wars fought over water or other resources, deprivation-induced refugee crises, or many of the other catastrophes that had been predicted.

As the economist Julian Simon put it in his 1981 book, *The Ultimate Resource*, "Are we now 'entering an age of scarcity'? You can see anything you like in a crystal ball. But almost without exception, the best data . . . suggest precisely the opposite." This had not always been his view. In the late 1960s Simon had, like Ehrlich, written about the dangers of unchecked population growth. But the continued improvement in human standards of living and lack of environmental catastrophes caused him to change his mind.

Simon eventually became a strong optimist because he came to have faith. Not in divine providence, but in human ingenuity. Population and economic growth bring with them challenges, but Simon argued that people are actually quite good at meeting challenges. We learn about the world via science, invent new tools and technologies, create institutions such as democracy and the rule of law, and do many other things that let us solve problems and create a better future.

Simon and his fellow optimists were well aware of the phenomena described by Jevons and Marshall, but were not convinced that they would lead to catastrophe. Instead, the optimists said, we'll find a way to deal with the challenges that come with the growth of populations and economies. Many of the voices prominent around Earth Day thought that humanity was growing and innovating its way into a terrible predicament. In sharp contrast, the optimists thought that we would grow and innovate our way *out* of one.

Simon's faith was buttressed by the evidence he and others collected about steady improvements throughout the Industrial Era
in human prosperity and health. He also found a second body of
evidence convincing—so much so that he was willing to make a
high-stakes public bet on it.

Betting the Planet

Simon looked at the evidence around the availability of natural
resources and concluded that we were in no danger of running
out of them anytime soon. His reasoning started with one of the
most basic facts of economics: scarcity causes prices to go up. As
fertilizers, metals, coal, or other resources become more rare, they
also get more expensive.

Simon saw, though, that this was not the end of the story. What
happened next was that the price surge activated human greed and
combined it with human ingenuity. This combination of self-interest
and innovativeness caused two things: a wide-ranging search for
more of the resource, and an equally ardent search for substitutes. As
one or both of these quests succeeded, Simon reasoned, the original
scarcity would be eased, and the resource's price would go back down.

In the most extreme and intriguing case, the substitute for the
resource would be . . . nothing at all. In his 1968 book, *Utopia or
Oblivion*, the architect and inventor R. Buckminster Fuller wrote,
"I made many calculations, and it seemed increasingly clear that
it was feasible for us to do so much with so little that we might be
able to take care of everybody. In 1927 I called this whole process
'Ephemeralization,'" by which he meant satisfying human desires
for consumption while using fewer resources from the physical
world—fewer molecules, in short.

The geodesic domes popularized and named by Fuller are a good
example of this phenomenon: they use fewer materials and weigh

a great deal less than conventional buildings of the same size, yet can support heavier loads. Fuller wrote, "Ephemeralization . . . is the number one economic surprise of world man." The word was eventually replaced by its synonym *dematerialization* in discussions of innovation, technological progress, and resource use.

Simon saw many examples of resource scarcity *not* being a permanent condition—from the discovery of huge new reserves of coal in Britain to kerosene taking over from whale oil for lighting homes in the middle of the nineteenth century. He became confident that the pattern of generally falling resource prices would continue in the years after Earth Day even as global population and affluence continued to increase much more quickly than ever before.

Paul Ehrlich was equally convinced of the opposite. Like the *Limits to Growth* authors and many others, he believed that the planet's large and rapidly growing population would cause an unprecedented and unquenchable thirst for resources, and that the coming scarcities would be permanent. This meant that prices would rise.

The two antagonists publicly stated and refined their positions for a decade after Earth Day. They then decided to put their money where their mouths were. In 1980, Julian Simon and Paul Ehrlich made one of the most famous bets in history.

Simon offered the following terms: Ehrlich could pick any resources he liked. He could also pick the time frame for the bet, as long as it was at least a year. If at the end of the chosen time frame the real price of the resources had risen, then Simon would pay Ehrlich the amount of the rise. If prices had fallen, Ehrlich would pay Simon.

Ehrlich accepted. He picked a decade for the duration of the bet and chose five resources: copper, chromium, nickel, tin, and tungsten. He virtually "bought" $200 of each on September 29, 1980, and waited for their prices to rise in the following years.

They didn't. The real price of all five metals had fallen by late September of 1990. Chromium declined by only a bit, from $3.90 per pound to $3.70, but the others became much cheaper. The price of tin, for example, collapsed from $8.72 per pound to $3.88. The overall value of Ehrlich's $1,000 resource portfolio declined by more than half. In October of 1990 he mailed Simon a check for $576.06.*

The Forecast Remains Gloomy

The results of the Simon-Ehrlich bet were far from a conclusive victory for the optimists. A number of analysts of the bet have concluded that Simon was "smart but lucky," as the investor and author Paul Kedrosky put it; smart because of Simon's insight about how high resource prices tend to lead to lower ones, and lucky because Ehrlich selected for their bet a time of particularly steep price drops in the chosen commodities.

Other times wouldn't have been so favorable to Simon. As Kedrosky wrote, "If you started the bet any year during the 1980s Simon won eight of the ten decadal start years. During the 1990s things changed, however, with Simon the decadal winner in four start years and Ehrlich winning six. . . . And if we extend the bet into the current decade . . . then Ehrlich won every start-year bet in the 2000s." In a world of rapidly growing populations and economies, falling commodity prices didn't seem guaranteed.

Nor, apparently, was dematerialization. The years after Earth Day saw many cases of specific products using less material: American-made cars, for example, generally got lighter after the Arab oil embargo of 1973. But the pattern that Jevons first noticed with coal kept repeating itself: greater efficiency led not to an overall

---

* The check was not accompanied by any note.

reduction in the use of a resource, but instead to greater total use. This pattern was observed so consistently that it acquired its own label: the rebound effect.

Research on this effect found that it was pervasive. A 2017 study by technology scholars Christopher Magee and Tessaleno Devezas found that "57 different cases clearly indicate that technological improvement has not resulted in 'automatic' dematerialization." The authors predicted, "The future is not highly likely to reverse this finding."

It seemed that Jevons and Marshall were still correct, well more than a century after they wrote. Our bottomless appetites and brilliant technologies were causing us to use up more of the world's bounty year after year.

CHAPTER 5

The Dematerialization Surprise

Well, when events change, I change my mind. What do you do?

—Paul Samuelson,
on *Meet the Press*, 1970*

U nlike Julian Simon and Paul Ehrlich, environmental scientist Jesse Ausubel didn't spend much time thinking about resource prices. But as the Simon-Ehrlich bet was coming to its final years, he started to take a keen interest in resource *quantities*—how much material of different kinds we humans were using as we went about building our economies and lives.

As Ausubel remembers it, his friend and colleague Robert Herman, a physicist with a wide range of interests, asked over dinner one night in 1987, "Are buildings getting lighter?" That apparently simple question led to a lot of investigations, not only of the weights of buildings but also of the "material intensity" of many other things. Along with the civil engineer Siamak Ardekani, they published their initial findings and proposed a research agenda in a 1989 paper called simply "Dematerialization." It concluded with a call for more research into "whether on a collective basis . . . forces drive society toward materialization or dematerialization."

---

* This quote has been attributed to many people, most often the economist John Maynard Keynes. But the website *Quote Investigator* found no reference earlier than Samuelson's.

Being Unaware of the Lightness

Ausubel continued to pursue the "Materialization or dematerialization?" question in subsequent years. The title of his 2015 essay
"The Return of Nature: How Technology Liberates the Environment" suggested his answer. Ausubel found substantial evidence
not only that Americans were consuming fewer resources per capita
(in other words, per person) but also that they were consuming
less *in total* of some of the most important building blocks of an
economy: things such as steel, copper, fertilizer, timber, and paper.
Total annual US consumption of all of these had been increasing
rapidly in the years prior to Earth Day. But since then, consumption
had reached a peak, then declined.

This was unexpected, to put it mildly. As Ausubel wrote, "The
reversal in use of some of the materials so surprised me that Iddo
Wernick, Paul Waggoner, and I undertook a detailed study of the
use of 100 commodities in the United States from 1900 to 2010. . . .
Of the 100 commodities, we found that 36 have peaked in absolute
use . . . Another 53 commodities have peaked relative to the size of
the economy, though not yet absolutely. Most of them now seem
poised to fall."

A few years earlier Chris Goodall had noticed something similar happening in the United Kingdom. Goodall, a writer and
researcher on environmental and energy issues, found an interesting pattern in the United Kingdom's Material Flow Accounts,
"a set of dry and largely ignored data published annually by the
Office for National Statistics," as the *Guardian* put it. He summarized his findings in a 2011 paper titled " 'Peak Stuff': Did the UK
Reach a Maximum Use of Material Resources in the Early Part
of the Last Decade?"

Goodall's answer to his own question was, essentially, yes:

"Evidence presented in this paper supports a hypothesis that the United Kingdom began to reduce its consumption of physical resources in the early years of the last decade, well before the economic slowdown that started in 2008. This conclusion applies to a wide variety of different physical goods, for example water, building materials and paper and includes the impact of items imported from overseas. Both the weight of goods entering the economy and the amounts finally ending up as waste probably began to fall from sometime between 2001 and 2003."

Goodall was eloquent about the significance of the demateri-alization of the United States or United Kingdom: "If correct, this finding is important. It suggests that economic growth in a mature economy does not necessarily increase the pressure on the world's reserves of natural resources and on its physical environment. An advanced country may be able to decouple economic growth and increasing volumes of material goods consumed. A sustainable economy does not necessarily have to be a no-growth economy."

I agreed with Goodall about the significance of economy-wide dematerialization, especially because the United Kingdom and United States were the leading economies of the Industrial Era—a period that, as we've seen, was defined by an unprecedented and extraordinary rise in the use of natural resources and other exploita-tions of the environment. If those two countries could reverse course and achieve substantial dematerialization, it would be a fascinating and hopeful development.

It would also be surprising because it would mean that something fundamental about the mainstream understanding of how growth works would be incorrect. Most of us carry around an implicit or explicit view of growth that combines the ideas of Alfred Marshall and William Jevons. We humans always want to consume more, according to this view, and will use more resources year after year to satisfy these wants. And technologies that allow us to make more efficient use of resources will *not* let us conserve resources because we'll just use the technologies to let us consume even more—so much more that overall resource use will continue to rise. This was the clear pattern from the time of Marshall and Jevons right through to Earth Day. What could possibly have caused it to change?

I thought this was a great question, so I decided to join Ausubel, Goodall, and others in investigating dematerialization. And if absolute dematerialization turned out to be a real and durable phenomenon, I wanted to identify its causes, discuss its implications, make testable predictions about its future, and suggest interventions—changes that individuals, communities, and governments can make—that would help accelerate and spread it.

The Great Reversal

Fortunately for anyone interested in dematerialization, a lot of high-quality evidence exists about resource consumption over time in America. Much of it comes from the US Geological Survey, a federal agency formed in 1879 and tasked by Congress with "classification of the public lands, and examination of the geological structure, mineral resources, and products of the national domain."

That "examination of . . . mineral resources" is a boon to anyone interested in dematerialization, because since the start of the twentieth century the USGS has been collecting data on the use of the most economically important minerals in America. Of particular interest is the survey's yearly estimate of "apparent consumption" of each mineral.

This consumption takes into account not only domestic production of the resource but also imports and exports. For example, to calculate America's total apparent consumption of copper in 2015, the USGS would take the amount of copper produced in the country that year, add total imports of copper, and subtract total copper exports.*

The Survey's data tell a fascinating story. To understand it, let's start with metals, one of the most obviously important materials for any economy. Here's total annual consumption from 1900 to 2015 of the five most important metals in the United States.[†] A reminder: This is not annual consumption per American. This is annual consumption by *all* Americans—the total tonnage used year by year of these metals.

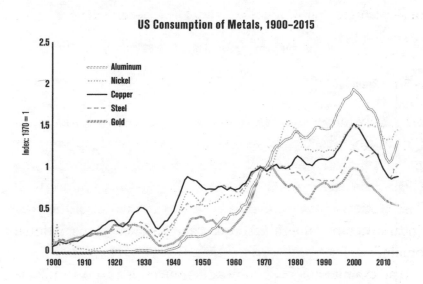

US Consumption of Metals, 1900–2015

---

* The USGS does *not* track imports or exports of resources contained within finished goods. So the copper found in computers and smartphones imported into America in 2015 is not included in the apparent consumption total for that year. Even if all this copper and other such resources could be tracked, they would not change the overall conclusions about dematerialization. Net imports of resource-heavy finished products are only a small part—less than 4 percent—of the overall US economy.

† The "most important" metals are defined as those on which the United States spent the most money between 2000 and 2015.

All of these metals are "post-peak" in America, meaning that the country hit its maximum consumption of each of them some years ago and has seen generally declining use since then. The magnitude of the dematerialization is large. In 2015 (the most recent year for which USGS data are available) total American use of steel was down more than 15 percent from its high point in 2000. Aluminum consumption was down more than 32 percent and copper 40 percent from their peaks.

This dematerialization becomes even more impressive when consumption of resources in the United States is compared to the country's economic growth. So here's the same graph again with one more line added to it—US real GDP:

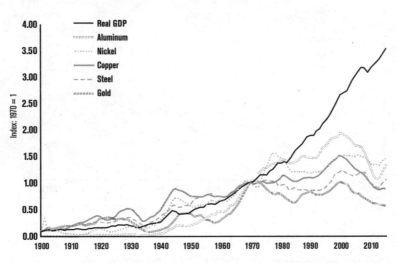

US GDP and Consumption of Metals, 1900–2015

This graph clearly shows that a huge decoupling has taken place. Throughout the twentieth century up to the time of Earth Day, consumption of metals in America grew just about in lockstep with the overall economy. In the years since Earth Day, the economy has continued to grow pretty steadily, but consumption of metals has reversed course and is now decreasing. We're now getting more "economy" from less metal year after year. We'll see a similar great reversal in the use of many other resources.

America is an agricultural powerhouse—the world's largest producer of both soybeans and corn, and fourth in wheat. Fertilizer is, as we've seen, essential for growing crops. So here's the country's total consumption over time of fertilizer, water, and cropland. And instead of GDP, this graph charts total US crop tonnage.

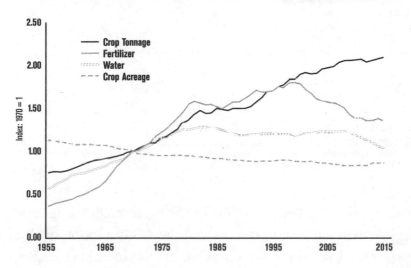

US Crop Tonnage and Consumption of Agricultural Inputs, 1955–2015

Here again, output (crop tonnage) used to be tightly linked to inputs (water and fertilizer). But then that relationship changed, and we're now getting more from less. Fertilizer use is down almost 25 percent from its 1999 peak, and by 2014 total water used for irrigation had decreased by more than 22 percent from its maximum in 1984. Total cropland has also fallen, to levels rivaling the lowest points of the previous century.

Building structures and infrastructure requires a lot of resources, so let's look at total consumption, according to the USGS, of the most important building materials. Let's also include data on timber use from the US Department of Agriculture and throw in paper for good measure because it, like timber, is a forest product.

US GDP and Consumption of Building and Wood Products, 1900–2015

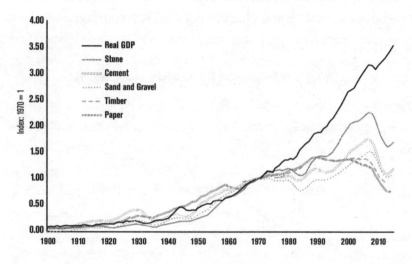

Here I see two different stories. The first is about building materials—cement, sand and gravel, and stone. Consumption of all of these peaked in 2007 and has dropped sharply since. But the sharp drop-off is surely because of the Great Recession, which hit the construction industries particularly hard. As construction recovers, we may find that we are not post-peak in these materials. But I predict that we're forever post-peak in our use of both wood and paper. Total timber use is down by a third, and paper by almost half, since their 1990 high points.

Are these graphs representative of what's been going on in the American economy as a whole? They are. Of the seventy-two resources tracked by the USGS, from aluminum and antimony through vermiculite and zinc, only six are not yet post-peak.* Of these, we spend by far the most on gemstones. We Americans apparently have a bottomless thirst for bling. If shiny ornamental stones are excluded from the analysis, then more than 90 percent of total 2015 resource spending in America was on post-peak materials.

American consumption of plastics, which is not tracked by the USGS, is an exception to the overall trend of dematerialization. Outside of recessions, the United States continues to use more plastic year after year in the form of trash bags, water bottles, food packaging, toys, outdoor furniture, and countless other products. But in recent years, there has been an important slowdown.

According to the Plastics Industry Trade Association, between 1970 and the start of the Great Recession in 2007 American plastic use grew at a rate of about 5.2 percent per year. This was more than 60 percent faster than the country's GDP grew over the same period. But a very different pattern has emerged in the years since the recession ended. The growth in plastic consumption has slowed down greatly, to less than 2.0 percent per year between 2009 and 2015. This is almost 14 percent slower than GDP growth over the same period. So while America is not yet post-peak in its use of plastic, it's quickly closing in on this milestone.

Finally, let's look at total energy consumption combined with greenhouse gas emissions, which are the most harmful side effect of generating energy from fossil fuels.†

* The six resources America is still using more of year after year are diatomite (fossilized algae skeletons) and industrial garnet (both of which are used as abrasives and filters), gemstones, salt, silver, and vanadium (a metal alloyed with steel to make everything from cutting tools to nuclear reactors).

† The "CO2 Emissions" on this graph are those calculated by the Global Carbon Project. They take into account the carbon from products that are produced outside the United States (in China and other countries), but consumed by Americans.

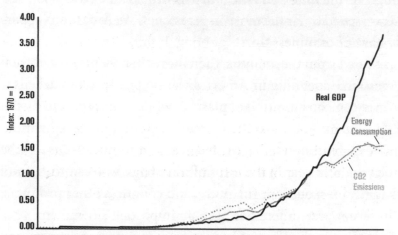

US Real GDP and Total Energy Consumption, 1800–2017

I was surprised to learn that total American energy use in 2017 was down almost 2 percent from its 2008 peak, especially since our economy grew by more than 15 percent between those two years. I had walked around with the unexamined assumption that growing economies must consume more energy year after year. This turns out not to be the case anymore, and it's a profound change. As we saw in the last chapter, energy use went up in lockstep with economic growth in America for more than a century and a half, from 1800 to 1970. Then growth in energy use slowed down, and then it turned negative—even as the economy kept growing. Over the last decade, we've gotten more economic output from less energy.

Greenhouse gas emissions have gone down even more quickly than has total energy use. This is largely because we have in recent years been using less coal and more natural gas to generate electricity (a switch we'll examine in chapter 7), and natural gas produces 50–60 percent less carbon per kilowatt hour than coal does.

The conclusion from this set of graphs is clear: a great reversal of our Industrial Age habits is taking place. The American economy is now experiencing broad and often deep absolute dematerialization. And is the entire world dematerializing? It's a hard question to answer definitively because there's no equivalent of the detailed and comprehensive USGS data for countries other than America. There is evidence, though, that other advanced industrialized nations are also now getting more from less. As we saw earlier in this chapter, Chris Goodall found that the United Kingdom is now past "peak stuff." And data from the Eurostat agency show that countries including Germany, France, and Italy have generally seen flat or declining total consumption of metals, chemicals, and fertilizer in recent years.

Developing countries, especially fast-growing ones such as India and China, are probably not yet dematerializing. But I predict that they will start getting more from less of at least some resources in the not-too-distant future. In the chapters ahead I'll explain why I believe this, and show how and why large-scale dematerialization has already taken place in America and other rich countries. First, though, let's return to the playbook for saving the planet that was developed around the time of the first Earth Day in 1970 and see how well it's been followed since then.

CHAPTER 6

CRIB Notes

*There is always a well-known solution to every human problem—
neat, plausible, and wrong.*

—H. L. Mencken,
"The Divine Afflatus," 1917

What's behind the broad and deep dematerialization of the American economy? Why are we now post-peak in our consumption of so many resources? In the next chapters I'll present my explanation of the causes of dematerialization. First, though, I want to give a short explanation of what the causes are *not*. In particular, I want to show that the CRIB strategies born around Earth Day and promoted since then for reducing our planetary footprint—consume less, recycle, impose limits, and go back to the land—have *not* been important contributors to the dematerialization we've seen.

Since Earth Day, we have demonstrably not consumed much less or gone back to the land in large numbers. We have recycled a lot, but this fact is irrelevant because recycling is a separate phenomenon from dematerialization. Much more relevant than recycling are the limits we've imposed in a couple of areas. The history of these limits is instructive because it helps us separate great ideas (limits on pollution and hunting animals) from truly terrible ones (limits on family size).

87

All, Consuming

The *C* part of the CRIB strategy—a plea for us to consume less for the planet's sake—has largely fallen on deaf ears. To see this, let's look at change in the real GDP of the United States. It grew by an average of 3.2 percent per year between the end of World War II and Earth Day. From 1971 to 2017, it grew by an annual average of 2.8 percent. Population growth also slowed down after the postwar baby boom, but it remained positive. America's population increased by an average of 1.5 percent a year from 1946 to 1970, and by 1 percent annually from 1971 to 2016. So while we have slowed down some, we certainly haven't come close to embracing degrowth in our population or consumption.

But the American economy *has* changed significantly since Earth Day and has become relatively less oriented around making and building things. Services, ranging from haircuts to insurance policies to concerts, now make up a much larger share of the economy than they did in 1970. US personal consumption of services has risen from 30 percent of GDP in 1970 to 47 percent in 2017. So, has the decline in resource use come about because we don't make or consume as many products as we used to?

No. While it's true that products have been declining in relative terms (in other words, as a percentage of total GDP) compared to services, our total consumption of products has still been increasing in absolute terms. So has our industrial production—the total amount of things made in America. What's more, the United States has not recently shifted away from "heavy" manufacturing. We still make lots of vehicles, machinery, and other big-ticket items, just as we used to.

But we don't make them the same way we used to. We now make them using fewer resources. To see this, let's add a line showing

US industrial production to our graph from the previous chapter of GDP and total metal consumption. This updated chart makes clear that the country hasn't stopped producing things. Instead, America's manufacturers have learned to produce more things from less metal.

US GDP, Industrial Production, and Consumption of Metals, 1900–2015

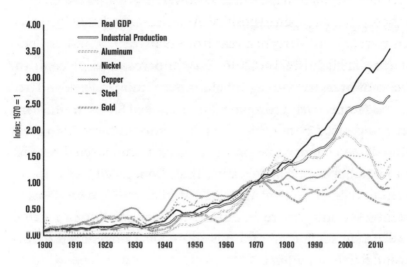

So to summarize, growth of consumption has in some cases slowed down in recent years. But growth in resource use has done much more than slow down—it has reversed course and is now generally negative. We have not as a society embraced degrowth. Instead, we've done something far stranger and more profound: we've decoupled growth—in consumption, prosperity, and our economy—from resource use.

Early in the Industrial Era, the French diplomat Alexis de Tocqueville published his 1835 book, *Democracy in America*. One of the first major investigations into the character of the then-young country, it remains one of the best.* De Tocqueville observed almost two centuries ago that the people of the United States liked their things: "In America, the passion for material well-being . . . is general. . . . Minds are universally preoccupied with meeting the body's every need and attending to life's little comforts." What's new is that providing for our needs and comforts now requires fewer materials, not more.

Recycling: Big, and Beside the Point

Recycling is big business: 47 percent, 33 percent, 68 percent, and 49 percent of all the tonnage of aluminum, copper, lead, and iron and steel (respectively) consumed in the United States in 2015 came from scrap metal rather than ore taken from the earth. Similarly, almost 65 percent of paper products came from recycled newspapers, pizza boxes, and so on rather than from felled trees.

Yet recycling is irrelevant for dematerialization. Why? Because recycling is about where resource-producing factories get their *inputs*, while dematerialization is about what's happened to total demand for their *outputs*.

Paper mills, for example, get their raw material from two main sources: recycling centers and forests. American consumption of output from all paper mills combined has been declining since 1990, the year of peak paper in the United States. This decline is purely a matter of how much total demand there is for paper; it has no direct relationship to the amount of recycling taking place.

But is there any indirect relationship? How much would our total consumption of resources such as paper or steel change without recycling? It's impossible to answer with certainty, but my intuition

---

* An unwritten law says that "serious" books about America must include a de Tocqueville quote. I've included two.

is that if recycling didn't exist, our total consumption of resources such as aluminum, copper, iron, and steel would be declining even more quickly.

This seems counterintuitive; the conclusion is supported by a simple chain of reasoning. Recycling metals makes economic sense exactly because it's cheaper to melt down and reuse scrap than it is to dig out and process ore. Without this scrap, a ton of metal would probably cost more, all other things being equal. And as a general rule, we use less of a thing when it costs more.

So it seems most likely to me that we'd use less metal overall in a hypothetical zero-recycling economy than we do in our actual enthusiastic-about-scrap-metal-recycling economy. This does *not* mean that I think metal recycling is bad. I think it's great, since it gives us cheaper metal products and reduces total greenhouse gas emissions (since it takes much less energy to obtain metal from scrap than from ore). But recycling, whatever its merits, is not part of the dematerialization story. It's a different story.

Back to the Land Is Bad for the Land

The back-to-the-land movement is a fascinating chapter in the history of American environmentalism, but a largely insignificant one. There were simply never enough homesteaders and others who turned away from modern, technologically sophisticated life to make much of a difference. Which is a good thing for the environment.

As Jeffrey Jacob documents in his book *New Pioneers*, the back-to-the-land movement in the United States began in the mid-1960s and continued into the next decade. According to one estimate, as many as 1 million North American back-to-the-landers were living on small farms by the end of the 1970s. This, though, was a weak current against the strong tide of urban growth; the number of American city dwellers increased by more than 17 million between

1970 and 1980. Going back to the land might have been widely discussed, but it was comparatively rarely practiced.

We should be thankful for this because homesteading is not great for the environment, for two reasons. First, small-scale farming is less efficient in its use of resources than massive, industrialized, mechanized agriculture. To get the same harvest, homesteaders use more land, water, and fertilizer than do "factory farmers." Farms of less than one hundred acres, for example, grow 15 percent less corn per acre than farms with more than a thousand acres. And bigger farms get better faster. Between 1982 and 2012 farms under one hundred acres grew their total factor productivity by 15 percent, whereas farms over a thousand acres grew theirs by 51 percent. So more homesteaders would have meant more land under cultivation, more water and fertilizer used, and so on.

Second, rural life is less environmentally friendly than urban or suburban dwelling. City folk live in high-density, energy-efficient apartments and condos, travel only short distances for work and errands, and frequently use public transportation. None of these things is true of country living. As economist Edward Glaeser summarizes, "If you want to be good to the environment, stay away from it. Move to high-rise apartments surrounded by plenty of concrete. . . . Living in the country is not the right way to care for the Earth. The best thing that we can do for the planet is build more skyscrapers."

And if homesteaders decide not only to ignore Glaeser's advice but also to leave modernity further behind and heat their homes with coal or wood, they do still more environmental harm. Coal home furnaces create lots of atmospheric pollution, much more than comes from other kinds of fuel. Poland, for example, today has 80 percent of all homes in Europe that burn coal, and thirty-three of the Continent's fifty most polluted cities. And burning wood means chopping down trees. A lot of them. It's almost certainly the case that the English turned to coal for home heating in the middle of the sixteenth century because they'd cut down such a huge percentage of their trees that the price of wood skyrocketed.

So if we care about the environment, we should probably be glad that the back-to-the-land movement stalled out, and that industrial-scale, high-yield agriculture has become the norm. A comprehensive review published in *Nature Sustainability* in 2018 concluded, "The data . . . do not suggest that environmental costs are generally larger for [high-yield] farming systems. . . . If anything, positive associations—in which high-yield, land-efficient systems also have lower costs in other dimensions—appear more common."

Imposing Limits: The Worst Idea, and the Best One

Of the four elements of the CRIB strategy, the drive to impose limits has by far the most checkered history. It yielded both the most harmful strategies, and the most helpful ones.

The Population Implosion

In 1979 the government of the People's Republic of China announced its new family planning policy, which soon became known as the one-child policy. It was enacted despite the steady decline in the country's birth rate throughout the 1970s. But after reading *Limits to Growth*, *A Blueprint for Survival*, and other books limning the looming dangers of unchecked population expansion, the missile scientist Song Jian came to believe that even faster birth rate reductions were required. He became the architect of the new policy, the main effect of which was to limit ethnic Han Chinese families to a single child. Exceptions to this restriction included giving some couples the right to a second child if their first was a girl, but the one-child policy soon became a central fact of Chinese family life.

It is hard to see it in a positive light. After the policy was officially abandoned in late 2015, journalist Barbara Demick wrote its unflattering obituary: "Family planning became a powerful bureaucracy, with officials who terrorized parents. They beat and burned down the houses of people who violated the family-planning limits. They snatched over-quota baby girls from the arms of their mothers and gave them to orphanages, which in turn put them up for adoption, earning a three-thousand-dollar 'donation' for each baby." The Chinese government maintains that approximately 400 million births were prevented by the one-child policy, but this is probably a large overestimate. As the economist Amartya Sen points out, "The additional contribution of coercion to reducing fertility in China is by no means clear, since compulsion was superimposed on a society that was already reducing its birth rate."

In their 2013 essay "How Will History Judge China's One-Child Policy?" the demographers Wang Feng, Yong Cai, and Baochang Gu compared the policy unfavorably to two of their country's great twentieth-century convulsions: the Cultural Revolution and the Great Leap Forward. They wrote, "While those grave mistakes both cost tens of millions of lives, the harms done were relatively short-lived and were corrected quickly afterward. The one-child policy, in contrast, will surpass them in impact by its role in creating a society with a seriously undermined family and kin structure, and a whole generation of future elderly and their children whose well-being will be seriously jeopardized." History, in short, will judge this government-imposed limit on family size harshly.*

---

* Yet this example of large-scale and largely unnecessary state-imposed coercion, entailing countless forced abortions, sterilizations, and other brutalities against women, retains some supporters, at least in the West. When China announced the formal end of the one-child policy in late 2015, Paul Ehrlich responded with a tweet: "China to End One-Child Policy, Allowing Families Two Children . . . GIBBERING INSANITY—THE GROWTH-FOREVER GANG."

Rational Restrictions

Imposing limits on family size is a terrible idea for reasons both practical and moral. But it's an excellent idea to impose limits on pollution, and on hunting some animals and selling products that come from their bodies. Such restrictions have yielded the great triumphs of the conservation and environmental movements in America and other countries.

In 1970, the same year as the original Earth Day festival, the United States established the federal Environmental Protection Agency and made major amendments to 1963's Clean Air Act. This was the start of a cascade of laws and regulations aimed at reducing pollution and other environmental harms. These have worked amazingly well. For example, atmospheric levels of sulfur dioxide in the United States have dropped to levels not seen since the first years of the twentieth century, and other kinds of air pollution have also dropped sharply. From 1980 to 2015, total emissions of six principal air pollutants decreased by 65 percent.

As lead was banned from paint and gasoline, the concentration of that element in the blood of young children dropped by more than 80 percent between 1976 and 1999. Because lead retards brain development during youth, these declines are tremendously important. According to one study, American children in 1999 had IQs that were on average 2.2 to 4.7 points higher than they would have been had lead concentrations remained at their 1970 levels. More work certainly remains, but thanks to the limits imposed on pollutants, America's soil, air, and water are all much cleaner than they were on Earth Day.

The conservationists who grew concerned in the early years of the twentieth century about what hunting was doing to the populations of many animals were the predecessors of Earth Day's environmentalists. Conservationists were spurred to action by the

shocking extinction of the passenger pigeon. That such an abundant bird could be eradicated stunned many and spurred new
laws restricting trade in animal products. The first of these was the
Lacey Act, passed by Congress in 1900 and named for John Lacey,
a Republican representative from Iowa. As he said during debate
on the bill, "The wild pigeon, formerly in flocks of millions, has
entirely disappeared from the face of the earth. We have given an
awful exhibition of slaughter and destruction, which may serve
as a warning to all mankind. Let us now give an example of wise
conservation of what remains of the gifts of nature."

The Lacey Act and its successors imposed three kinds of limits
on taking and consuming animals. First, hunting of some animals
was fully banned. Protected species include the sea otter, which
was protected by a 1911 international moratorium; the snowy egret,
which was ruthlessly hunted for its gorgeous plumes until passage
of the Weeks-McLean Law Act in 1913; and dolphins and manatees,
which were sheltered by 1972's Marine Mammal Protection Act.

Second, many limits have been imposed on when and where
animals can be hunted. Sport and food hunting are illegal in most
national parks, for example, and duck, bear, deer, and many other
animals have well-defined hunting seasons. Third, bans have been
imposed on the commercial trade in many animal products. The
most sweeping of these is probably the nationwide ban on the sale
of hunted meat. You may see venison or bison meat at a butcher's
counter or on a menu in America, but it always comes from a
ranch, not a hunt.

These imposed limits have brought many iconic American animals back from the brink of extinction. North America now has
more than half a million bison, for example, and over three thousand
sea otters live off the coast of Northern California. Some previously
threatened animals have come back so well that they're now widely
considered pests. People in many American neighborhoods today

feel that there are too many white-tailed deer, Canada geese, and beaver.

The story of dematerialization is not the story of following the CRIB strategies. Except for the excellent idea of imposing limits on polluting and pursuing animals, these strategies were ignored (we didn't embrace degrowth and stop consuming), abandoned (we stopping going back to the land), irrelevant (dematerialization has nothing to do with recycling), or deeply misguided (China's attempt to limit family size was a huge mistake). So how did we finally start getting more from less? How did we become post-peak in our use of so many resources? The next three chapters will take up this critical question.

CHAPTER 7

What Causes Dematerialization?
Markets and Marvels

*The triumph of the industrial arts will advance the cause of
civilization more rapidly than its warmest advocates could have
hoped.*

—Charles Babbage, *The Exposition of 1851;
or, Views of the Industry, the Science, and
the Government of England*, 1851

If CRIB strategies aren't responsible for the large-scale dematerialization of the American economy that has taken place since Earth Day, then what *is*? How have we got more from less? I believe that four main forces are responsible, and that it's helpful to think of them as two pairs. In this chapter we'll look at the first pair, then take up the second in chapter 9.

Capitalism and technological progress are the first pair of forces driving dematerialization. This statement will come as a surprise to many, and for good reason. After all, it's exactly this combination that caused us to massively increase our resource consumption throughout the Industrial Era. As we saw in chapter 3, the ideas of William Jevons and Alfred Marshall point to the distressing conclusion that capitalism and tech progress always lead to more from more: more economic growth, but also more resource consumption.

So what changed? How are capitalism and tech progress now getting us more from *less*? To get answers to these important questions, let's start by looking at a few recent examples of dematerialization.

Fertile Farms

America has long been an agricultural juggernaut. In 1982, after more than a decade of steady expansion due in part to rising grain prices, total cropland in the country stood at approximately 380 million acres. Over the next ten years, however, almost all of this increase was reversed. So much acreage was abandoned by farmers and given back to nature that cropland in 1992 was almost back to where it had been almost twenty-five years before. This decline had several causes, including falling grain prices, a severe recession, over-indebted farmers, and increased international competition.

A final factor, though, was the ability to get ever-more corn, wheat, soybeans, and other crops from the same acre of land, pound of fertilizer and pesticide, and gallon of water. The material productivity of agriculture in the United States has improved dramatically in recent decades, as we saw in chapter 5. Between 1982 and 2015 over 45 million acres—an amount of cropland equal in size to the state of Washington—was returned to nature. Over the same time potassium, phosphate, and nitrogen (the three main fertilizers) all saw declines in absolute use. Meanwhile, the total tonnage of crops produced in the country increased by more than 35 percent.

As impressive as this is, it's dwarfed by the productivity improvements of American dairy cows. In 1950 we got 117 billion pounds of milk from 22 million cows. In 2015 we got 209 billion pounds from just 9 million animals. The average milk cow's productivity thus improved by over 330 percent during that time.

Thin Cans

Tin cans are actually made of steel coated with a thin layer of tin to improve corrosion resistance. They've been used since the nineteenth century to store food. Starting in the 1930s, they began also to be used to hold beer and soft drinks.*

In 1959 Coors pioneered beer cans made of aluminum, which is much lighter and more corrosion resistant than steel. Royal Crown Cola followed suit for soda five years later. As Vaclav Smil relates, "A decade later steel cans were on the way out, and none of them have been used for beer since 1994 and for soft drinks since 1996. . . . At 85 g the first aluminum cans were surprisingly heavy; by 1972 the weight of a two-piece can dropped to just below 21 g, by 1988 it was less than 16 g, a decade later it averaged 13.6 g, and by 2011 it was reduced to 12.75 g."

Manufacturers accomplished these reductions by making aluminum cans' walls thinner, and by making the sides and bottom from a single sheet of metal so that only one comparatively heavy seam was needed (to join the top to the rest of the can). Smil points out that if all beverage cans used in 2010 weighed what they did in 1980, they would have required an extra 580,000 tons of aluminum. And aluminum cans kept getting lighter. In 2012 Ball packaging introduced into the European market a 330 ml can that held 7.5 percent less than the US standard, yet at 9.5 g weighed 25 percent less.

Gone Gizmos

In 2014 Steve Cichon, a "writer, historian, and retired radio newsman in Buffalo, NY," paid $3 for a large stack of front sections of the *Buffalo*

---

* The first versions didn't include any built-in way to open the container, so anyone seeking liquid refreshment needed a can opener.

News newspaper from the early months of 1991. On the back page of the Saturday, February 16, issue was an ad from the electronics retailer Radio Shack. Cichon noticed something striking about the ad: "There are 15 electronic gimzo type items on this page. . . . 13 of the 15 you now always have in your pocket."

The "gizmo type items" that had vanished into the iPhone Cichon kept in his pocket included a calculator, camcorder, clock radio, mobile telephone, and tape recorder. While the ad didn't include a compass, camera, barometer, altimeter, accelerometer, or GPS device, these, too, have vanished into the iPhone and other smartphones, as have countless atlases and compact discs.

The success of the iPhone was almost totally unanticipated. A November 2007 cover story in *Forbes* magazine touted that the Finnish mobile phone maker Nokia had over a billion customers around the world and asked, "Can anyone catch the cell phone king?"

Yes. Apple sold more than a billion iPhones within a decade of its June 2007 launch and became the most valuable publicly traded company in history. Nokia, meanwhile, sold its mobile phone business to Microsoft in 2013 for $7.2 billion to get "more combined muscle to truly break through with consumers," as the Finnish company's CEO Stephen Elop said at the time of the deal.

It didn't work. Microsoft sold what remained of Nokia's mobile phone business and brand to a subsidiary of the Taiwanese electronics manufacturer Foxconn for $350 million in May of 2016. Radio Shack filed for bankruptcy in 2015, and again in 2017.

From Peak Oil to . . . Peak Oil

In 2007 US coal consumption reached a new high of 1,128 million short tons, over 90 percent of which was burned to generate electricity. Total coal use had increased by more than 35 percent since

1990, and the US Energy Information Administration (the official energy statisticians of the US government) forecast further growth of up to 65 percent by 2030.

Also in 2007 the US Government Accountability Office (GAO), a federal agency known as "the congressional watchdog," published a report with an admirably explanatory title: "Crude Oil: Uncertainty about Future Oil Supply Makes It Important to Develop a Strategy for Addressing a Peak and Decline in Oil Production." It took seriously the idea of "peak oil," a phrase coined in 1956 by M. King Hubbert, a geologist working for Shell Oil. As originally conceived, peak oil referred to the maximum amount of oil that we could annually produce for all of humanity's needs.

The first oil wells pumped out the crude oil that was closest to the earth's surface or otherwise easiest to access. As those wells dried up, we had to drill deeper ones, both on land and at sea. As the world's economies kept growing, so did total demand for oil, which kept getting harder and harder to obtain. *Peak oil* captured the idea that despite our best efforts and ample incentive, we would come to a time after which we would only be able to extract less and less oil year after year from the earth. Most of the estimates summarized in the GAO report found that peak oil would occur no later than 2040.

The report did not mention fracking, which in retrospect looks like a serious omission. *Fracking* is short for "hydraulic fracturing" and is a means of obtaining oil and natural gas from rock formations lying deep underground. It uses a high-pressure fluid to cause fractures in the rock, through which oil and gas can flow and be extracted.

The United States and other countries have long been known to have huge reserves of hydrocarbons in deep rock formations, which are often called shales. Companies had been experimenting with fracking to get at them since the middle of the twentieth century, but had made little progress. In 2000 fracking accounted for just 2 percent of US oil production.

That figure began to increase quickly right around the time of the GAO report. Not because of any single breakthrough, but instead because the suite of tools and techniques needed for profitable fracking had all improved enough. A gusher of shale oil and gas ensued.

Thanks to fracking, US crude oil production almost doubled between 2007 and 2017, when it approached the benchmark of 10 million barrels per day. By September of 2018 America had surpassed Saudi Arabia to become the world's largest producer of oil. American natural gas production, which had been essentially flat since the mid-1970s, jumped by nearly 43 percent between 2007 and 2017.

As a result of the fracking boom the United States has experienced peak coal rather than peak oil. And the peak in coal is not in total annual supply, but instead in demand. Fracking made natural gas cheap enough that it became preferred over coal for much electricity generation. By 2017 total US coal consumption was down 36 percent from its 2007 high point.

The phrase *peak oil* is still around, but, as is the case with coal, it usually no longer refers to supply. As a 2017 *Bloomberg* headline put it, "Remember Peak Oil? Demand May Top Out Before Supply Does." Even though the extra supply from fracking has helped push down oil and gas prices, many observers now believe that energy from other sources—the sun, wind, and the nuclei of uranium atoms—is getting cheaper faster and becoming much more widely available. So much so that, as a 2018 article in *Fortune* about the future of oil hypothesized, "This wouldn't be just another oil-price cycle, a familiar roller coaster in which every down is followed by an up. It would be the start of a decades-long decline of the Oil Age itself—an uncharted world in which . . . oil prices might be 'lower forever.'" Analysts at Shell, the company from which the phrase *peak oil* originated, now estimate that global peak oil demand might come as soon as 2028.

Taking Stock of Rolling Stock

My friend Bo Cutter started his career in 1968 working for Northwest Industries, a conglomerate that owned the Chicago and North Western Railway. One of his first assignments was to help a team tasked with solving a problem that sounds odd to modern ears: figuring out where CNW's railcars were.

These cars are massive metal assemblies, each weighing thirty tons or more. In the late 1960s CNW owned thousands of them, representing a huge commitment of both material and money. Across the railroad industry, the rule of thumb then was that about 5 percent of a company's railcars moved on any given day. This was not because the other 95 percent needed to rest. It was because their owners didn't know where they were.

CNW owned thousands of miles of track in places as far from Chicago as North Dakota and Wyoming. Its *rolling stock* (as locomotives and railcars are called) could also travel outside the company's network on tracks owned by other railroads. So these assets could be almost anywhere in the country.

When the railcars weren't moving, they sat in freight yards. At the time Cutter started his job, freight yards didn't keep up-to-date records of the idle rolling stock they contained because, in the days before widespread digital computers, sensors, and networks, there was no way to cost-effectively know or communicate the location of each car. So it was impossible for CNW or any other railroad to systematically track its most important inventory, even though doing so would be hugely beneficial to the company's bottom line. For example, Cutter's team knew that if they could increase the percentage of cars moving each day from 5 percent to 10 percent, they would need only half as many of them. Even a single percentage point increase in freight-car use would yield major financial benefits.

When Cutter started his assignment, CNW and all other railroads employed spotters, who visited yards and watched trains pass, then telegraphed their findings to the head office. Other railroads passed on similar information to collect the demurrage charges they were owed for each CNW car on their tracks and in their yards. Cutter's team improved on these methods by making them more systematic and efficient. They put in place a better baseline audit of where railcars were, employed more spotters, painted CNW cars differently so they were easier to see, and explored how to make more use of a new tool for businesses: the digital computer.

That tool and its kin are now pervasive in the railroad industry. In the early 1990s, for example, companies started putting radio-frequency identification tags on each piece of rolling stock. These tags would be read by trackside sensors, thus automating the work of spotting. At present over 5 million messages about railcar status and location are generated and sent throughout the American railway system every day, and the country's more than 450 railroads have nearly real-time visibility over all their rolling stock.

The Rare Earth Scare

In September of 2010 the Japanese government took into custody the captain of a Chinese fishing boat that had collided with Japanese patrol vessels near a group of uninhabited islands in the East China Sea claimed by both countries. China responded by imposing an embargo on shipments of rare earth elements (REE) to the Land of the Rising Sun.

Even though Japan relented almost immediately and released the captain, a global panic began. This is because rare earths are "vitamins of chemistry," as USGS scientist Daniel Cordier puts it.

"They help everything perform better, and they have their own unique characteristics, particularly in terms of magnetism, temperature resistance, and resistance to corrosion."

By 2010 China produced well over 90 percent of the world's REE. Its actions in the wake of the maritime incident convinced many that it could and would take unilateral action to control the flow of these important materials, and panicked buying soon followed (along with its close cousin rampant speculation). A bundle of REE that would have sold for less than $10,000 in early 2010 soared to more than $42,000 by April of 2011. In September of that year the US House of Representatives held a hearing called "China's Monopoly on Rare Earths: Implications for US Foreign and Security Policy."

China didn't attain its near monopoly because it possessed anything close to 90 percent of global reserves of REE. In fact, rare earths aren't rare at all (one, cerium, is about as common in the earth's crust as copper). However, they're difficult to extract from ore. Obtaining them requires a great deal of acid and generates tons of salt and crushed rock as by-products. Most other countries didn't want to bear the environmental burden of this heavy processing and so left the market to China.

In the wake of the embargo, this seemed like a bad idea. As Representative Brad Sherman put it during the congressional hearing, "Chinese control over rare earth elements gives them one more argument as to why we should kowtow to China." But there was never much kowtowing. By the time of the hearing, prices for REE were already in free fall.

Why? What happened to the apparently tight Chinese stranglehold over REE? Several factors caused it to ease, including the availability of other supply sources and incomplete maintenance of the embargo. But as public affairs professor Eugene Gholz noted in a 2014 report on the "crisis," many users of REE simply innovated their way out of the problem. "Companies such as Hitachi Metals [and its subsidiary in North Carolina] that make rare earth magnets found ways to make equivalent magnets using smaller amounts of rare earths in the alloys. . . . Meanwhile, some users remembered that they did not need the high performance of specialized rare earth magnets; they were merely using them because, at least until the 2010 episode, they were relatively inexpensive and convenient."

Overall, the companies using REE found many inexpensive and convenient alternatives. By the end of 2017 the same bundle of rare earths that had been trading above $42,000 in 2011 was available for about $1,000.

What's Going On?

There is no shortage of examples of dematerialization. I chose the ones in this chapter because they illustrate a set of fundamental principles at the intersection of business, economics, innovation, and our impact on our planet. They are:

> *We do want more all the time, but not more resources.* Alfred Marshall was right, but William Jevons was wrong. Our wants and desires keep growing, evidently without end, and therefore so do our economies. But our use of the earth's resources does not. We do want more beverage options, but we don't want to keep using more aluminum in drink cans. We want to communicate and compute and listen to music, but we don't want an arsenal of gadgets; we're happy with a single smartphone. As our population increases, we want more food, but we don't have any desire to consume more fertilizer or use more land for crops.
>
> Jevons was correct at the time he wrote that total British demand for coal was increasing even though steam engines were becoming much more efficient. He was right, in other words, that the price elasticity of demand for coal-supplied power was

greater than one in the 1860s. But he was wrong to conclude that this would be permanent. Elasticities of demand can change over time for several reasons, the most fundamental of which is technological change. Coal provides a clear example of this. When fracking made natural gas much cheaper, total demand for coal in the United States went down even though its price decreased.*

With the help of innovation and new technologies, economic growth in America and other rich countries—growth in all of the wants and needs that we spend money on—has become decoupled from resource consumption. This is a recent development and a profound one.

Materials cost money that companies locked in competition would rather not spend. The root of Jevons's mistake is simple and boring: resources cost money. He realized this, of course. What he didn't sufficiently realize was how strong the incentive is for a company in a contested market to reduce its spending on resources (or anything else) and so eke out a bit more profit. After all, a penny saved is a penny earned.

Monopolists can just pass costs on to their customers, but companies with a lot of competitors can't. So American farmers who battle with each other (and increasingly with tough rivals in other countries) are eager to cut their spending on land, water, and fertilizer. Beer and soda companies want to minimize their aluminum purchases. Producers of magnets and high-tech gear run away from REE as soon as prices start to spike. In the United States, the 1980 Staggers Act removed government subsidies for freight-hauling railroads, forcing them into competition and cost

---

* In the decade leading up to 2018, for example, Central Appalachian coal prices declined by more than half.

cutting and making them all the more eager to not have expensive railcars sit idle. Again and again, we see that competition spurs dematerialization.

There are multiple paths to dematerialization. As profit-hungry companies seek to use fewer resources, they can go down four main paths. First, they can simply find ways to use less of a given material. This is what happened as beverage companies and the companies that supply them with cans teamed up to use less aluminum. It's also the story with American farmers, who keep getting bigger harvests while using less land, water, and fertilizer. Magnet makers found ways to use fewer rare earth metals when it looked as if China might cut off their supply.

Second, it often becomes possible to substitute one resource for another. Total US coal consumption started to decrease after 2007 because fracking made natural gas more attractive to electricity generators. If nuclear power becomes more popular in the United States (a topic we'll take up in chapter 15), we could use both less coal *and* less gas and generate our electricity from a small amount of material indeed. A kilogram of uranium-235 fuel contains approximately 2–3 *million* times as much energy as the same mass of coal or oil. According to one estimate, the total amount of energy that humans consume each year could be supplied by just seven thousand tons of uranium fuel.

Third, companies can use fewer molecules overall by making better use of the materials they already own. Improving CNW's railcar utilization from 5 percent to 10 percent would mean that the company could cut its stock of these thirty-ton behemoths in half. Companies that own expensive physical assets tend to be fanatics about getting as much use as possible out of them, for clear and compelling financial reasons. For example, the world's commercial airlines have improved their load factors—essentially the percentage of seats occupied on flights—from 56 percent in 1971 to more than 81 percent in 2018.

Finally, some materials get replaced by nothing at all. When a telephone, camcorder, and tape recorder are separate devices, three total microphones are needed. When they all collapse into a smartphone, only one microphone is necessary. That smartphone also uses no audiotapes, videotapes, compact discs, or camera film. The iPhone and its descendants are among the world champions of dematerialization. They use vastly less metal, plastic, glass, and silicon than did the devices they have replaced and don't need media such as paper, discs, tape, or film.

If we use more renewable energy, we'll be replacing coal, gas, oil, and uranium with photons from the sun (solar power) and the movement of air (wind power) and water (hydroelectric power) on the earth. All three of these types of power are also among dematerialization's champions, since they use up essentially no resources once they're up and running.

I call these four paths to dematerialization *slim, swap, optimize,* and *evaporate*. They're not mutually exclusive. Companies can and do pursue all four at the same time, and all four are going on all the time in ways both obvious and subtle.

Innovation is hard to foresee. Neither the fracking revolution nor the world-changing impact of the iPhone's introduction were well understood in advance. Both continued to be underestimated even after they occurred. The iPhone was introduced in June of 2007, with no shortage of fanfare from Apple and Steve Jobs. Yet several months later the cover of *Forbes* was still asking if anyone could catch Nokia.

Innovation is not steady and predictable like the orbit of the Moon or the accumulation of interest on a certificate of deposit. It's instead inherently jumpy, uneven, and random. It's also combinatorial, as Erik Brynjolfsson and I discussed in our book *The Second Machine Age.* Most new technologies and other innovations, we argued, are combinations or recombinations of preexisting elements.

The iPhone was "just" a cellular telephone plus a bunch of sensors plus a touch screen plus an operating system and population of programs, or apps. All these elements had been around for a while before 2007. It took the vision of Steve Jobs to see what they could become when combined. Fracking was the combination of multiple abilities: to "see" where hydrocarbons were to be found in rock formations deep underground; to pump down pressurized liquid to fracture the rock; to pump up the oil and gas once they were released by the fracturing; and so on. Again, none of these was new. Their effective combination was what changed the world's energy situation.

Erik and I described the set of innovations and technologies available at any time as building blocks that ingenious people could combine and recombine into useful new configurations. These new configurations then serve as more blocks that later innovators can use. Combinatorial innovation is exciting because it's unpredictable. It's not easy to foresee when or where powerful new combinations are going to appear, or who's going to come up with them. But as the number of both building blocks and innovators increases, we should have confidence that more breakthroughs such as fracking and smartphones are ahead. Innovation is highly decentralized and largely uncoordinated, occurring as the result of interactions among complex and interlocking social, technological, and economic systems. So it's going to keep surprising us.

As the Second Machine Age progresses, dematerialization acceler- *ates.* Erik and I coined the phrase *Second Machine Age* to draw a contrast with the Industrial Era, which as we've seen transformed the planet by allowing us to overcome the limitations of muscle power. Our current time of great progress with all things related to computing is allowing us to overcome the limitations of our mental power and is transformative in a different way: it's allowing us to reverse the Industrial Era's bad habit of taking more and more from the earth every year.

Computer-aided design tools help engineers at packaging companies design generations of aluminum cans that keep getting lighter. Fracking took off in part because oil and gas exploration companies learned how to build accurate computer models of the rock formations that lay deep underground—models that predicted where hydrocarbons were to be found.

Smartphones took the place of many separate pieces of gear. Because they serve as GPS devices, they've also led us to print out many fewer maps and so contributed to our current trend of using less paper. It's easy to look at generations of computer paper, from 1960s punch cards to the eleven-by-seventeen-inch fanfold paper of the 1980s, and conclude that the Second Machine Age has caused us to chop down ever more trees. The year of peak paper consumption in the United States, however, was 1990. As our devices have become more capable and interconnected, always on and always with us, we've sharply turned away from paper. Humanity as a whole probably hit peak paper in 2013.

As these examples indicate, computers and their kin help us with all four paths to dematerialization. Hardware, software, and networks let us slim, swap, optimize, and evaporate. I contend that they're the best tools we've ever invented for letting us tread more lightly on our planet.

All of these principles are about the combination of technological progress and capitalism, which are the first of the two pairs of forces causing dematerialization.

Technology: The Human Interface with the Material World

One of my favorite definitions of technology comes from the philosopher Emmanuel Mesthene, who called it "the organization of knowledge for the achievement of practical purposes." Sometimes that knowledge is crystallized into products such as hammers and iPhones, and sometimes it exists as techniques such as those for fracking or precision agriculture.

Like knowledge itself, technologies accumulate. We haven't forgotten about the lever, the plow, or the steam engine in the Second Machine Age, and we haven't had to give them up to use cloud computing or drones. Like innovation itself, technologies are combinatorial; most of them are combinations or recombinations of existing things. This implies that the number of potentially powerful new technologies increases over time because the number of available building blocks does.

These facts help me understand why we didn't start to dematerialize sooner. It could simply be that we didn't have the right technologies, or enough building blocks, to allow large-scale dematerialization. We had technologies that made it feasible and profitable for us to grow by taking more and more from the earth—more and more metals, fuels, water, fertilizers, and so on—but not ones that made it possible to profitably grow while taking less and less. In the Second Machine Age, that has changed.

My other preferred definition of technology comes from the great science fiction author Ursula K. Le Guin, who wrote, "Technology is the active human interface with the material world. Its technology is how a society copes with physical reality: how people get and keep and cook food, how they clothe themselves, what their power sources are (animal? human? water? wind? electricity? other?), what they build with and what they build, their medicine—and so on and on. Perhaps very ethereal people aren't interested in these mundane, bodily matters, but I'm fascinated by them." So am I, because these "mundane matters" have twice reshaped the world—first during the Industrial Era, when technological progress allowed us to prosper by taking more from the planet, and now in the Second Machine Age, when we've finally figured out how to prosper while taking less.

Capitalism: Means of Production

Capitalism and religion are the two subjects that leave the fewest people on the sidelines. People have *very* firmly held opinions on both topics, and few change their minds no matter what evidence and arguments are presented to them. Yet despite this clear history of intransigence, many thinkers and writers have tried to bring others around to their point of view on both topics. Most have failed.

I'm going to join this long sad parade by arguing in favor of capitalism. Before I do that, though, I want to define what I'm talking about. Even more than is the case with *technology*, clear definitions are important with *capitalism* because it's such a triggering word. As the psychologist Jonathan Haidt has pointed out, some hear it as a synonym for *liberation*, others for *exploitation*.

But let me put the dictionary before the thesaurus and offer a definition of what capitalism is before suggesting what it's like. For our purposes, capitalism is a way to come up with goods and services and get them to people. Every society that doesn't want its people to starve or die of exposure has to accomplish this task; capitalism is simply one approach to doing it. The important features of this approach are:

Profit-seeking companies. Under capitalism, most goods and services are produced by for-profit companies rather than nonprofits, the government, or individuals. Companies can be owned by only a few people (such as the partners in a law firm) or a great many (publicly traded companies have shareholders all over the world) and are assumed to last over time; they don't have a predefined end date.

Free market entry and competition. Companies can go after one another's markets and customers; there are few if any protected monopolies. It might not be legal to completely copy a rival's patented product, but it's perfectly legal to try to come up with something better. In economist-speak, markets are *contested*. Similarly, people can take their skills from one market to another; they're not tied to a single geography or job.

Strong property rights and contract enforcement. Patents are a form of *intellectual property*. They can be bought and sold just as other kinds of property—from land to houses to cars—can. Laws and courts ensure that none of these kinds of property can be stolen or destroyed, even by large, powerful entities such as billionaires, giant corporations, or the government. Similarly, if a small company and a big one sign a contract to work together, neither party gets to unilaterally walk away from the agreement without fear of getting sued.

Absence of central planning, control, and price setting. The government does not decide what goods and services are needed by people, or which companies should be allowed to produce them. No central body decides if there is "enough" volume and variety in smartphones, caffeinated beverages, steel girders, and so on. The prices of these and most other goods and services are allowed to vary based on the balance of supply and demand, rather than being set in advance or adjusted by any central authority.

Private ownership of most things. Smartphones, cups of coffee, steel girders, and most other products are owned by the people or companies that bought them. The companies that produced these things are also owned by people. Many shares of Apple, Starbucks, US Steel, and other public companies are held by mutual funds, pension funds, and hedge funds, but all these funds are themselves ultimately owned by people. Most houses, cars, land, gold, Bitcoin, and other assets are also owned by people rather than the government.

Voluntary exchange. The phrase most closely associated with capitalism is *voluntary exchange.* People can't be forced to buy specific products, take a certain job, or move across the country. Companies don't have to sell themselves if they don't want to. They also don't have to make some products and not others, or stay within specific markets. The Waffle House chain doesn't have any of its breakfast restaurants in my state of Massachusetts, but that's not because lawmakers there are keeping it out. The legislature in Boston doesn't have that power.

I want to highlight a couple of things about this definition. First, capitalism is not without oversight. The government has clear roles to play in establishing laws and settling disputes (to say nothing of setting tax rates, controlling the money supply, and doing other things of critical economic importance). As we'll see in the next two chapters, every sane advocate of capitalism also recognizes that while voluntary exchange and free market entry are great, they don't create utopia. Some important "market failures" need to be corrected by government action.

The second thing I want to point out is that *all of today's rich countries are capitalist,* by this definition. This is not to say that all capitalist countries are alike. Denmark, South Korea, and the United

States are very different places. They have dissimilar trade policies, tax systems, social safety nets, industrial structures, and so on. But they all have all of the things listed above; they are all inherently capitalist. Denmark's economy is not planned and controlled out of Copenhagen, people in Korea own their own houses and furniture,* and contracts in America are generally respected and enforced.

Today's poorer countries, in sharp contrast, reliably do *not* have all of the things listed above. Their governments tend to run such things as airlines and telephone networks that are run by private companies in rich countries. It's generally much harder to start a company in less affluent countries, so free market entry and competition are constrained. According to the World Bank, in 2017 it took less than six days to start a business in America, Denmark, Singapore, Australia, and Canada, and seventy days or more in Somalia, Brazil, and Cambodia. The world champion of entrepreneurial sclerosis was Venezuela (a country we'll talk more about in the next chapter), at two hundred and thirty days. In poorer countries, it's also often not clear who owns what. Things that are taken for granted in the rich world, such as unambiguous land registries and clear title to houses and other property, are problematic in many developing countries.

The biggest difference between rich and poor countries might be whether laws are clearly and consistently enforced. Poorer countries don't lack laws; they often have extensive legal codes. What's in short supply is justice for all. Officials are corrupt; the elite get special treatment and rarely lose in court; police, regulators, and inspectors can expect bribes; and contested markets, property rights, and voluntary exchange suffer in countless other ways. It's not that these abuses don't occur in rich countries, but they occur much, much less often.

---

* Unless they rent or borrow them.

I'll make some more points about capitalism in the next chapter. To wrap up this one, I want to emphasize how well technological progress and capitalism work together.

Overcoming the Limits

A great way to see what happens when capitalism and tech progress combine is to look back at 1972's *The Limits to Growth*, which we first came across in chapter 4. It's a fascinating document for two reasons. First, it's one of the most Malthusian books written since Malthus. It's far gloomier than anything Jevons came up with. The team behind *The Limits to Growth* tried to model the future of the exponentially growing world economy and concluded, "We can thus say with some confidence that, under the assumption of no major change in the present system, population and industrial growth will certainly stop within the [twenty-first] century, at the latest. The system . . . collapses because of a resource crisis."

Second, *The Limits to Growth* provided an invaluable service by recording what the known global reserves of important resources were in 1972. "Known global reserves" are the deposits of a resource that can be profitably extracted given the prevailing knowledge and state of technology. The authors of *The Limits to Growth* included the known reserves of many resources to show how inadequate they were in the face of exponential growth of both output and resource consumption. The authors had little reason to suppose in the early 1970s that either kind of growth would stop on its own. As we saw in chapter 4, resource consumption went up in lockstep with overall economic output all throughout the twentieth century up to Earth Day. Few people expected that to change. The team behind *The Limits to Growth* certainly didn't.

The most generous estimate of future resource availability included in *The Limits to Growth* assumed that exponential consumption would continue, and that proven reserves were actually five times greater than commonly assumed. Under these conditions, the team's computer models showed that the planet would run out of gold within twenty-nine years of 1972; silver within forty-two years; copper and petroleum within fifty; and aluminum within fifty-five.

These weren't accurate predictions.

We still have gold and silver, and we still have large reserves of them. In fact, the reserves of both are actually much bigger than in 1972, despite almost half a century of additional consumption. Known global reserves of gold are almost 400 percent larger today than in 1972, and silver reserves are more than 200 percent larger. And it's probably not too early to say that we're not going to run out of copper, aluminum, and petroleum as quickly as estimated in *The Limits to Growth*. Known reserves of all are much larger than they were when the book was published. Known aluminum reserves are almost twenty-five times what they were in the early 1970s.

How could these predictions about resource availability, which were taken seriously when they were released, have been so wrong? Because the *Limits to Growth* team pretty clearly underestimated both dematerialization and the endless search for new reserves. Capitalism and tech progress combine to drive both of these trends—the use of fewer resources and the hunt for more of them—and neither of these two drivers is about to become less powerful. So we'll continue to innovate our way to greater dematerialization while we keep finding more reserves.

The counterintuitive conclusion from this line of reasoning is that resource scarcity isn't something we need to worry about. The earth is finite, so the total quantity of resources such as gold and petroleum is limited. But the earth is also very, very big—big enough to contain all we need of these and other resources, for as long as we'll need them. The image of a thinly supplied Spaceship Earth hurtling through the cosmos with us aboard is compelling, but deeply misleading. Our planet has amply supplied us for our journey. Especially since we're quickly slimming, swapping, optimizing, and evaporating our way to dematerialization.

The Second Enlightenment

Abraham Lincoln, the only US president to hold a patent,* had a deep insight about capitalism. He wrote that the patent system "added the fuel of interest to the fire of genius in the discovery and production of new and useful things." "The fire of genius" is a wonderful label for technological progress. "The fuel of interest" is equally good as a summary of capitalism. They interact in a self-reinforcing and ever-expanding cycle, and they're now creating a dematerializing world.

Innovators come up with new and useful technologies. They then partner with entrepreneurs or become entrepreneurs themselves as James Watt did. A new company is the result. Investors such as steam-engine backer Matthew Boulton often join in to provide the capital needed for growth in its early days. The start-up enters a market and takes on incumbents like the Newcomen steam engine. Customers like the new technology better and are free to choose it. Rivals can't just copy the new technology because it's protected by patents. So they either have to license it or come up with innovations themselves. The start-up grows and prospers and eventually becomes the new incumbent. Its success inspires the next round of innovators, entrepreneurs, and investors, who once again take aim at the incumbent by offering something better to their customers.

Because of free market entry, the next innovators and start-ups can come from anywhere. And because innovation is such a distributed, dynamic, and unpredictable activity, it often comes from an

---

* Lincoln's patent was for a flotation system that lifted riverboats stuck on sandbars.

unexpected place. It's not necessary to plan this process. In fact, it's a terrible idea to try to do so. Any central planner will miss many of the actual innovators or actively try to squelch them to protect the status quo of which the planners themselves are a part.

This cycle of capitalist, technology-rich "creative destruction" was beautifully described in the middle of the twentieth century by the Austrian economist Joseph Schumpeter. But since the late nineteenth century and the work of Alfred Marshall and William Jevons, we've believed that this cycle would cause us to use up more and more of our planet's resources. This was true throughout the Industrial Era, and especially in the years around Earth Day and the birth of the modern environmental movement. Environmentalists' urgent cautions about resource use and planetary depletion were born out of an awareness of how powerfully technological progress and capitalism interacted.

But then, for the reasons described in this chapter, that interaction changed. Tech progress and capitalism continued to reinforce each other, and to cause economies to get bigger and people to become more prosperous. But instead of also causing greater use of natural resources, they instead sparked dematerialization, something truly new under the sun. The fuel of interest in eliminating costs was added to the fire of the computer revolution, and the world began to dematerialize.

The economic historian Joel Mokyr argues that the Industrial Era was made possible by the values of the Enlightenment. This intellectual movement began in the second half of the eighteenth century with many societies in the West embracing what Steven Pinker characterizes as four values: reason, science, humanism, and progress. According to Mokyr, the Enlightenment created a "culture of growth" that let both capitalism and technological progress flourish.

I see an interesting inversion taking place now. If the Enlightenment led to the Industrial Era, then the Second Machine Age has led to a Second Enlightenment—a more literal one. We are now lightening our total consumption and treading more lightly on our planet. In America, the United Kingdom, and other rich countries, we are past "peak stuff" and are now using fewer total resources year after year. We're accomplishing this because of the combination of technological progress and capitalism, which now let us get more from less.

A complete Second Enlightenment requires more. It also requires that we not only use fewer resources but also generate less pollution and take better care of our fellow creatures. As powerful as they are, tech progress and capitalism won't accomplish these goals on their own. To accomplish them, we need another pair of forces. Before we examine them, though, we need to talk about capitalism a bit more because it's so important and so widely misunderstood.

CHAPTER 8

Adam Smith Said That:
A Few Words about Capitalism

The impulse to acquisition, pursuit of gain, of money, of the greatest possible amount of money, has in itself nothing to do with capitalism. This impulse exists and has existed among waiters, physicians, coachmen, artists, prostitutes, dishonest officials, soldiers, nobles, crusaders, gamblers, and beggars. One may say that it has been common to all sorts and conditions of men at all times and in all countries of the earth, wherever the objective possibility of it is or has been given. It should be taught in the kindergarten of cultural history that this naïve idea of capitalism must be given up once and for all.

—Max Weber, *The Protestant Ethic
and the Spirit of Capitalism*, 1905

Capitalism is not popular these days. In a 2016 survey, a majority of Americans between the ages of nineteen and twenty-eight said that they didn't support it; in a follow-up survey, capitalism found majority support only among Americans over fifty. Clearly, many people feel that this system for producing goods and services is no longer working well, or that the flaws it's always had have finally become unignorable.

I believe something very different. I argued in the previous chapter that capitalism is one of the main forces driving the dematerialization of our economies. As we'll see a bit later in this book, I also believe it's a main reason why we're seeing an unprecedented global rise in prosperity, health, and other critical aspects of well-being.

So I should explain myself. To do so, I'm going to enlist the support of the eighteenth-century Scottish economist and political theorist Adam Smith. Why am I reaching so far back? For the same reasons Nobel Prize winner George Stigler did.

In 1977, Stigler published in the normally staid *Journal of Political Economy* his article "The Conference Handbook." It grew out of his frustration at how often discussions at economics conferences kept going over the same topics. So Stigler proposed shortening these repetitious conversations by replacing the sentences heard most often with numbers, thereby saving everyone involved a lot of time. "The Conference Handbook" thus presents his list of the most heard phrases in economics. The first item in the list is "Adam Smith said that."

Stigler's point was twofold: that Smith figured out many things over two centuries ago, and that we keep going over topics he covered, often without adding much (if anything) new. I couldn't agree more. Even though he never used the word *capitalism*, Smith was its first great analyst. The definition I offered in the previous chapter relies heavily on his insights. He recognized both capitalism's great strengths and its weaknesses and discussed both at length.

Half-Right: Current Critiques of Capitalism

A lot of the criticisms of capitalism I come across read as if their authors haven't taken Smith's ideas into account, much less the more than two centuries of intense debate, refinement, and research that they sparked. That's a shame. Keeping Smith's insights in mind lets us see why this system for organizing economic activity works so well at delivering prosperity. It also lets us see where capitalism's fault lines lie and helps us in evaluating arguments against it.

So, with Adam Smith as a guide, let's look at three valid critiques of capitalism, and three invalid ones.

First, the valid criticisms:

Capitalism is selfish. Yes, it absolutely is. But as Smith points out, this is a good thing. One of the most quoted passages from his 1776 masterpiece, *The Wealth of Nations*,* is "It is not from the benevolence of the butcher, the brewer, or the baker that we expect our dinner, but from their regard to their own interest." The profit motive is an extremely powerful incentive for people and companies to create goods and services others will want to buy. Self-interest is not a flaw in capitalism, it's a central feature.

In most societies and religious traditions selfishness is held to be a vice, so the notion that the profit motive is beneficial fights against long traditions and deeply ingrained assumptions. The New Testament, for example, holds that "the love of money is the root of all evil."† This view is persistent. For example, after conducting seven studies of Americans' views of the profit motive, researchers Amit Bhattacharjee, Jason Dana, and Jonathan Baron concluded in 2017, "Even in one of the most market-oriented societies in history, people doubt the contributions of profit-seeking industry to societal progress." Yet nothing works better. As Smith observed, "Nobody but a beggar chooses to depend chiefly upon the benevolence of his fellow-citizens."

Capitalism is amoral. This is also true, and it's a much harder criticism to dismiss than selfishness. "Will somebody buy this?" (or even worse, "Can we convince somebody to buy this?") is one of a producer's most frequently asked questions, and it's bad

---

* The book's full title is *An Inquiry into the Nature and Causes of the Wealth of Nations.*

† King James Version, 1 Timothy 6:10.

for society if it's the only one that gets asked. People will buy
child pornography, the feathers of desperately endangered birds,
pajamas that catch on fire easily, stolen goods, and many other
things that are *malum in se*—bad in and of themselves. Countless other popular goods and services occupy moral gray areas:
such offerings include foods full of sugar, fat, and salt; cigarettes;
powdered infant formula marketed to mothers in regions where
it's unsafe to drink the water; assault rifles; and so on. People will
readily buy these, too.

Capitalism is not going to host the debate about which of these
offerings are to be permitted. That essential debate needs to happen
elsewhere in a society. Smith got right the fundamental principle we
should apply: "The interest of the producer ought to be attended to
only so far as it may be necessary for promoting that of the consumer."
We also need to attend to the interests not only of the producer or
the consumer but also of the people (such as slaves or children)
and the animals that are used in production but don't want to be.

Capitalism is unequal. Without question, it is. As Smith observed,
"Wherever there is great property, there is great inequality." Land,
mineral rights, and shares in a company are all forms of property
under capitalism, and ownership of most of these is far from equal
in most societies. The dominant belief among American economists
in the decades after World War II was that inequality in capitalist
countries would decrease as prosperity spread, but that view is
now shifting. Both current trends and newly available historical
data indicate that high levels of inequality might well be the norm.

In chapters 12 and 13 we'll look more closely at the rise of
inequality and consider its harms. For now, I just want to note
how insightful Smith was about one of inequality's most serious
consequences: a feeling of not belonging and not participating, of
being shut out of larger communities. Smith was right to stress

that this aspect of falling behind is of great concern. As he wrote in his other great work, *The Theory of Moral Sentiments*, "The poor man goes out and comes in unheeded, and when in the midst of a crowd is in the same obscurity as if shut up in his own hovel." In chapter 13 we'll see how harmful this feeling of disconnection can be.

Now here are three invalid critiques of capitalism, each refuted by Smith long ago:

Capitalism is cronyism. Smith knew that competition was essential for capitalism to function well. He also knew that companies don't want real competition because it drives down profits. Another of his most famous observations is "People of the same trade seldom meet together, even for merriment and diversion, but the conversation ends in a conspiracy against the public, or in some contrivance to raise prices." Smith saw that government had a role to play in making sure that competitors don't become cronies—close friends who collude to all get rich together by simultaneously raising prices.

Many of the complaints I hear about our current economic system aren't complaints about capitalism. Instead, they're complaints about perversions of it. Collusion and crony capitalism, as described by Smith in the paragraph above, are dangers. So is corporatism: favors done for large, established companies by the government. Smith also realized the danger of what is now called regulatory capture—where instead of acting in the best interests of the public, regulators or elected officials instead take care of incumbent companies. As he wrote, "The member of parliament who supports every proposal for strengthening [a] monopoly, is sure to acquire not only the reputation of understanding trade, but great popularity and influence with an order of men whose numbers and wealth render them of great importance."

Capitalism is anarchy. No, it's not. Yet another of Smith's most famous observations, taken from a lecture he gave more than twenty years before *The Wealth of Nations* appeared, is that "little else is requisite to carry a state to the highest degree of opulence from the lowest barbarism, but peace, easy taxes, and a tolerable administration of justice." Capitalism will cause great prosperity to blossom, but only in a properly tended garden. Laws and courts are needed to protect the rights, property, and contracts of society's weaker members; violence and the threat of violence can't be tolerated; and taxes are necessary even though they're unwelcome.

Taxation needs to be done carefully (it needs to be "easy") because it can (and often does) distort incentives. But it does need to be done; as the US Supreme Court justice Oliver Wendell Holmes Jr. put it, "Taxes are what we pay for civilized society." We need them to pay not only for armies and courts but also, as Smith realized, for infrastructure that improves both daily life and the economy. He wrote about the government's "duty of erecting and maintaining certain public works and certain public institutions, which it can never be for the interest of any individual, or small number of individuals, to erect and maintain."

Capitalism is oppression. Perhaps the single most unfair, inaccurate, and ignorant critique of capitalism is that it is bad for the workers who help create it. Karl Marx was confident that workers under capitalism would be trampled and impoverished until they threw off their shackles and embraced communism, but as we saw in chapter 2 this is not what happened. Despite its many flaws, the Industrial Era increased the prosperity and quality of life for average people more quickly than ever before. As we'll see later, progress in many important areas has sped up in recent decades as capitalism and tech progress have both spread around the world.

Adam Smith realized that capitalism's greatest virtue was that it improved the lives of not only the elite but also of people born into modest circumstances. He saw much more clearly than Marx or Malthus what the future held as long as capitalism was allowed to operate properly. And throughout his writing, he's concerned with what we might today call social justice. Smith believed deeply that workers deserved a high and rising standard of living. As he wrote in *The Wealth of Nations*, "They who feed, clothe, and lodge the whole body of the people, should have such a share of the produce of their own labor as to be themselves tolerably well fed, clothed, and lodged." He believed, as I do, that capitalism is the best means to accomplish that goal.

Somewhere on the Spectrum

One criticism of capitalism I hear a lot is that it doesn't provide a social safety net for everyone. This is true, but it's like complaining that a ship doesn't fly. And just as a transportation system can have both ships and airplanes, a society can have both all of capitalism's elements and a social safety net. As I said in the previous chapter, all of the rich countries that meet my definition of *capitalist* have welfare systems that include support for the poor and unemployed, subsidized health care for at least some groups, child and elder care, and so on. Advanced capitalist countries have tremendous variations in their social safety nets—Norway's, for example, is very different from America's—but all such countries have one.

Much of the confusion stems from a caricature. *Market fundamentalism* describes the belief that capitalism *alone* is sufficient to ensure well-being of all members of a society, and that social safety nets are wasteful and unnecessary. Or, even worse, that they're counterproductive because they reduce people's incentive to work. The term is associated with the writings of the mid-twentieth-century novelist and political theorist Ayn Rand. The investor and philanthropist George Soros and others have used the term in connection with the policy agendas, initiated around 1980, of Ronald Reagan and Margaret Thatcher.

But while Reagan and Thatcher clearly worked to shrink and change the welfare systems in their countries, they never sought to completely eliminate them. Market fundamentalism is a theoretical condition—a society with capitalism, but without welfare—that doesn't exist in reality. Few people think that it should, outside of a few right-wing pundits in America (as the antitax crusader Grover Norquist said in 2001, "I don't want to abolish government. I simply want to reduce it to the size where I can drag it into the bathroom and drown it in the bathtub").

Market fundamentalism is still a useful concept, though, because it anchors one end of the spectrum of belief about how much a government should rely on capitalism to ensure the well-being of its people. Market fundamentalists believe that capitalism by itself is enough. Social democrats, who occupy the next position on the spectrum, believe that it's not. They believe that government should play an active role in helping out people who are temporarily or permanently left behind by capitalism, and in reducing its inequalities. The more people identify as social democrats, the more they tend to favor high tax rates, more regulation, and larger welfare systems. Scandinavian countries are often held up as the clearest examples of social democracies, while America almost never is, since the safety net in America is smaller and less elaborate than in Sweden or Denmark. However, Sweden, Denmark, and America are all clearly capitalist countries.

The real difference comes when we take the next step along the spectrum, from "social democracy" to "socialism." The similarity in labels is unfortunate, since they're completely different ideas about how to run a country. Socialism rejects just about all the pillars of capitalism. Under socialism, most companies and industries are owned or controlled by the government, and much economic activity—who makes what, who gets what, who works where, what the prices are—is centrally planned. Property rights are fewer because there's less private property; the state owns more of the things that matter. When socialist governments come to power via an election rather than a revolution, the result is "democratic socialism." Which only deepens the confusion around labels.

The far end of the spectrum, past socialism, is communism. Communism, as envisioned by Marx, was a kind of self-organizing, egalitarian global utopia for workers. There would be no inequality, no money, no private property, no companies, no bosses, no governments, and no borders between nations. Marx provided few details on how a planetary communist economy would work—how goods and services would be produced and allocated to people—but he was sure that it would arise. He considered communism a historical inevitability, and socialism a kind of stepping-stone on the way to it.

Market fundamentalism and communism are as different as it's possible to imagine, but they do have one important thing in common: neither has ever existed in the real world. Countries that adopted Marx's ideas never reached full communism; they instead remained at socialism (the full name of the Soviet Union—the Union of Soviet Socialist Republics—acknowledges this). North Korea still has money, private companies are allowed to operate in Cuba, and many sectors of the Chinese economy have a great deal of competition.

Not That We Needed Another One: An Experiment in Socialism

So as regards how capitalistic a country is, all the action seems to be in the middle of the spectrum. The real fault line is right down the center: between social democracy and democratic socialism.

I can't imagine a clearer demonstration of how much it matters whether a word is used as an adjective or a noun. *Social* is fine. *Socialism* is a catastrophe.

I thought the historical record on this point, written from Moscow to Beijing to Havana, was quite clear, and that we didn't need any more demonstrations of socialism's too-numerous-to-list shortcomings. We didn't even need to keep debating whether a socialist economy could work in theory (regardless of what had happened in practice) because the great Austrian British economist Friedrich Hayek laid that issue to rest.

Hayek realized that fluctuating prices for such things as aluminum and wheat are signals about scarcity and abundance. These signals cause people who buy and sell to take action (to slim, swap, optimize, evaporate, and so on). So free-floating prices in capitalist economies do an important double duty: they provide both information and incentives. Prices fixed by a socialist government do neither of those things. Hayek used this insight to shoot down the idea of socialism in 1977: "I've always doubted that the socialists had a leg to stand on intellectually. . . . Once you begin to understand that prices are an instrument of communication and guidance which embody more information than we directly have, the whole idea that you can bring about the same order . . . by simple direction falls to the ground. . . . I think that intellectually there is just nothing left of socialism."

But in some quarters, socialism is cool again. The good news is that even as this is happening, we're getting a detailed look, aided by all the technologies of modern media, at yet another socialist experiment as it unfolds and falls apart. The bad news is how much the people of Venezuela are suffering as they provide this lesson.

Venezuela, South America's richest country as recently as 2001, elected the ardent socialist Hugo Chávez in 1998. He was succeeded after his 2013 death by his vice president, Nicolás Maduro. Both men gained and held on to power via elections rather than military coups or popular revolutions. For twenty years, then, the country has been a clear example of democratic socialism.

Both Chávez and Maduro closely followed the Socialism 101 playbook. They nationalized companies in industries from oil services to fertilizer production to banking to glassmaking. Instead of relying on markets to bring goods and services to the poor, the government established and ran *misiones* that provided meals and groceries. The state also bought food on international markets then sold it internally at subsidized prices (in other words, at a loss). Currency controls were put in place for most businesses, which meant the end of free markets for other moneys such as the US dollar. A set of "fair price" laws set not only prices but also acceptable profit margins and products. And so on.

Chávez and Maduro thus chipped away at or knocked over all the pillars of capitalism within their country. A team of economic researchers could hardly have created a better field experiment on the effects of socialism. However, no ethical team would have tried to run such an experiment because of the damage it would likely cause. Any economist or historian who wasn't a committed Marxist could have predicted at least some of the results of Venezuela's plunge into socialism. However, I think few would have predicted the actual scale of the economic catastrophe and the accompanying human suffering.

Socialism can be slow-acting poison, and the first decade of "Chavism" wasn't too bad (at least in comparison to what came later). Along with much of the rest of the world Venezuela entered a recession in 2009. It recovered by 2011, however, mainly because of the strength of its oil industry, which accounts for 95 percent of its total exports. Venezuela has the largest proven oil reserves in the world and so benefited greatly from oil prices that largely stayed above $100 per barrel. High oil prices allowed the government to subsidize many other things and kept its socialist experiment going.

Oil prices plummeted in 2014, however, and things began to fall apart quickly. Food became scarce because the government could no longer afford to buy as much of it on international markets. Many private companies had stopped making food products that were being given away for free by the state. Other producers had been crippled by currency and price controls or were badly mismanaged after nationalization.

The grim consequences of bungling a nation's food supply were quick to appear. By mid-2017 Venezuelans were referring to being on an involuntary "Maduro diet"; adults lost an average of nearly twenty pounds in a year. Malnutrition among children was already widespread in 2016; but according to one doctor, "In 2017 the increase in malnourished patients has been terrible. Children arrive with the same weight and height of a newborn."

In early 2016 oil prices more than doubled from their low point, leading many to hope that Venezuela could recover. The price rise did little good, though, because the country had lost the ability to produce oil. Total output dropped by 29 percent in 2017, a decline greater than that experienced by Iraq after the American invasion in 2003. A former director of the state-run oil company explained, "In Venezuela, there is no war, nor strike. What's left of the oil industry is crumbling on its own" because of incompetence and corruption.

Other industries didn't fare much better. The IMF estimated that the country's GDP dropped 35 percent between 2013 and 2017. According to economist Ricardo Hausmann, this is the largest economic collapse ever seen in the history of not only Latin America but also Western Europe and North America. It dwarfed even the Great Depression. The government tried to make up for this huge fall in output by printing a great deal of money. As is always the case, this did nothing except cause prices to spike. The IMF predicted that Venezuelan inflation could hit 13,000 percent in 2018, but this estimate proved far too conservative. By November of that year, the annual inflation rate was 1,290,000 percent. Three months later, the IMF estimated that it was 10 million percent.

As economic mismanagement at every level intensified, so did human misery. Crime skyrocketed; by 2016 Venezuela had the second-highest homicide rate in the world after El Salvador. The government resorted to increasingly brutal measures to fight crime and shore up support in the poor neighborhoods that had been the base of Chavism. One investigation tallied more than eight thousand extrajudicial killings by Venezuelan police and soldiers in less than three years.

The neutron bomb was a nuclear weapon designed to kill as many people as possible while minimizing damage to buildings and other physical infrastructure. Socialism in Venezuela functioned as a kind of inverse neutron bomb: it didn't kill people directly, but inflicted massive damage on societal infrastructure. Everything from health care to money to the production of goods and services to public safety was devastated by it.

As socialism's detonations continued, Venezuelans fled their country in ever-larger numbers. By early 2018 at least five thousand people a day were streaming into Colombia and other neighboring countries. Unable to find work and desperate to feed their families, many women turned to prostitution. "We've got lots of teachers, some doctors, many professional women, and one petroleum engineer," reported a brothel owner in a Colombian border town. "All of them showed up with their degrees in hand."

Back in Venezuela conditions continued to worsen. The country was increasingly referred to as a war zone, but that comparison is in some ways too kind. The government went to great lengths to hide the true magnitude of its health crises, but even official statistics put its infant mortality rate higher than that of Syria in 2016.

In a May 2018 election that was boycotted by the main opposition party and widely regarded as far from free and fair, Maduro was reelected with 68 percent of the vote. By early 2019, though, his presidency was in trouble. More than 80 percent of Venezuelans wanted him to resign, in large part because of his government's terrible mismanagement of the economy. Hyperinflation and other self-inflicted wounds had reduced almost 90 percent of the population to poverty. Opposition leader Juan Guaidó declared himself the interim president of the country on January 23, 2019. By mid-February more than fifty countries had recognized him as the rightful president of Venezuela.

UK prime minister Margaret Thatcher famously observed in 1976, "The trouble with socialism is that eventually you run out of other people's money." Maduro eventually faced a related crisis: his country ran out of food and other goods because its money and just about everything else related to its socialist economy ran out of credibility.

The Problem with Capitalism Is That There Isn't Enough of It

But hasn't capitalism also let people down in Latin America and the world's other less developed regions? Perhaps its failures haven't been as rapid and grotesque as socialism's in Venezuela, but hasn't it still failed? Ricardo Hausmann argues that it hasn't. It's worked quite well where it has taken hold. The problem, he points out, is that it hasn't been allowed to spread widely. As he puts it, "The capitalist reorganization of production petered out in the developing world, leaving the vast majority of the labor force outside its control. The numbers are astounding. While only one in nine people in the United States are self-employed, the proportion in India is nineteen out of twenty. Fewer than one-fifth of workers in Peru are employed [in] private businesses. . . . In Mexico, about one in three are." In the rich world self-employed people are often freelancers or consultants, interacting professionally with companies when they choose to. In the developing world, however, the great majority of the self-employed would love to have a job with a company, but none are available. So people have to try to make a living as solo farmers, merchants, or tradespeople.

Hausmann has observed that different regions in developing countries have different economies, and he notes a fascinating pattern: where there is more capitalism, there is more prosperity. In the Mexican state of Nuevo León, for example, two-thirds of the people are employed by companies. In Chiapas, meanwhile, fewer than 15 percent are. Average incomes in Nuevo León are nine times higher. Hausmann doesn't think this is a coincidence: "The developing world's fundamental problem is that capitalism has not reorganized production and employment in the poorest countries and regions, leaving the bulk of the labor force outside its scope of operation."

In the next chapter we'll look at why capitalism has petered out in some places. We'll also examine what else needs to be in place, in addition to capitalism and tech progress, to ensure that we humans will tread more lightly on our planet even as we become more numerous and prosperous. The point of this chapter was simply to be clear on what capitalism is, and why it works so well. As Adam Smith said it did.

CHAPTER 9

What Else Is Needed? People and Policies

The legitimate object of government, is to do for a community
of people, whatever they need to have done, but can not do at
all, or can not, so well do, for themselves—in their separate, and
individual capacities.

—Abraham Lincoln,
"Fragment on Government," 1854

As we've seen, ongoing innovation and contested markets full of competitors seeking to reduce the money they spend on materials have combined to bring us past peak stuff and let us get more from less. This process is accelerating as we move deeper into the Second Machine Age, since computers and their kin are the most powerful tools for dematerialization that we've ever seen. They're taking us out of the gloomy Malthusian world conjured by the ideas of Marshall and Jevons and instead bringing us into a Second Enlightenment.

So is the virtuous cycle created by tech progress and capitalism all that's needed to let us tread more lightly on the planet in all the ways that matter? No, for two straightforward reasons. The first is covered in every decent introductory economics course; the second in every ethics seminar. The economic consideration is the negative externality of pollution. The ethical one combines two questions: *How should we treat animals?* and *Which products should not be traded in markets?*

The Negatives of Capitalism

As every Economics 101 student learns, an *externality* is a cost or a benefit that arises from a transaction, but that does not go to the people directly involved in that transaction. A lot of economic transactions don't have significant externalities. When I walk to the store in my neighborhood to buy milk, the store owner and I both benefit, and nobody else much cares.

But if the dairy that produces the milk doesn't properly clean up after its cows, the smell will start to bother the neighbors, even if these people don't drink milk. The neighbors can't take their business elsewhere if they're not doing any business with the dairy, but they're still suffering from the stench. Examples like this are always part of Econ 101 to drive home the point that pollution is a classic *negative externality*—that the dairy's neighbors are bearing the cost of the smell even though they're not buying or selling any milk.*

Markets do a lot of important things spectacularly well, but they tend not to take care of negative externalities. If a factory's owner and its customers both live far from the facility, they'll have little incentive to make sure it's not contaminating the air, land, and water nearby. So while the first principle of Econ 101 is that markets work and should be left alone by governments, the second principle is that markets don't deal with negative externalities, and so the government needs to intervene.

Governments can handle the negative externality of pollution by simply forbidding it—in the United States, for example, it is illegal to dump most kinds of waste at sea—or by attaching a cost to it.

---

* The nineteenth-century British economist and philosopher Henry Sidgwick is usually credited with introducing the concept of externalities. They were originally called *spillovers*. Later economists apparently decided that that term was too clear and stopped using it in favor of the more opaque word *externalities*.

Some people find it distasteful to let companies pollute as long as they're willing to pay for it, but the logic is sound. If pollution has a cost, companies will spend time and effort and innovate to lower it, just as they do all kinds of clever things to lower their spending on materials and resources. If pollution is costly instead of free, companies will work hard to "de-pollute," just as they work hard to dematerialize.

Markets for Pollution!?!?

If companies can buy and sell the right to pollute, things will get even better. This is the conclusion of a line of thinking kicked off by the legendary and Nobel Prize–winning economist Ronald Coase in his 1960 paper "The Problem of Social Cost." Coase argued that since markets work so well, the smart thing to do with externalities such as pollution is to make them tradable in a market.

"Let's allow companies to buy and sell pollution" struck many at the time as even more strange and distasteful than "let's allow companies to pollute for a fee." Amazingly enough, though, in the 1980s an alliance of market-loving conservatives and liberal environmentalists found common ground around using Coase's ideas to reduce pollution, and a "cap-and-trade" program for air-polluting emissions began in the United States with the Clean Air Act of 1990. Under cap-and-trade, the government declares an overall limit, or cap, on the amount of pollution allowed, then lets companies trade the right to pollute within that limit. The cap is reduced over time to bring total pollution down.

The basic idea behind cap-and-trade programs is that some companies can reduce their pollution more cheaply than others. So rather than mandating that each and every company reduce its pollution by the same amount—say 10 percent per year—the government instead mandates that the entire industry reduce its total pollution by 10 percent per year and lets companies trade with each other for the right to pollute up to that total.

To see how this works, consider two companies in the same industry called Brown and Green. Brown knows it'll have a hard time reducing its pollution (perhaps because it uses older technology), and so it will seek to buy the right to pollute more as long as buying that right is cheaper than upgrading all necessary equipment. Green, on the other hand, can inexpensively reduce its pollution. So it will happily sell the right to pollute to Brown as long as the price of that right is higher than Green's (low) cost of pollution reduction.

In a well-designed pollution-trading market Green and Brown find each other, settle on a price, and both walk away happy. So do all the rest of us, because total pollution decreases. Green reduces its pollution by a lot while getting paid by Brown. Brown reduces pollution only a little while paying Green. The total amount of pollution emitted stays under the 10 percent cap.

The cap-and-trade approach to reducing pollution has been a huge success. As *Smithsonian* magazine summarized in 2009, it "continues to let polluters figure out the least expensive way to reduce their . . . emissions. As a result, the law costs utilities just $3 billion annually, not $25 billion [as they originally estimated]. . . . It also generates an estimated $122 billion a year in benefits from avoided death and illness, healthier lakes and forests, and improved visibility on the Eastern Seaboard."

The story of atmospheric pollution reduction in the United States and elsewhere via cap-and-trade systems illustrates why capitalism and tech progress, as powerful a combination as they are, aren't enough. They don't deal with negative externalities such as pollution on their own. We learned in chapter 7 that they can be relied on to cause dematerialization simply because resources cost money. But pollution, a material we'd very much like to see less of, doesn't naturally have a price.

Of the People and for the People

So we need another pair of forces to enter the picture. This second pair consists of *public awareness* and *responsive government*. As we saw in chapter 3, public awareness in America of the serious health problems caused by air pollution was slow to come, but events such as the 1948 calamity in Donora, Pennsylvania, and frequent "killer smogs" in major cities showed us that something needed to be done. In events around the country on Earth Day and afterward, people demanded action.

They eventually got it from responsive governments. I mean *responsive* here in three senses. The first and most obvious is "responsive to the will of the people." After Earth Day America and other countries passed a series of landmark antipollution laws because people demanded action on the issue and got it from their elected officials, who wanted to be reelected. Democracies tend to be more attentive to the desires of their people than do other forms of government (although, as we'll see, exceptions exist in both directions).

The second sense of *responsive* is "responsive to good ideas." The US federal government put in place a cap-and-trade system, which has worked out extremely well. In this case, elected officials became convinced that an odd-sounding idea from an academic economist—*Create a market . . . for pollution?*—would be a smart thing to do.

Third, I mean *responsive* in the way that a good car is responsive: it's able to do what the driver wants it to do. A synonym here is *effective*. A cap-and-trade system or any other pollution-control effort won't work if the government is weak, corrupt, or otherwise unable to enforce its laws. It's not too cynical to say that polluters won't stop simply because they're asked to or because a law has been passed. They need to be confident that there will be penalties, and that the cost of these penalties will be greater than the cost of being clean and green. So governments need to have high-quality monitoring and enforcement capabilities.

Greens Aren't Always Democrats

In recent years China, despite not being a democracy, has proven to be responsive in all three senses when it comes to air pollution. There has long been anecdotal evidence that Chinese families were trying hard to escape the country's most polluted cities. One mother was quoted in 2013 as saying, "I hope in the future we'll move to a foreign country. Otherwise we'll choke to death."

In 2017 economists Shuai Chen, Paulina Oliva, and Peng Zhang moved past anecdotes and found systematic evidence of migration away from pollution. They matched up severe pollution events in China (similar to the one in 1948 in Donora, Pennsylvania) with migration patterns throughout the country and came to a striking conclusion. As they put it, "We found that a county that experienced an increase in pollution of 10 percent in the last year (everything else constant) would also experience a reduction in its population of about 2.7 percent."

The Communist Party censored attempts to highlight the air-pollution problem, including a 2015 documentary that was viewed online 200 million times before it disappeared. But it also took action. In March of 2014 Premier Li Keqiang announced to the National People's Congress, "We will resolutely declare war against pollution as we declared war against poverty."* The government mandated that coal plants reduce their emissions, shelved plans to build new ones in highly polluted regions, and even removed coal furnaces from many homes and small businesses (without, in some cases, providing anything to replace them).

---

* As we'll see in chapter 11, the Chinese war on poverty has also been hugely successful.

These efforts worked. Using data from both official Chinese sources and from America's network of consulates around the country, economist Michael Greenstone found reductions in fine-particulate pollution of more than 30 percent throughout the country by 2018. He estimated that these reductions, if they were maintained, would add 2.4 years to the life of the average Chinese citizen. As Greenstone wrote, "It took about a dozen years [after passage of the 1970 Clean Air Act] and the 1981–1982 recession for the United States to achieve the 32 percent reduction China has achieved in just four years."

Democrats Aren't Always Green

The democracy of India, meanwhile, hasn't been nearly as responsive to its terrible air-pollution problems. By 2018 the country had the fourteen most-polluted cities in the world, yet public outcry remained muted and the government took some steps that were actually counterproductive, such as allowing construction sites to generate more dust.

The biggest problem, though, was probably that India's government wasn't responsive in the third sense of the word: it was not able to take effective action. As the *New York Times* explained in 2017, "India has never been able to boss around its population like China does. India's political system is much freer, and messier: a decentralized democracy covering 1.3 billion people rife with all sorts of regional and political rivalries. . . . On Nov. 8, after NASA satellite imagery showed a huge smog smudge swallowing northern India, what did the chief ministers of Delhi and Punjab do? Did they rush to meet the prime minister? No, they started tweeting each other."

In November of 2017, during an annual period of heavy pollution, the air in Delhi turned bad enough to cause traffic accidents.

As was the case in Donora almost seventy years earlier, drivers couldn't see one another through the gray haze. Schools were finally shut down, but not as a result of any coordinated government action. The shutdown happened only because the deputy chief minister of Delhi State saw children vomiting out the windows of their school bus.

We see far too many examples of governments that have laws but are ineffective at enforcing them. Clearing land for crops by setting fires—so-called slash-and-burn agriculture—is generally illegal in Indonesia, but the practice still occurs on a vast scale. When the fall burns coincide with an El Niño weather pattern, the result can be a haze that blankets large portions of Southeast Asia for days. Environmental activists have experimented with a Singaporean law that allows companies listed on the stock exchange there to be sued if they're involved in illegal land clearing in Indonesia. The hope is that the combination of Singapore's more responsive and effective government and companies' desire not to pay lawsuit damages will have an effect on this pollution.

The Globalization of Pollution

Unresponsive governments and pollution that can travel around the world are a terrible combination. Many of us have heard of the Great Pacific Garbage Patch, a massive gyre of plastic debris concentrated in the Pacific by ocean currents. It has become a symbol of the constantly increasing amount of long-lived plastic trash in the world's waters.

Yet this global problem does not have global sources. A study published in 2017 by researchers Christian Schmidt, Tobias Krauth, and Stephan Wagner found that 88–95 percent of all plastic garbage that flowed into the world's oceans from rivers came from just ten of them, of which eight were in Asia and two in Africa. The developed economies of North America and Europe were as a group contributing little to the problem of river-sourced plastic trash in our oceans. This is because these countries have laws about pollution that aren't only strict but also enforced. The United States, for example, which accounts for approximately 25 percent of the world's overall economy, contributes less than 1 percent of total global river-sourced plastic ocean trash. China, meanwhile, is responsible for about 15 percent of the world's economy, yet contributes 28 percent of total oceanic plastic trash from rivers.

Multicountry cooperation around pollution (or anything else) is difficult, but history gives us some hope that it can be done. In 1974 the chemists Mario Molina and F. Sherwood Rowland published in *Nature* their research showing that a group of industrial chemicals called chlorofluorocarbons were causing a hole in the earth's ozone layer. This was a serious problem since the ozone layer is our primary shield from the sun's cancer-causing ultraviolet radiation. It would also be a difficult problem to solve. CFCs were widely used around the world as everything from refrigerants in air conditioners to propellants in aerosol spray cans.

The research wasn't conclusive, but still reached a large audience. Public awareness about the threats posed by a hole in the ozone layer grew quickly, and consumers in several countries organized boycotts of CFC-containing spray cans and other products. Producers of the chemicals flatly denied that they were causing any harm. In 1979, DuPont maintained, "No ozone depletion has ever been detected. . . . All ozone depletion figures to date are based on a series of uncertain projections." The Association of European Chemical Companies cautioned that economies around the world would be harmed by a CFC ban.

Despite such denials and cautions, governments around the world responded with speed and a sense of purpose that make an observer nostalgic. After a series of meetings and negotiations, twenty-four countries and the European Economic Community signed on to a set of protocols for reducing their use of CFCs and other ozone-depleting chemicals. The signing ceremony took place in September 1987 at the headquarters of the International Civil Aviation Organization in Montreal, Canada. Eventually every country in the United Nations agreed to the "Montreal Protocol," which initially specified global CFC reductions of 50 percent within twelve years.

That goal proved far too modest, not least because chemical companies soon saw that a phaseout of existing chemicals gave them a great chance to profit from patents on new ones. At post-Montreal meetings signatories agreed to reduce use of the chemicals by 75 percent, then 100 percent, and to reduce the time to do so to ten years. In addition to the profit motive, the fact that CFCs were produced by a relatively small group of companies and industries helped in accomplishing these milestones. While the chemicals themselves spread around the world, their sources were easy to pinpoint and ultimately amenable to persuasion.

UN secretary-general Kofi Annan said, "Perhaps the single most successful international agreement to date has been the Montreal Protocol." He's perhaps right. In 2016 a team of researchers reported that largely due to CFC reductions the hole in the ozone layer was closing more quickly than initially expected. Since 2000, it had shrunk by over 4 million square kilometers, an area larger than India. Along with Paul Crutzen, who did pioneering work on how human activity could affect the ozone layer, Molina and Rowland were awarded the Nobel Prize in chemistry in 1995.

In chapter 15 we'll look at why it's been so much harder to build international agreements to reduce the greenhouse gas emissions responsible for global warming.

Duty and the Beasts

A lot of us like animals and feel protective toward them. We especially like them if they're iconic, majestic, photogenic, or cuddly. If the lamprey—a (disgusting) primitive parasitic fish that's basically a tooth-filled circular mouth with a digestive system attached to it—were in danger of extinction, I doubt many people would care, but the annual harp seal hunt in Canada and other countries evokes outrage and protests around the world. This isn't because the species is endangered; it's classified by the Canadian government as abundant. It's because snow-white, huge-eyed harp seal pups are the cutest things ever.

I don't want to debate here whether our notions of protectiveness and stewardship toward our fellow creatures are properly calibrated. I just want to point out that most of us do feel a moral obligation to at least some other living things, and especially an obligation to not cause them to vanish forever from the earth. Human-caused extinctions are irreversible (so far), and repugnant to many of us.

Someone who has studied the bet between Julian Simon and Paul Ehrlich might respond that whatever our feelings and beliefs toward animals, there's no reason to be too concerned about extinctions. After all, according to this logic, animal products such as meat, hide, and feathers are resources just as aluminum, copper, and potash are. As Simon pointed out, when resources become scarce, their prices go up. This rise spurs an intense search, aided by the twin forces of capitalism and tech progress, for alternatives. The search succeeds and markets turn away from the original resource. If this resource is an animal, it then repopulates itself, safe from the predations of the market.

But we shouldn't get complacent about the power of capitalism and tech progress to prevent the complete dematerialization of species, for two reasons. The first is biology. By the time high prices or other factors lead us to stop killing animals, there may simply not be enough left to allow their population to rebound. This happened to the passenger pigeon in America. Their apparently endless flocks were reduced so much that breeding ceased even after the hunts did. Mating programs in zoos didn't work, and Martha, the last known member of the species, died in her Cincinnati cage in 1914.

Fighting Our Animal Urges

The other reason high prices might not rescue animals is that we humans sometimes *like* high prices. With most products, demand goes down when prices go up, all other things being equal. But with "Veblen goods," something very different happens: higher prices cause demand to go *up*. Such products are named for Thorstein Veblen, the American economist and sociologist who coined the phrase *conspicuous consumption*. Veblen goods such as luxury cars, designer clothes, and fine art are valued in large part because they're expensive. They signal the affluence and high status of their owners.

Some animal products are Veblen goods, which is bad news for the animals. As we saw in chapter 3, sea otters became so scarce in the late nineteenth century that prices for their pelts rose tenfold. But this didn't cause a search for replacements because people didn't *want* a replacement; they wanted the otter pelt more than ever. The inverted economics of Veblen goods would probably have doomed the species if not for the international moratorium on sea otter hunting signed in 1911.

Bison faced the same problem as their numbers cratered. In the 1890s buffalo heads sold for as much as $1,500, which is equivalent to more than $40,000 today. I'm confident that some time around the turn of the twentieth century some knave would have sold to some fool the right to kill the last few North American bison on Earth for a huge sum of money, had that been allowed.

Fortunately for us, it wasn't. The bison were rescued by a combination of public awareness and responsive government. An odd coalition of interest groups formed to protect the American bison and bring it back from the brink of extinction. Its members included ranchers, sport hunters, romantics who were nostalgic for the rough frontier of the early nineteenth century, and entrepreneurs who wanted to attract the nature-hungry tourists of the early twentieth. Together they successfully pressed the government to toughen and enforce the laws against bison hunting in Yellowstone National Park, establish more preserves for the animals, and take other effective steps.

As we saw earlier, we have had similar successes with the beaver, snowy egret, white-tailed deer, and other animals that we cared about. In each case conservationists realized that the species was in trouble and built public awareness of the problem. Governments became responsive to their concerns and to good solutions and put in place effective measures to reverse the situation. Animals that were threatened by some combination of their own reproductive biology and humans' Veblenian tastes were saved from an unnecessary end.

I hope we'll save the elephants, too. Africa had an estimated 26 million elephants when Europeans started exploring and exploiting the continent in the 1500s. Our fondness for ivory products and hunting trophies reduced the population to about 10 million by 1913 and 1.3 million by 1979. Weak enforcement of antipoaching laws, large-scale illegal trade in ivory, and rapidly rising incomes in China (the world's largest ivory market) continued to drive down populations; the comprehensive Great Elephant Census, completed in 2016, counted just over 350,000 animals across the continent.

The good news is some African countries such as Kenya, Zambia, and Botswana are effectively managing their herds, and seeing stable or growing elephant populations. The even better news is that China put in place an almost complete ban on the sale of ivory at the end of 2017. Public support for the ban was surely increased by the seven-foot-six-inch basketball superstar Yao Ming, who starred in a 2014 documentary about elephant poaching and decline. He felt a bond with Africa, he said, because "many animals there are bigger than me."

Strong signs indicate that public awareness and responsible government might be combining to decrease Chinese demand for ivory. The Kenyan conservation organization Save the Elephants found in 2017 that wholesale prices in Chinese markets for new ivory had dropped more than 50 percent in three years. There's little point in purchasing ivory to carve if people don't want to buy it and the government won't let you sell it.

When the Partnership Fails

Public awareness and responsive government are the essential partnership for dealing with the externality of pollution and taking care of our fellow creatures. When one of the partners isn't doing its job, progress and the environment can suffer.

One of the clearest recent examples of a breakdown in the partnership is the history of public resistance to glyphosate, a "very toxicologically and environmentally safe" weed killer that has been called "a once-in-a-century herbicide" because of its excellent properties. Introduced in 1974, it has become the most widely used herbicide in the world. With this popularity came scrutiny, but not alarm. A comprehensive review of its safety conducted in 2000 had a straightforward conclusion: "Under present and expected conditions of use, [glyphosate] herbicide does not pose a health risk to humans."

By that time, however, the first crops that were genetically modified to be resistant to glyphosate had appeared on the market. They were developed and marketed by Monsanto, a St. Louis–based company that for many reasons is among the world's most disliked and mistrusted.* Monsanto's version of the herbicide was called Roundup, and its genetically modified crops (of which corn and soybeans were the first to market) were marketed as "Roundup Ready."

Since the introduction of these crops, many people have decided that they're no longer ready for Roundup. The herbicide has been caught up in the resistance to genetically modified organisms (GMOs) and has come under attack from many environmental groups.† By 2016 two-thirds of people across the EU's five biggest countries supported a ban on glyphosate. They nearly got one. After a bitter public relations battle that pitted Greenpeace, green parties, and other environmental groups against most farmers, an EU committee voted in late 2017 to continue to allow use of the herbicide within the EU for five more years. French president Emmanuel Macron disagreed with the ruling and announced that France would ban glyphosate within three years.

---

* Monsanto began to acquire its bad name in the 1960s and 1970s when it (along with other chemical companies) produced Agent Orange, a powerful herbicide that was widely used by the US military during the Vietnam War. Agent Orange caused serious health problems in humans. Later, Monsanto mishandled the launch of GMOs in Europe. The company's reputation never recovered. It was acquired by Bayer in 2018.

† Their arguments received a boost in 2015 when the International Agency for Research on Cancer (IARC), which is part of the World Health Organization, categorized glyphosate as "probably carcinogenic." As the author and environmentalist Mark Lynas points out, this is less alarming than it sounds since "red meat, wood smoke, manufacturing glass processes, drinking very hot beverages over 65C and even the occupation of being a hairdresser" have the same IARC designation. Confusion arises because the IARC considers *hazards*, while previous investigations of glyphosate had assessed its *risks*. This difference in terminology isn't small. As toxicologist David Eastmond points out, sharks are a hazard to people, but a shark in an aquarium poses no risk to visitors. Cancer researcher Geoffrey Kabat says flatly, "The problem with using *hazard* is that it may bear no immediate relation to anything in the real world."

Macron was being responsive to the sentiments of his electorate, but not to the strong scientific consensus. Unfortunately, this is not rare. Politicians tend to follow their people, even when they've settled on beliefs that are contradicted by available evidence and logic and even when the environment and our health will suffer as a result. We see this all too clearly with GMOs themselves.

GM NOs

The scientific consensus about the safety of GMO foods is overwhelming. In 2016, after reviewing approximately one thousand studies, a committee of the US National Academy of Sciences "concluded that no differences have been found that implicate a higher risk to human health safety from these [genetically engineered] foods than from their non-GE counterparts." The UK Royal Society; the African, French, and German academies of science; the American Medical Association; and several other bodies have also studied the issue. All have reached the same conclusion. Even the European Commission, which nearly banned glyphosate, agrees:

> "The main conclusion to be drawn from the efforts of more than 130 research projects, covering a period of more than 25 years of research, and involving more than 500 independent research groups, is that biotechnology, and in particular GMOs, are not per se more risky than e.g. conventional plant breeding technologies."

Yet thirty-eight countries don't allow their farmers to grow GMO crops, according to the Genetic Literacy Project website. These include most EU countries (except for Spain and Portugal), Russia, and much of Africa. This collective refusal represents a great triumph of ideology over evidence, and also over the environment. GMO crops have been developed to resist viruses and other pests, better withstand drought and heat, require less fertilizer, and so on. They're a powerful way to continue the Green Revolution, and to continue the recent trend of dematerializing agriculture—of getting larger and larger harvests from smaller and smaller amounts of land, water, fertilizer, and herbicide.

Forbidding GMOs is bad not only for the environment but also for people. This is probably easiest to see in the case of golden rice, a strain of rice genetically modified to produce beta-carotene, a precursor to vitamin A. Vitamin A is critically important for young children, yet many Asian and African infants weaned on rice gruel don't get enough of it. UNICEF estimates that approximately half a million children become blind each year because of vitamin A deficiency, half of whom die within a year of losing their sight. In total, the deficiency is thought to cause more than a million deaths annually.

Golden rice, named for its color, has been available for years. It has been approved as safe by the US FDA, the food standards bodies in Australia and New Zealand, and Health Canada. It is patented, but free licenses are available to developing countries. However, many groups remain adamantly opposed to it. Greenpeace, for example, holds that releasing golden rice would be "environmentally irresponsible and could compromise food, nutrition and financial security."

Evidence and Public Opinion Get Trumped

The United States is the world's largest producer of GMOs, and more than half of Americans believe they're as safe or safer than conventional crops. But it would be wrong to conclude from this that in America the partnership between responsive government and public awareness is currently working flawlessly. On the critical topic of pollution caused by greenhouse gases, the United States is failing badly.

The scientific consensus that carbon dioxide and other gases from human activities are causing global average temperatures to rise is overwhelming; it's at least as strong as the agreements on glyphosate and GMO safety. In every state in America in 2017, a majority of people supported the country's participation in the Paris Agreement on climate change. Yet President Donald Trump pulled the United States from that agreement, even though it was nonbinding and allowed its members to set their own goals. Under Trump, the federal government was responsive neither to the best available evidence on climate change nor to the will of its people. It was instead apparently guided by Trump's belief that "the concept of global warming was created by and for the Chinese in order to make U.S. manufacturing non-competitive," as he tweeted in 2012.

In chapter 15 we'll take up how to best respond to climate change. It is dismaying how badly public awareness and governmental response have been warped away from science and evidence on this topic, and on issues such as glyphosate and GMOs.

The Four Horsemen of the Optimist

I call technological progress, capitalism, responsive government, and public awareness the "four horsemen of the optimist." When all four are present, we tread more lightly on our planet. We progressively dematerialize our consumption, reduce pollution, and take better care of our fellow creatures.

That may sound naive and utopian, but the evidence convinces me that it's not. Countries that have all four horsemen working in concert are accomplishing something unprecedented in human history—they're decoupling economic growth from resource consumption, from pollution, and from land use. They're becoming better stewards of the planet, and the life on it. No society is doing this perfectly, but many *are* doing it, and doing it better.

A critic might respond that caring about the environment is a luxury that only rich countries can afford. While there's some truth to this, it dodges a fundamental question: Why did some countries become rich, but not others?

Institutionalizing Progress

In my view the best answer to this question comes from the work of the economist Daron Acemoglu and political scientist James Robinson, summarized in their book *Why Nations Fail*. They argue that the differences between rich countries and poor ones, between those that maintain growth over long periods and those that can only accomplish it fitfully (if at all), stem from differences in their institutions.

Institutions are the "rules of the game" for a society. They are, to use the more precise definition offered by the economic historian Douglass North, "the humanly devised constraints that shape human interaction." Three key things to keep in mind about institutions are that they're devised by humans (so America's courts and labor unions are institutions, but its weather and mountain ranges aren't), that they impose constraints (in America speed limits constrain how fast you can drive, and standards of politeness usually keep you from burping loudly at the dinner table), and that they shape incentives (I don't speed too much when I drive because I don't want to lose my license or go to jail, and I don't burp at the dinner table because I don't want to eat alone all the time).

Acemoglu and Robinson divide economies into two broad categories. The first is economies that have *inclusive* institutions, "those that allow and encourage participation by the great mass of people in economic activities that make the best use of their talents and skills." A key feature of inclusive institutions is that they allow people to keep what they earn or acquire, no matter who they are.

As the authors put it, "To be inclusive, economic institutions must feature secure private property, an unbiased system of law, and a provision of public services that provides a level playing field in which people can exchange and contract."

The second category of economy, as I'm sure you've guessed, has the opposite kind of institutions, which Acemoglu and Robinson call *extractive*. In these economies most people have no real chance of getting ahead (slaves are the clearest example of this wretched lot in life) and a small group of elites find ways to keep or take—to extract—most of the gains that are generated.

Many countries that look inclusive on paper are actually extractive in practice. As Acemoglu and Robinson point out, the United States and many Latin American countries have similar constitutions and written laws, but throughout parts of Latin America formal laws don't mean much because courts are weak or biased, bureaucracies are vast and unresponsive, and corruption is widespread. As a result, only the elites have a real chance at success.

These ideas help us tie together dematerialization, the four horsemen of the optimist, and prosperity. I argued previously in chapter 7 that some economies have left behind the consumption patterns of the Industrial Era and started to dematerialize because of the combination of capitalism and technological progress. My definition of capitalism corresponds closely to Acemoglu and Robinson's definition of inclusive institutions. Key to both are the notions that most people have the opportunity to advance and flourish, that they have a fair shot in the marketplace, and that they get to keep what they earn and build.

People hate pollution, especially as they become aware of the great harm it does them. The historical pattern has been that as people become wealthier, they demand cleaner air, land, and water. Capitalism alone won't provide these because pollution is an externality (a highly negative one). So a clean environment has to come from the laws and regulations of a responsive government. This is similar to Acemoglu and Robinson's "provision of public services," which is a feature of inclusive institutions.

Finally, public awareness and responsive government need to come together to place some animals outside the market. Otherwise capitalism will eat all of them. The efforts of Yao Ming and others to change Chinese attitudes toward buying ivory and the recent ban in that country on the ivory trade are both attempts to change institutions in China. The first is an attempt at public awareness, the second at responsive government.

I'll finish this chapter with one example that shows what happens when the four horsemen are all present, and another example that illustrates what happens when they're largely absent.

The Horsemen and the Automobile

The 1970 Clean Air Act in the United States gave the EPA authority to regulate pollution emitted by cars and trucks. The measures put in place since then have been extraordinarily successful at reducing vehicle emissions. As the EPA notes on its website, "Compared to 1970 vehicle models, new cars, SUVs and pickup trucks are roughly 99 percent cleaner for common pollutants (hydrocarbons, carbon monoxide, nitrogen oxides and particle emissions). New heavy-duty trucks and buses are roughly 99 percent cleaner than 1970 models." The author and self-described "rational optimist" Matt Ridley makes a stark comparison: "A car today emits less pollution traveling at full speed than a parked car did from leaks in 1970."

While these improvements were taking place, cars were also getting more fuel efficient. The push for better gas mileage in the United States started after the Arab oil embargo of 1973. The high gas prices caused by the boycott led many Americans to turn away from bigger, less fuel-efficient cars. It also led to government action:

in 1975 Congress put in place the Corporate Average Fuel Economy (CAFE) standards, which mandated that automakers had to make their entire fleets more fuel efficient.

They did. Overall vehicle fuel efficiency improved from less than 15 miles per gallon in 1975 to approximately 25 miles per gallon by 1983, essentially meeting the CAFE standard set for 1985. Average horsepower went down over this period as engine designers made trade-offs to meet the imposed fuel-efficiency goals. Once this happened and no new CAFE improvements were immediately put in place, carmakers turned back to power: median horsepower almost doubled between 1983 and 2007.

In that year, however, the first in a new set of CAFE standards was put in place. These were intended not only to decrease reliance on foreign oil but also to reduce greenhouse gas emissions. Automakers once again turned their attention to fuel efficiency and improved overall gas mileage by more than five miles per gallon between 2007 and 2016. This time, however, they didn't have to turn away from also making cars more powerful; median horsepower increased by more than 10 percent over the same period.

The technologies of the Second Machine Age—digital and otherwise—allowed designers to make engines that were simultaneously more efficient and more powerful. And all throughout this time, engines themselves were dematerializing. As Bloomberg put it in a 2017 story, "Combustion engines on America's roads are about 42 percent smaller than they were 40 years ago."

All four horsemen are clearly present in this story. The public wanted cleaner air and got it via a responsive government. We also wanted faster and more fuel-efficient cars and got them because of capitalism and tech progress. We eventually even got them simultaneously, after technologies had progressed enough. And the history of the CAFE standards shows how powerful government intervention can be for directing change. Automakers as a group showed little enthusiasm for increasing fuel efficiency when no unmet mandate was in place.

Fewer Horsemen? Fewer Whales

The history of Soviet whaling in the second half of the twentieth century, which would be farcical if it weren't so tragic, shows something very different. The USSR was part of the 1946 International Convention for the Regulation of Whaling, which came about only after the industrial whaling described earlier in chapter 3 had killed millions of the world's largest mammals and almost exterminated several species. Under the convention, the Soviet Union—like other signatories—received a small annual hunt quota* and reported against it every year.

According to research by biologists Yulia Ivashchenko and Phillip Clapham, however, the Soviets actually killed 180,000 more whales than they reported between 1948 and 1973. The timing of this sustained illegal hunting was disastrous, since it came when many populations were already severely depleted after a half century of continuous large-scale hunting. The North Pacific right whale, for example, was almost eradicated by only three years of Russian whaling in the 1960s. That species might never recover.

The only thing worse than the scale and timing of the Soviet whale hunt was its utter pointlessness. Russians have never had a taste for whale meat. So while Japanese whalers turned 90 percent of the whales they harpooned into products, Soviet crews only took the animals' blubber (approximately 30 percent of its weight) and tossed the rest of the carcass back into the sea.

The blubber was converted into oil, but the Soviet Union had huge conventional oil reserves and was already self-sufficient in

---

* The initial global quota under the treaty was sixteen thousand whales per year.

energy. Then why the huge sustained hunt? Alfred Berzin, a Russian scientist who worked on Soviet whaling ships, offered in his memoir a clear, convincing, and heartbreaking reason: "The plan—at any price!"

In *The Truth About Soviet Whaling: A Memoir*, Berzin documented how the USSR's extensive and unresponsive economic planning bureaucracy doomed so many whales. Whaling was considered part of the fisheries industry, and fishing ships were evaluated not on market demand for their catch—Soviet central planners loudly and proudly rejected market signals such as supply, demand, and price as valid elements of an economy—but instead on gross tonnage, or the total weight of whales killed. So plans for growth in USSR fisheries were simply plans for more and more dead whales, no matter their use.

The USSR minister of fisheries during the time of the whale hunts was Aleksandr Ishokov, who was named a Hero of Socialistic Work for his ability to execute plans. As Berzin wrote in his memoir, "On one occasion a scientist was trying to protect the whale resources from destructive whaling and he reminded the Minister about his descendants. Ishokov returned an abominable, criminal, and chilling response that should be carved upon the gravestone of the Soviet economic system: 'These descendants will not be the ones to fire me from my job.'"

The only one of the four horsemen present at all in this story is tech progress. Explosive harpoons, spotter helicopters, and factory ships made Russian whaling brutally effective. But capitalism, tech progress's partner in dematerialization, was totally absent. In the Soviet economy ship captains didn't have to sell their catch (they just had to weigh it) and so received no signal from anything we'd recognize as a customer or market. Whalers also couldn't fish for anything else or switch to another career. Jobs for people and uses for things were centrally planned, and professional autonomy and property rights were heretical bourgeois ideas.

Public awareness and responsive government, the tandem defense against environmental harms, were also absent. Having no free press, the Soviet people were kept in the dark about whaling and countless other things, and the USSR succeeded in keeping international monitors off its boats until 1972, by which time most of the damage had been done. And the Soviet government was spectacularly unresponsive to the will of its people, and to good ideas such as letting supply and demand play a role in production. Or not killing all the whales.

CHAPTER 10

The Global Gallop of the Four Horsemen

*I have seen the darkness gradually disappearing, and the light
gradually increasing. One by one, I have seen obstacles removed,
errors corrected, prejudices softened, proscriptions relinquished,
and my people advancing in all the elements that make up the
sum of general welfare.*

—Frederick Douglass,
speech given in Washington DC, 1890

I've argued in the past few chapters that tech progress, capitalism,
responsive government, and public awareness—the four horsemen
of the optimist—are largely responsible for the broad and deep
dematerialization of our consumption and our economies we've
experienced since Earth Day. They're also behind other positive
changes we've made in the way we produce things. These changes
include not enslaving people or forcibly taking their land, ending
industrialized child labor, bringing many species back from the
brink of extinction, and greatly reducing pollution.

What else have the four horsemen done recently? What other
important changes have they helped bring about? I see three, which
I'll discuss in the following chapters. First, though, I want to make
the case that all four horsemen have been advancing quickly over
the past few decades—that tech progress has been quite rapid by
historical standards, and that capitalism, responsive government,
and public awareness have also been spreading quickly around the

world. I've found that these trends are underappreciated—just as dematerialization is—so it's important to document them clearly. Once we've done that, we can talk about their effects with greater confidence.

This Is for Everyone

In 2016, more people in the world had a phone than a flush toilet or piped water. The next year, the *Economist* reported, "In much of [Africa] people with mobile phones outnumber those with electricity, never mind that many have to walk for miles to get a signal or recharge their phones' batteries." These developments reveal that in much of the world the Second Machine Age has arrived before the Industrial Era did, even though the Industrial Era had a two-century-plus head start.

Mass electrification and citywide indoor plumbing are over a century old, yet they haven't yet made it to a substantial portion of the world's population. Digital communication in the form of a mobile phone, meanwhile, is now everywhere; the World Bank estimates that in 2016 the world had more mobile phone subscriptions than people on the planet.* This technology has spread around the world with astonishing speed: in 2000, there were only twelve mobile subscriptions for every hundred people on Earth.

Digital devices are not only spreading quickly; they're also getting much more sophisticated. Instead of simple mobile phones, more than 1.5 billion smartphones were sold globally in 2017 (versus 450 million non-smartphones). These miniature computers are powerful. India's most popular smartphone in 2018 was the Lyf

---

* Obviously, many people have more than one mobile phone subscription. In the developing world it is common to switch among subscriptions to take advantage of low prices and special offers.

Jio F90M. It is powered by a 1.2 GHz quad-core processor and has 512 MB RAM and internal storage of up to 128 GB. These specs are comparable to those of the main line of MacBook laptops sold by Apple in the United States in 2006.

People with access to a device such as this can do much more than just communicate. They can also compute and access the substantial portion of humanity's accumulated knowledge that's now available for free on the Internet.* These are powerful capabilities, reserved until recently for the global elite. As the author and entrepreneur Peter Diamandis observed in 2012, "Right now, a Maasai warrior on a mobile phone in the middle of Kenya has better mobile communications than the president did twenty-five years ago. If he's on a smartphone using Google, he has access to more information than the US president did just fifteen years ago."

Many of the world's poorest and most vulnerable people now have that access to information. The World Bank estimated that in 2016 more than 45 percent of the world's population used the Internet, including 55 percent of non-high-income people in Latin America and the Caribbean, 43 percent of the same group in the Middle East and North Africa, and 20 percent in sub-Saharan Africa. Twelve percent of the world's lowest-income people got online that year. We'd like those percentages to be higher, and history gives us great confidence that they will be. After all, as recently as 2000 fewer than 7 percent of all the people on the planet, rich or poor, used the Internet.

I believe that technological progress today is faster than ever before in our history. In less than a generation we've gone from a largely unconnected to a deeply interconnected world, increasingly underpinned by artificial intelligence and other fundamentally important innovations such as powerful and tiny sensors, cloud

---

* Or, to be more precise, at zero marginal cost.

computing, the Global Positioning System, and ever-faster and ever-cheaper processors. Once again new technologies are remaking our world, as they did during the Industrial Era. This time, it's happening with head-spinning speed.

Massive Market Entry

Has capitalism also spread around the world in recent years? Yes. In 1978, two years after Mao Zedong died, the Central Committee of China's Communist Party convened to decide on the country's economic strategy. Paramount leader Deng Xiaoping persuaded his colleagues to adopt an approach radically different from the Marxist path of strong central planning and hostility to private property and international trade that had prevailed up to that point.

The new approach was called "reform and opening up." It was also referred to as "socialism with Chinese characteristics," but a better label for it might be "Chinese authoritarianism with some capitalist characteristics." The first reforms allowed farmers to own and sell their own crops, opened up the country to foreign investment, and let entrepreneurs start businesses.

With these changes, the People's Republic of China, a country of more than 950 million people in 1978, took its first steps toward joining the capitalist economic order. In a 1985 interview with *Time* magazine Deng made the remarkable statement, "There are no fundamental contradictions between socialism and a market economy."

Mikhail Gorbachev began openly discussing economic openness and restructuring at about the same time as Deng. In 1985 Gorbachev, then the general secretary of the Communist Party of the Soviet Union, gave a notably frank speech in Leningrad acknowledging that the country's growth was slowing and that too many people remained too poor. His solution, like Deng's, was to push for less central planning and more international trade and market-based enterprise. A cascade of reforms followed. The most radical was 1988's Law on Cooperatives, which allowed private businesses to exist in the country for the first time since Stalin forbade them in 1928.

These changes weren't enough to save the Soviet Union from all the forces pulling it apart. The hammer-and-sickle flag that flew over the Kremlin was lowered for the last time on Christmas Day 1991. Soon after, Gorbachev signed a document giving up his presidency and returning self-government, after more than six decades, to the fifteen republics that had made up the USSR. During the ceremony the Russian-made felt pen Gorbachev tried to use didn't work, so he borrowed a fountain pen from CNN president Tom Johnson. Once the signing was completed, Soviet-style socialism ended for the more than 400 million people who'd been living behind the Iron Curtain.

Also in 1991 India's finance minister, Manmohan Singh, presented a budget that would radically change his country. He took advantage of dire fiscal circumstances. Because of oil-price shocks, heavy public spending, slowing economic growth, and other factors, the Indian government was almost out of money. Delhi had only enough foreign reserves to last two weeks and had been put in the humiliating position of having to airlift forty-seven tons of gold to England (its colonial master until 1947) as collateral for a loan.

Singh proposed deep changes to the way his country's economy worked. To make Indian products more competitive in international markets, the rupee would be devalued. Foreigners would find it much easier to invest. The elaborate system of licenses that determined who'd be allowed to produce what goods and services would be simplified, as would the dense tangle of regulations that confronted prospective and existing businesses.

When introducing these reforms, Singh paraphrased Victor Hugo by stating, "No power on earth can stop an idea whose time has come." That idea was for India to become more capitalist. Even after it did, many restrictions and regulations remained, but the country was forever a different place. As the *Economist* put it, "1991 . . . deserves its spot in the annals of economic history alongside December 1978, when China's Communist Party approved the opening up of its economy, or even May 1846, when Britain voted to repeal the Corn Laws." India's 840 million people quickly found themselves operating in a transformed economic environment—one with a great deal less central planning and more free-market entry, competition, and voluntary exchange.

Between 1978 and 1991, then, more than 2.1 billion people—about 40 percent of the world's 1990 population—began living within substantially more capitalist economic systems. This is certainly the largest and fastest shift toward economic freedom that the world has ever seen. It's even bigger and more abrupt than the adoption of communism by the Soviet Union and China, which unfolded over the more than three decades between Lenin's 1917 Bolshevik Revolution and the final victory of Mao's army in 1949.

And what's been happening since 1991? Has capitalism continued to spread? As we see with the tragic example of Venezuela, socialist experiments have continued. But they're the exception, not the rule. Since 1995 the Heritage Foundation has compiled an Index of Economic Freedom for virtually all the world's countries. This index attempts to quantify four "pillars of economic freedom": rule of law, government size, regulatory efficiency, and open markets.

Globally, this index has increased by 6 percent since 1995, from a score of 57.6 to 61.1. This growth is largely driven by Europe, where formerly communist countries have continued to become more capitalist. Europe's overall score increased by almost 20 percent between 1995 and 2018. Other regions in the world improved much more slowly, but they did improve. The only exception is Central and South America, which saw a slight overall decline in economic freedom over the twenty-three-year period.

As we saw in chapter 7, tech progress and capitalism are natural partners, combining the fuel of interest with the fire of genius. The technology analyst Benedict Evans illustrates how well this partnership has worked in recent years to bring mobile communication and computing to people around the world. In particular, he demonstrates how the lack of competition present in countries with a government-run monopoly on telecommunications held back progress. He uses the example of Brazil, which privatized its Telebrás monopoly in 1998.

As Evans writes, "When Tele São Paulo was privatized, with Telefónica buying it, there was a waiting list of 7 million lines, out of a population of 20 million. . . . As well as the 7 million people waiting for a line, it was routine for your number to be swapped with someone else, just because." Telebrás also appeared to be padding its payrolls by more than a bit: "Telefónica worked out there wasn't enough room in the headquarters building for all the people listed as working there to physically fit." Meanwhile, an estimated 45 percent of São Paulo's businesses didn't have a telephone line.

Evans summarized the importance of combining tech progress with capitalism: "80–90% of earth's population is under mobile coverage, and 50% and growing have a phone. Would [Tele São Paulo] . . . et al. have done that? Never. . . . That 5 billion people have a phone and 2.5 billion already have a smartphone is a huge achievement of, mostly, free markets and permissionless innovation."

I completely agree.

The Global Good-Government Movement

We saw in the previous chapter with the example of Chinese air-pollution reduction that autocratic regimes *can* be responsive to the desires of their people. But more often, they pursue objectives without much regard for the popular will. So a broad decline in authoritarianism and growth in democracy around the world is a strong sign that governments are becoming more responsive.

Economist Max Roser calculates that in 1988 41.4 percent of humanity lived in a democracy. Within eighteen years that figure increased almost 40 percent. Democracy has retreated a bit since then—to 55.8 percent of all people in 2015—but the recent trend toward representative government remains strong. Although autocracies still governed more than 23 percent of the global population in 2015, there are fewer and fewer of them over time. And as Roser says, "It is worth pointing out that four out of five people in the world that live in an autocracy live in China."

Some democracies, though, have become more authoritarian in recent years. Such countries as Hungary, Poland, Turkey, the Philippines, and America have elected leaders with clear authoritarian leanings. This is bad news, which we'll discuss further in chapter 13. The good news is that most democracies are holding strong. As the foreign-policy researchers Bruce Jones and Michael O'Hanlon pointed out in 2018:

> "Much as we might regret partial setbacks to liberal democracy in Hungary, population 10 million, developments there pale in significance when compared with democratic progress in Indonesia, population 261 million. . . . Witness South Korea, which impeached a president earlier this year but seems no worse for the wear. Or Brazil, dealing with similar political problems in an ugly yet still constitutional manner. Or India, where a strongman leader is nonetheless checked in some of his ambitions by a balance-of-powers system. . . . Democracy is fragile and can never be taken for granted. But declarations about democracy's demise, or even its significant decline, go too far."

Are governments of the world, whether or not they're democracies, doing a better job of being responsive to the will of their people? The evidence here is mixed. Since 1996 the World Bank has maintained governance indicators for virtually all countries. Two of these are "voice and accountability" and "control of corruption," which seem like good measures of governmental responsiveness (after all, who wants to pay a bribe?). Across all regions and income groups, these two indicators have changed remarkably little over more than twenty years. Looking at the World Bank data, it's hard to conclude that the world's governments have been getting better at listening to their own people.

Other data, however, show that governments *are* doing much better by their people. Political scientists Christopher Fariss and Keith Schnakenberg developed a "human rights protection" score that captures whether people are free from political repression, false imprisonment, torture, and related violations. They found that the world as a whole did a better job at protecting people in 2014 than did 80 percent of individual countries studied between 1949 and 2014.

In the previous chapter I defined three ways that governments could be responsive. In addition to being responsive to the will of their people, they could also be responsive to good ideas (such as allowing GMO crops and glyphosate, taking steps to limit greenhouse gas emissions, or protecting endangered species) and responsive in the sense of being effective and therefore able to accomplish their goals. The strong and steady rise in the global human rights protection score indicates to me that governments are becoming more responsive in all three ways.

Torture and false imprisonment are self-evidently bad ideas, and governments are engaging in them less. Protecting human rights is hard work, requiring effective government. Some police officers will always find it expedient to extract confessions by beating up suspects, and some local officials will always break up protests with too much force. These things still happen all over the world far too often, but they're happening less often. Governments abuse their own people less and have become more effective at halting abuses.

You Have Our Sympathies

The last of the four horsemen of the optimist is public awareness: awareness both that we should take better care of each other and of our planet, and of good ways to do so. In *Enlightenment Now* Steven Pinker uses the image of an expanding "circle of sympathy" to convey that the first kind of public awareness is increasing. He makes an optimistic argument:

"Given that we are equipped with the capacity to sympathize with others, nothing can prevent the circle of sympathy from expanding from the family and tribe to embrace all of humankind, particularly as reason goads us into realizing that there can be nothing uniquely deserving about ourselves or any of the groups to which we belong. We are forced into cosmopolitanism: accepting our citizenship in the world."

Recent evidence from around the world backs up Pinker's claim. Since 1980, for example, both use of the death penalty and the prosecution of homosexuality have rapidly decreased in countries around the world. These steps probably wouldn't be surprising to the political scientist Christian Welzel, who has documented a steady rise in what he calls "emancipative values" such as gender equality, personal choice, freedom of speech, and political voice. Drawing on the World Values Survey, which since the early 1980s has asked questions of as many as 150,000 people in ninety-five countries that together contain 90 percent of the planet's population, Welzel documents a startling trend: all regions of the world, without exception, are embracing more and more of these values.

The cumulative changes are huge. As Pinker writes, "Young Muslims in the Middle East, the world's most conservative culture, have values today that are comparable to those of young people in Western Europe, the world's most liberal culture, in the early 1960s." How did this huge change come about? Welzel's theory is that as opportunities widen for people (as their incomes rise, for example, and their governments become less restrictive), they tend to support wider opportunities for others. Or, as the playwright Bertolt Brecht wrote in 1928 in *The Threepenny Opera*, "First comes a full stomach, then comes ethics." We saw in chapter 2 how much more full stomachs got during the Industrial Era, and we'll see in the next chapter how quickly nutrition and other measures of a healthy life have been improving as we move deeper into the Second Machine Age. So perhaps it's no wonder that around the world people's ethical senses are broadening.

The second kind of public awareness—awareness of effective approaches for dealing with our challenges—is generally improved by education. Here again the trends are encouraging. As recently as 1980, almost 44 percent of all people at least fifteen years old were illiterate. By 2014, the figure had dropped to less than 15 percent. And investment in education is increasing. Max Roser points out that of the eighty-eight countries for which public education spending data is available in both 2000 and 2010, three-quarters increased the percentage of GDP they were devoting to education over that time.*

So tech progress, capitalism, responsive government, and public awareness have all advanced strongly in recent decades. As they have, they've helped us humans tread more lightly on our planet by dematerializing our consumption and reducing pollution and species loss. What else have these four horsemen done?

---

* Keep in mind also that for most if not all of these countries, GDP itself also increased substantially over the decade. So the total increases in educational spending are quite large.

Three main things, which we'll examine in the next three chapters. First, they've contributed to widespread *improvement* in both the human condition and the state of nature. Second, they've contributed to *concentration* of economic activity: more and more output coming from a smaller and smaller number of counties, farms, and factories, and more and more gains going to fewer and fewer companies and people. Third, they've helped create increasing *disconnection* among people and declines in social capital. As we'll see, the improvement is great news, concentration is a mixed blessing, and disconnection is a frightening trend.

CHAPTER 11

Getting So Much Better

Once you have these tools, you can't not use them. . . . You can delete the clichéd image from your brain of supplicant impoverished people not having control of their own lives. That's not true.

—Bono, TED Talk, 2013

Max Roser's *Our World in Data* is one of my favorite websites, for two reasons. The first is that it contains a lot of valuable information. The second is that it tells an invaluable story—an optimistic and hopeful one. The evidence presented in *Our World in Data* and in books like Julian Simon's *The Ultimate Resource*, Bjørn Lomborg's *Skeptical Environmentalist*, Steven Pinker's *Enlightenment Now*, and Hans Rosling's *Factfulness* shows clearly that most of the things we should care about are getting better. Not all, but most. This happy fact applies both to the state of nature and the human condition.

The Power of Negative Thinking

But do your friends and family believe that a lot of important things are getting better? Do you? If not, they and you are far from alone. Most people don't appreciate that things are improving as the four horsemen advance. For example, Rosling writes, "Over the past 20 years, the proportion of people living in extreme poverty has almost halved. But in online polls, in most countries, fewer than 10 percent of people knew this." Most people believe things are getting worse. Across all countries surveyed in 2017, only 20 percent of people correctly answered that poverty rates have declined over the previous twenty years.*

Why isn't the good news sinking in? A few factors are at work. One is our basic human "negativity bias": bad news makes a bigger impression on us and stays with us longer than does neutral or good news. Another factor is that the press tends to emphasize sensationalistic news, which is often negative. Journalism's jaded motto is "If it bleeds, it leads."

One other important factor, I think, was identified by the British philosopher John Stuart Mill in an 1828 speech: "I have observed that not the man who hopes when others despair, but the man who despairs when others hope, is admired by a large class of persons as a sage." In many elite circles and publications negativity seems to be a sign of seriousness and rigor, while optimism and positivity seem naive and under-informed.

Simon, Rosling, Pinker, Roser, and others have pushed back against this institutional negativity bias. They've done work that is both rigorous *and* positive. In fact, they've shown that doing rigorous work—looking systematically at the best available evidence—often compels you to be positive about many things because the evidence is so encouraging.

In this chapter I'll use the information collected in Our World in Data and elsewhere to show some of the big improvements in important measures we've seen in recent decades. As I said in the last chapter, I don't think it's a coincidence that these large and fast improvements are occurring at the same time that the four horsemen of the optimist are galloping quickly around the world. Instead, it's a story of cause and effect: the four horsemen are among the most important reasons that things are getting better.

---

* The country in which the most people are correctly informed about global poverty trends is China. Forty-nine percent of people surveyed there said poverty had declined around the world.

Before I show the evidence, I want to be clear about one thing: I'm not trying to make the case that things today are good enough. Because they're certainly not. The world has too many poor, hungry, and sick people. Too many children are malnourished and uneducated. Too many people, despite the laws on the books, are forced into indentured servitude and slavery. We continue to pump greenhouse gases into the atmosphere, dump plastic into the oceans, kill rare animals, cut down tropical forests, and otherwise befoul our planet.

But we can document improvements without saying or implying that everything's okay now. We *should* document the improvements because they tell us something critically important: *what we're doing is working* and therefore we should keep doing it instead of contemplating huge course changes. As Lomborg wrote in *The Skeptical Environmentalist*, "When things are improving we know we are on the right track. . . . Maybe we can do even more to improve . . . but the basic approach is not wrong."

The basic approach we've taken in recent decades—letting the four horsemen of the optimist gallop faster around the world—is far from wrong. It's causing some startlingly fast and broad improvements. So we need to encourage them to ride faster and farther. We need to step on the accelerator, not yank the steering wheel in a different direction.

The State of Nature

Let's first consider our impact on our planet and start with one of humanity's greatest harms: causing other species to go extinct.

In addition to the passenger pigeon, we humans have entirely wiped out hundreds of other animal species. Our appetite for destruction has led some observers to warn that we're facing a sixth "mass extinction" event, comparable to five previous episodes over the past 450 million years when at least half of all species on Earth vanished.

In an essay for the online magazine *Aeon*, however, Stewart Brand explained how implausible this is: " If *all* [currently threatened species] went extinct in the next few centuries, *and* the rate of extinction that killed them kept right on for hundreds or thousands of years more, *then* we might be at the beginning of a human-caused Sixth Mass Extinction." However, Brand points out that documented extinctions are relatively rare (with about 530 recorded within the past five hundred years) and appear to have slowed down in recent decades; for example, no marine creatures have been recorded as extinct in the past fifty years.

The good news is that we humans are pushing back against our own tendencies toward annihilation in four main ways. First (and closest to science fiction), research is taking place on how to bring back extinct animals by making use of the DNA that remains in their corpses. Brand is a prominent exponent of this "de-extinction" movement and is working with the geneticist George Church and others to adapt an elephant into a species more akin to a woolly mammoth.* Second, we're fighting to preserve some of the most threatened species living on islands (where a disproportionate number of extinctions take place) by removing imported predators. To date, at least eight hundred islands have been protected in this way.

Third, we humans have *created* a great many new species around the world. We do this both deliberately by crossbreeding, as with the cattle-bison hybrid "beefalo," and inadvertently. Many animals have tagged along with us on our journeys around the world and have both speciated (evolved into new species) and hybridized (interbred with local creatures). Some people believe that, over the Industrial Era, our activities have led to a net *gain* in biological variety in many parts of the world. As the ecologist Chris Thomas

---

* This is more than just a science project. As we'll see in the conclusion, having mammoths roam once more could have important climate benefits.

puts it, "It appears to be empirically true that, over the last couple of hundred years, those parts of the world that we know about as regions have increased numbers of species."

Brand argues, though, that the biggest threat to animal species isn't absolute extinction, but instead huge declines in population size due to overhunting and habitat loss. Here, recent news is mixed. Overhunting continues, especially of marine life. As Jesse Ausubel points out, "Fish biomass in intensively exploited fisheries appears to be about one-tenth the level of the fish in those seas a few decades . . . ago."

Ocean overfishing is a classic example of the "tragedy of the commons," an unhappy phenomenon named in a 1968 *Science* article by the ecologist Garrett Hardin. Hardin defined a *commons* as a shared resource, such as a pasture or a body of water, that is available to many but owned by none. That open access sounds great but has a big problem: everyone has ample incentive to exploit the commons (by grazing cows on the pasture or taking fish from the water), but because no one owns it, no one has the incentive to protect or sustain it. So the strong tendency is for everyone to do the economically rational thing, which is to try to exploit it before it's stripped bare. As they do this, they help strip it bare.*

We have many ways to deal with the tragedy of the commons. Elinor Ostrom, to date the only woman to win the Nobel Prize in economics, developed principles for managing commons successfully. One of the most fruitful for helping severely depleted species, and the fourth way that we're helping our fellow creatures survive and thrive, is to simply declare by law that large areas of land or water—large commons—can't be exploited. As we saw in chapter 6, this is in large part how the conservation movement succeeded in protecting bison,

---

* Hardin thought that the planet Earth was the greatest commons of all (he was right about that), and that we'd ruin it via overpopulation (he was wrong about that).

beaver, and other species around the turn of the twentieth century. As we move deeper into the twenty-first century, this approach is quickly spreading around the world. Parks and other protected areas made up only 4 percent of global land area in 1985, but by 2015, this figure had almost quadrupled, to 15.4 percent. At the end of 2017, 5.3 percent of the earth's oceans were similarly protected.

Green Acres

Declaring that a piece of land or water is a park isn't the only way to help out its living things. We can also interact with them less, which seems to suit them just fine. For example, both the demilitarized zone between North and South Korea and the exclusion zone around the still-radioactive Chernobyl nuclear plant in Ukraine have seen animals thrive because humans are absent.

The most important way that we're absenting ourselves from the land at present is by no longer farming it. As we saw in chapter 7, for example, the amount of land used for farming in the United States has declined since 1982 by a Washington State–sized amount. After we stop farming the land, it eventually reverts to forest. Throughout the developed world this process is now dominating any and all tree felling that is taking place, and overall reforestation has become the norm.

Most countries in the developing world, meanwhile, are still experiencing net deforestation as trees are cut down for plantations, farms, and pastureland. We often see this pattern: richer countries have turned the corner, lessening their overall planetary footprint and reversing previous environmental harms, while poorer ones have not yet.

This isn't because poor people are indifferent to the environment. Instead, it's because poorer countries tend to have weaker institutions and less responsive governments, as discussed in chapter 9. It's also because people in poor countries generally have access to less advanced and dirtier technologies; they heat their homes and cook their meals with dung or wood instead of natural gas and light them with kerosene lamps instead of solar-powered LEDs. Finally, some countries have decided to accept higher levels of pollution, deforestation, and other harms in order to grow more quickly.

Even with continued deforestation in developing countries and other challenges, a critical milestone has been reached: across the planet as a whole we have, as an international research team concluded in 2015, experienced a "recent reversal in loss of global terrestrial biomass." For the first time since the start of the Industrial Era, our planet is getting greener, not browner. Since 2003, large-scale reforestation in Russia and China, growth in African and Australian savannas, and slowing tropical deforestation have combined to increase the amount of carbon-storing vegetation on Earth. This increase is nowhere near enough to offset all the greenhouse gases we humans are putting into the atmosphere, but it's still great news.

Turning Down the Heat

The planet's most worrisome environmental issue is global warming. Sustainability scientist Kim Nicholas has beautifully summarized key points about climate change on a sign she takes to marches and rallies. Titled "Climate Science 101," it reads:

1. It's Warming
2. It's Us
3. We're Sure
4. It's Bad
5. We Can Fix It*

---

* In the best scientific tradition, each of the statements on Nicholas's sign is supported with a footnote.

The only thing an economist might want to add to this sign is "It's Pollution," because that label immediately indicates both how to think about global warming and what to do about it. As we saw in chapter 9, pollution is the classic negative externality—a cost caused by an economic activity that is not directly and immediately borne by the people engaged in that activity. For all the things that competitive markets and voluntary exchange do well, they don't deal well with externalities. In fact, they often cause them.

Since 1800, the earth's level of atmospheric carbon dioxide (CO_2) has increased from 283 ppmv* to 408 ppmv in 2018. Just about all of this rise is due to human economic activity (It's Us). Carbon dioxide is a "greenhouse gas," which keeps heat in the atmosphere instead of letting it escape into space (It's Warming). Large enough increases in global temperatures raise ocean levels (by melting the ice sheets that cover Greenland and Antarctica); cause heat waves that are bad for crops, animals, and people; and shift the geographic areas in which many species can live. Higher levels of atmospheric CO_2 also cause the world's oceans to become more acidic, which is poisonous to coral reefs and other critical habitats. So It's Bad. And, yes, We're Sure.

We Can Fix It because It's Pollution, and we know how to deal with that negative externality. As we saw in chapter 9, we've greatly reduced CFCs, smog, SO_2, and many other atmospheric pollutants. So why should greenhouse gases be different or more difficult?

Largely because they're generated by so much of our economic activity. Worldwide, over 20 percent of greenhouse gas emissions come from industry, 6 percent from buildings, 14 percent from transportation, 24 percent from agriculture, and 25 percent from electricity and heat production. The major contributors to global warming thus include the most fundamental things that we people

---

* Parts per million by volume.

do—make things, shelter ourselves and keep warm, get from place to place, and eat—all around the world.

This helps us understand why we haven't seen more cap-and-trade programs or carbon taxes established for greenhouse gases. Cap-and-trade has worked extremely well for reducing SO2 and other particulate pollution in the United States and elsewhere, as we saw in chapter 9. It was politically feasible because atmospheric particulate pollution immediately affected everyone in a region, yet was mainly generated by a small group of coal-burning electricity generation plants and factories. Their objections at being taxed were overruled. It's much harder, though, to push through a carbon tax when just about everyone is going to have to pay it, and when the harms are far enough in the future that they can be ignored or downplayed.

A related problem is that while most other kinds of atmospheric pollution stay local, greenhouse gases are global—they diffuse throughout the earth's atmosphere no matter where they're generated. So if only a single country puts in place a carbon cap-and-trade system, it could be described as taxing its people to do all other nations a favor, yet getting nothing back from them. That's a hard sell.

A final reason that greenhouse gases have been so hard to curtail is simple chemistry. They're generated every time anyone burns any fossil fuel anywhere, for any purpose—they're an inevitable by-product of combustion. And they're hard to capture as they're being generated. Modern air filters that trap all the tiny pollution particles generated by a car's internal combustion engine are small, light, inexpensive, and safe. A "carbon capture" system for a car, on the other hand, would have to include a system to separate out the CO2 from the rest of the exhaust stream and a pressurized tank to hold it until it could be disposed of. This would be both expensive and impractical, and to my knowledge it has never been seriously suggested.

So without broad taxes or broadly effective capture technologies, greenhouse gas pollution continues to rise around the world. However, there are a couple of exceptions. The United States has reduced its total emissions in recent years because of the huge rise in fracking discussed in chapter 7. Burning natural gas releases much less CO_2 (per unit of energy) than does burning coal, so as the fracking revolution led America to shift from coal to gas for generating electricity, total greenhouse gas (GHG) emissions decreased.

In other words, we got lucky. The recent decline in US CO_2 emissions wasn't caused by adopting a cap-and-trade system or any other deliberate reduction policies. It happened largely because tech progress and capitalism caused a shift from coal to natural gas, and natural gas emits fewer GHG pollutants.

Overall, we humans haven't yet done a great job of dealing with GHG pollution, even though it's conceptually no different from other types of pollution. In chapter 15 we'll look at ways to address this situation, and to more quickly bring down levels of atmospheric carbon. It's urgent that we do so because, unlike particulate matter and most other kinds of air pollution, carbon sticks around for a long time. As a result, the total amount of carbon in the atmosphere will keep increasing for many years to come, even after we pass peak GHG pollution and start emitting less of it year after year.

To see why this is, assume that CO_2 lasts in the atmosphere for one hundred years. Let's say that 2017 turns out to be the peak year for total US CO_2 emissions at 5,140 million tons, and that in 2018 we emit less, say, 5,100 million tons. Then the relevant calculation for the planet in 2018 is to add these 5,100 million tons to the atmosphere but only subtract 1,750 million tons—the amount of carbon added by America one hundred years ago, in 1918, when there were many fewer people and much less human economic activity. So while the year-over-year reduction is great, it does *not* cause a decrease in total atmospheric GHG. To accomplish that goal, much bigger and more sustained reductions are necessary. In chapter 15 we'll look at how we can use the four horsemen to maximize our chances of getting there.

Cleaning Up Our Acts

Happily, the situation with other kinds of air pollution is much better. They're much less long-lived, and the four horsemen have combined to bring them down sharply in much of the world. Public awareness of the harms of pollution has spread, and responsive governments have mandated reductions. Tech progress has responded to these mandates by creating internal combustion engines and other products that pollute less, and capitalism has spread these products around the world, even to countries with weak pollution-control regimes.

As a result of all this, air-pollution death rates since 1990 have fallen in most countries, and years of life lost have fallen even more quickly. But even though death rates have decreased, growing populations mean that the total number of annual deaths attributable to air pollution has been rising in India and other countries with relatively poor pollution controls. I predict, though, that as these countries become more prosperous, this situation will change, and they'll move past peak deaths from air pollution. As India's Indira Gandhi said in 1972 at the United Nation's first conference on the environment, "Poverty is the biggest polluter." So as poverty declines, so, too, will pollution.

The situation with water pollution is more mixed. As we saw in chapter 9, some countries are still dumping huge amounts of plastic and other garbage into their rivers. This trash then flows into the oceans, which are a commons for the whole planet. Here again the divide between developed countries and developing ones is sharp. Poverty pollutes, while affluence cleans up from its prior mistakes via public awareness and responsive government. A clear example of this is the effort by both government and industry in the United

States to clean up the country's lakes, ponds, streams, and rivers after the passage of 1972's Clean Water Act. Economists David Keiser and Joseph Shapiro brought together 50 million pollution readings from 170,000 sites across the country and concluded that "water pollution has declined dramatically over time and that the Clean Water Act . . . contributed to this decline."

After ocean acidification and plastic trash, nitrogen pollution might well be the most serious problem facing the world's waters. Nitrogen fertilizer that isn't absorbed by crops can wash into rivers and oceans. There it causes a number of harms including large "dead zones" of oxygen-poor water that can suffocate fish and other marine life.* As we saw in chapter 2, the Industrial Era saw massive increases in the amount of nitrogen fertilizer used around the world. This means that the amount of nitrogen pollution also increased.

The problem is a serious one, but there are two hopeful signs. First, as shown in chapter 5, the United States (which remains a farming powerhouse) is now post-peak in its total use of nitrogen and other fertilizers even as its agricultural output grows. As the two horsemen of tech progress and capitalism continue to gallop, this will be the case for more and more countries. The second hopeful sign is that responsive government can make a large difference in fertilizer use. Between 2005 and 2015 the Chinese government taught more than 20 million small farmers about efficient use of fertilizer. The results of this intervention were impressive: average yields across all crops increased by about 10 percent, while total application of nitrogen decreased by about 15 percent. These two examples show that neither pollution of water nor anything else is a fixed price that must be paid for human prosperity.

---

* This phenomenon, called *eutrophication,* happens when the fertilizer in the water causes large amounts of plants and algae to grow. This growth uses up so much of the oxygen in the water that fish don't have enough.

The Human Condition

In 2016 the economist and columnist Noah Smith reviewed the evidence on poverty around the world, and his conclusion was notably exuberant: "This is incredible—nothing short of a miracle. *Nothing like this has ever happened before in recorded history.*" A graph created by Max Roser clearly reveals the "miracle" Smith was talking about, and how right he was that the improvement is without precedent. The graph doesn't show the percentage of people living in poverty, but instead something even more important: the total number of extremely poor people on earth.

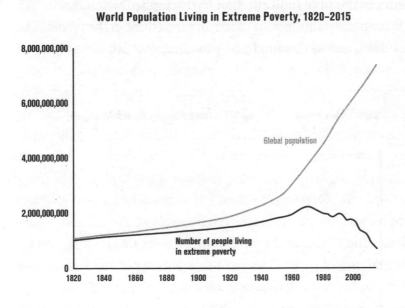

World Population Living in Extreme Poverty, 1820–2015

The World's War on Poverty

The total number of poor people in the world peaked right at the time of the first Earth Day in 1970, then started to slowly decrease.

But the real miracle came when this happy decline accelerated during the twenty-first century. In 1999, 1.76 billion people were living in extreme poverty. Just sixteen years later, this number had declined by 60 percent, to 705 million. Hundreds of millions fewer people are living in poverty now than in 1820, when the world's total population was seven times smaller than it is today.

Much of this decline is reflective of what occurred in China, which, as we saw in the previous chapter, threw off economic socialism beginning in 1978 and let capitalism work its poverty-reducing miracles. But the story of global poverty reduction isn't a purely Chinese one. As the graph below shows, every region around the world has seen large poverty reductions in recent years. The speed of the recent decline indicates that it's no longer ridiculous to talk about completely eliminating extreme poverty from the planet. The World Bank thinks this might be possible by 2030.

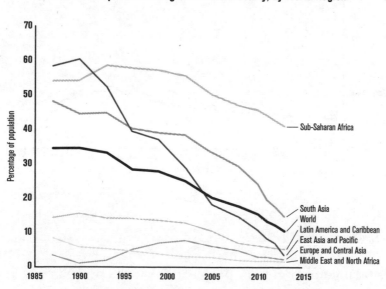

Share of the Population Living in Extreme Poverty, by World Region

It's not just incomes that have improved. As I consult Our World in Data and other comprehensive sources of evidence, I struggle to find even a single important measure of human material well-being that's not getting better in most regions around the world.

Here are recent trends in a few key areas.

Daily Bread

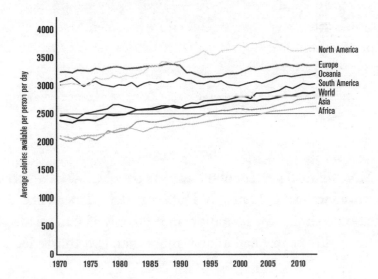

Food Supply by Region in Kilocalories per Person per Day, 1970–2013

As recently as 1980, the global average number of available daily calories wasn't enough to permit an active adult male to maintain his body weight. Less than thirty-five years later, however, every region in the world met this standard of twenty-five hundred daily calories.

Clean Living

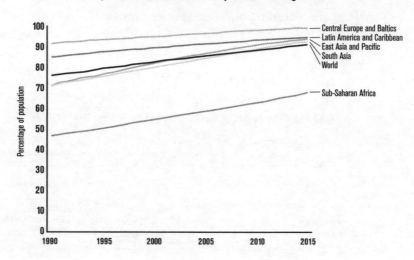

Share of the Population with Access to Improved Drinking Water

More than 90 percent of the world's people now have access to improved water;* in 1990 only a bit more than 75 percent did. The situation is similar for sanitation: in 1990 only a bit more than half of the world's people had it; now, more than two-thirds do.

---

* As Our World in Data explains, "An improved drinking water source includes piped water on premises (piped household water connection located inside the user's dwelling, plot or yard), and other improved drinking water sources (public taps or standpipes, tube wells or boreholes, protected dug wells, protected springs, and rainwater collection)."

Young Minds

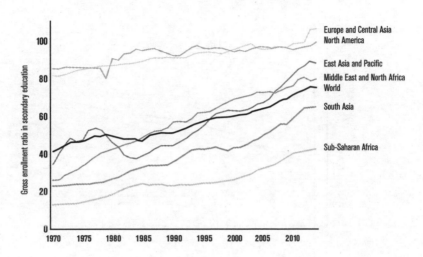

Gross Enrollment Ratio in Secondary Education

The trend in secondary education enrollment around the world is similar to the one for sanitation, but even sharper: in 1986 fewer than half of the world's teenagers were in school; at present, more than 75 percent are.

By now the pattern should be familiar: life expectancy at birth has gone up around the world in recent decades:

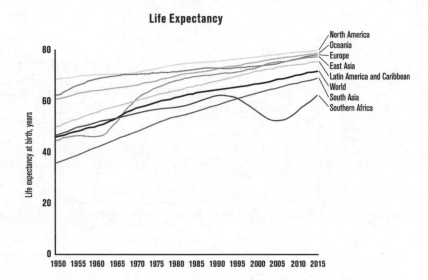

As we saw in chapter 1, global life expectancy was about 28.5 years in 1800. Over the next 150 years, that number increased by 20 years. Then, in the years between 1950 and 2015, it increased by 25 more. These gains are now universal; Southern Africa has regained the 10 years of expected life lost during its terrifying AIDS crisis.

One of the reasons life expectancy has gone up so quickly is the collapse in both child and maternal mortality around the world:

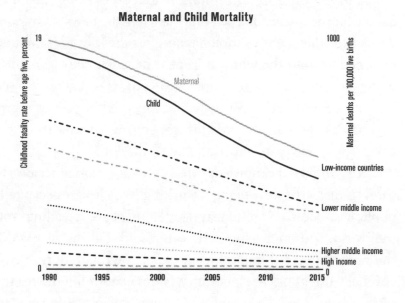

Maternal and Child Mortality

I find these mortality declines especially fast, large, and broad. Today, we still have desperately poor regions, failed states, and the decimations of war. But in no region today is the child mortality rate higher than the world's average rate was in 1998.

Convergent

Trends in maternal and child mortality highlight a critical fact that's often overlooked: around the world, inequality in most important measures of human material well-being is decreasing. Poor countries are catching up to rich ones, and gaps that were once large are shrinking. Inequalities in income and wealth dominate the news, and in many places these gaps are large and growing. They're also important, so we'll look at economic inequality in the next two chapters.

But it's true, too, that there are other kinds of inequality that we should care about as we examine the human condition: inequalities in health, education, diet, sanitation, and other things that matter deeply for the quality of a person's life. Here the news is profoundly good; these inequalities are collapsing. As the four horsemen have galloped around the world in recent decades, they've made life better not only for those people and countries that were already rich but for just about everyone else. Everywhere, fewer mothers and babies are dying, more kids are getting an education, more people have adequate nutrition and sanitation.

It's essential to acknowledge these global victories because they show us that what we're doing is working. Tech progress, capitalism, public awareness, and responsive government are spreading around the world, and improving it. It's often said that insanity is doing the same thing over and over but expecting different results. The corollary might be that ignorance is not examining the results of what's being done. Over and over, when we look at the evidence, we see that the four horsemen are improving our world.

CHAPTER 12

Powers of Concentration

With the invention of the city and its powerful combination of economies of scale coupled to innovation and wealth creation came the great divisions of society.

—Geoffrey West, *Scale*, 2017

It's pretty well known that around the world societies are urbanizing; people are leaving the countryside and moving to cities. What's much less well-known is that this process might be nearly complete.

In 2018, the United Nations estimated that 55 percent of the world's population lived in urban areas, and that the figure would rise to 68 percent by 2050. Also in 2018, however, economist Lewis Dijkstra of the European Commission (EC) concluded, "Everything you heard about urbanization is wrong." Dijkstra and his colleagues found that by 2015 the world was already 84 percent urbanized, and that contrary to previous estimates Asia, Africa, and Oceania were already more urbanized than both North America and Europe.

The huge differences from prior estimates came about because the EC researchers used satellite imagery to identify urban areas (those with both large populations and high population density), whereas earlier estimates had relied on countries' own lists of their cities. These lists used incompatible definitions and were often incomplete. After standardizing what *urban* meant and looking at the entire planet using satellite data, a very different picture emerged of where people live. We're not on our way to becoming a city-dwelling species—we're already largely there.

This recent, fast, and deep urbanization is a clear example of a broad trend: that of greater *concentration* of people and their economic activities. Concentration is "close gathering" (for example, people are gathered much more closely in cities than in villages), so increases in concentration mean closer gathering of that which used to be more spread out. We saw in the previous chapter that as the four horsemen of the optimist gallop around the world, they're improving it. They're also concentrating it.

Where the Action Is

Urbanization illustrates how this works. During the past couple of centuries capitalism and tech progress combined to make agriculture far less labor-intensive, so farms didn't need as many workers. The factories of the Industrial Era did, though, so people in search of work moved from the countryside to the cities and towns with manufacturing. As the Industrial Era gave way to the Second Machine Age, factories, too, began to require fewer people overall even as their total output increased. Again, this was due to the first two horsemen: tech progress offered opportunities to save on labor, and the competition inherent in capitalism led companies to accept this offer. First agriculture, then manufacturing, hit "peak jobs," followed by a decline in total employment even as the industries themselves grew.

The service industries, meanwhile, continued to need ever-more people. "Service industry" is a category so broad as to be almost meaningless: it includes everything from investment banking to software programming to dry cleaning to dog walking. Most service industries do have two important things in common: many of their jobs have been harder to automate (no dog-walking robot is commercially available yet, as far as I know), and they rely heavily on in-person interactions. You can't get your dry cleaning done via telepresence, and investment bankers like being around other investment bankers.

The in-person nature of service jobs matters for concentration. Because cities are where the people are, they're also where the service jobs are. Because people are aware of where the jobs are, they move to cities. Responsive governments contribute to urbanization by building public transportation and other infrastructure, helping to clear a path for dense housing, and fighting crime and promoting public safety. All four horsemen thus contribute to the recent self-reinforcing cycle of urbanization, and the increasing concentration of human population.

The US presidential election of 2016 provided a vivid illustration of concentration—both of the country's population and its economy. Despite winning almost 3 million more votes than Republican candidate Donald Trump, Democratic candidate Hillary Clinton won a majority of the vote in fewer than five hundred counties. These counties, however, together generated 64 percent of the country's economy. The more than twenty-five hundred counties won by Trump were responsible for only a bit more than a third of the American economy.

More from Fewer

Capitalism and tech progress have another fundamental effect. They don't just lead to fewer people working on farms and in factories; they also lead to fewer farms and factories in total. We saw in chapter 7 that since the early 1980s the total acreage of cropland in the United States has been reduced by a Washington State–sized amount, even as total crop tonnage greatly increased. Over the same time the number of farms in the country decreased by an even larger percentage, from about 2.5 million in 1982 to fewer than 2,050,000 in 2017.

The pattern in manufacturing is the same: more production from fewer factories. While America's manufacturing output increased by more than 43 percent between 1994 and 2016, the number of establishments in the industry—or physical locations where manufacturing happens—decreased by almost 15 percent. So it's not just that economic activity is concentrating geographically; it's also concentrating organizationally. In industries including agriculture and manufacturing, all the work is being done by a smaller and smaller number of entities.

Titans of Industries

We're also seeing a clear close gathering of sales and profits around the world in most industries. This is the type of concentration that economists have traditionally focused on the most: when they describe an industry as "concentrated," they're not talking about geography or the number of locations. Instead, they mean that most of the total sales or profits come from only a small number of companies (rather than being spread more equally across all competitors in the market).

Economists and policy makers pay attention to concentration for many reasons, one of the most important of which is vigilance against monopolies—situations in which an industry has only one company (which would obviously get *all* of the sales and profits). A monopoly is the most concentrated industry possible. Monopolies can come about in several ways, but once they exist, they strongly tend to exhibit certain behaviors, none of which are good for customers (or for society as a whole). Monopolies tend to raise prices simply because they can—after all, they have no competitors to lure away customers by offering a lower price—thereby increasing their revenues and profits in the easiest way possible. They also tend to innovate less, again because no rivals exist to take away their market by offering a better product.

Because of their effect on prices and innovation, monopolies have long been opposed both by professional economists and many consumers. The American board game Monopoly traces its roots to 1903, when the Landlord's Game was invented by Elizabeth Magie to illustrate the problems of concentrating land ownership. The game eventually became quite popular. It was played frequently and earnestly during the 1970s by a group of students at the University of Chicago. When one asked the free-market-loving (and Nobel Prize–winning) economist Milton Friedman to sign the player's Monopoly set, Friedman obliged, but also wrote "down with" before the game's title.

This anecdote illustrates that monopolies are a serious departure from real capitalism, which as we saw in chapter 7 depends on healthy competition among companies to deliver its benefits. So a trend of greater concentration in many of a country's industries could be worrying, since it could be creating lots of monopolies. Recent changes in industry concentration are so important that they were the topic of the Federal Reserve Bank of Kansas City's 2018 Economic Policy Symposium in Jackson Hole, Wyoming, an event that has been called "Woodstock for central bankers."

One of the main papers for that conference was written by the economist John Van Reenen. He looked at a great deal of evidence and research and found that concentration has been on the rise around the rich world in recent decades. As he writes, "The data show sharp increases in concentration across the whole US economy in the last 30 years, with the growth generally stronger in the second half of the sample. . . . Within the 9 EU countries where comprehensive data is available, sales concentration has risen since 2000. This remains true when adding other non-EU OECD countries such as Australia, Japan and Switzerland."

Tech Winners Take All

So does this mean that competition and capitalism are in decline and in trouble in many countries? Many have argued that this is the case, but Van Reenen's analyses point to a different conclusion. His work suggests that industrial concentration is rising globally not because of a decline in capitalism and tech progress, but rather because of an *increase* in them. Recent tech progress is so profound that it's changing the nature of competition, and this change is reflected in the concentration evidence. So it's not that competition is decreasing (due to bad government policies, weak antitrust enforcement, or other causes) and a new crop of lazy monopolists is being grown. Instead, technology-fueled competition is fierce, and a new generation of sophisticated leading firms is being forged.

Van Reenen reaches this conclusion by noting that around the world in recent decades companies within the same industry have become more dissimilar from one another. In particular, differences have increased in productivity and in pay. A few companies have become much more productive and have started paying much higher salaries (two developments that are closely related), while the rest have seen near-stagnant productivity and pay. The leading firms have been able to capture more of their industry's total sales and profits, while their rivals simply lumber along. I call this situation one of *superstars and zombies* within an industry; the more common phrase for it within economics is *winner take all* or *winner take most*.

Van Reenen writes, "Many of the patterns are consistent with a . . . view where many industries have become 'winner take most/ all' due to globalization and new technologies rather than a generalized weakening of competition due to relaxed antitrust rules or rising regulation."

Erik Brynjolfsson and I agree with this view.* We argued in 2008 that concentration was increasing because of tech progress, and that it would continue to do so.

We made a simple point supported by a great deal of historical evidence: it's extremely difficult for companies, even well-managed ones, to understand and extract the full value of powerful new technologies such as the steam engine, electrification, the smartphone, or artificial intelligence. Many companies are willing to spend money on the new technology, but surprisingly few are ready, willing, or able to make the changes required to fully exploit it.

These changes, if and when they're successfully put into practice, are called intangible assets,† and they're what allow a company to put new technologies to work, obtain higher productivity, pay more, and gain competitive advantage over rivals in an industry. So a period of broad, deep, and fast tech progress such as we're experiencing during this Second Machine Age should be expected to generate both superstars and zombies in industries around the world. In an era where few companies succeed at the difficult work of not only acquiring powerful new technologies but also the right intangible assets, the superstars pull ahead. Concentration thus increases.

The World's Wealthiest

It's easy to see how increased industrial concentration of the kind described by Van Reenen would lead to increased concentration in people's wealth and incomes. The share prices of publicly traded superstar firms become valuable and so increase the wealth of their

---

* As do many other researchers on the impact of technological change.

† They're called this because you can't see or touch them as you can machinery and buildings.

founders and investors. This has happened during previous bursts of tech progress—as we saw in chapter 2, both James Watt and Matthew Boulton became wealthy because of the steam engine—but wealth creation in the Second Machine Age is exceptional.

Since 1925 (when systematic data collection began), six of the eight highest public-market valuations ever recorded for American companies have belonged to modern high-tech superstars such as Amazon, Alphabet (Google's parent company), Intel, and Microsoft. The people who were smart or lucky enough to acquire large amounts of stock in these companies have become fantastically affluent. Amazon founder Jeff Bezos, for example, became known as the "richest man in modern history" in July of 2018, when his wealth passed $150 billion.

Most Americans, however, don't own stock in Amazon. Or in any other company. Economist Edward Wolff found that, in 2016, 50.7 percent of US households owned no stocks at all, either directly or in retirement accounts. So all stock market wealth is concentrated in less than half of America's households. Even within this group, there's a lot of concentration: Wolff found that the top 10 percent of US households owned 84 percent of total stock market wealth in 2016. High concentration here means high inequality; when stock ownership is closely held by a relatively small group of people and share prices increase, members of that group become much wealthier than everyone else.

Few disagree that wealth and income have become more concentrated in recent decades; just about every legitimate researcher I'm aware of has concluded that they have. But the causes and the consequences of rising inequality are much debated. Van Reenen and others believe that the main causes are structural. The two tectonic forces of globalized capitalism and tech progress are creating more winner-take-all or winner-take-most industries characterized by a few superstar companies and many zombies.

People associated with the superstars see their wealth and pay grow quickly, while those who work in or around the zombies see their fortunes stagnate. At the heart of this explanation are large differences among companies during this period of great technological upheaval.

Other explanations for rising inequality focus not on differences across companies, but instead on broad changes that have affected the entire economy (or at least large parts of it). Many such changes have been proposed. They include increased corporate short-termism and "financialization" of the economy; the decline of labor unions; declining labor mobility (caused in part by burdensome occupational licensing requirements); increasing use by businesses of noncompete agreements that limit employees' options when they leave; and the rise of regions with at most one employer per industry (which, facing no competition, doesn't have to pay much).

I side with Van Reenen and others who believe that differences across companies are the main (although certainly not the only) driver of income and wealth concentration and inequality. Some of the strongest evidence in support of this view is that income and wealth are becoming more concentrated in just about all the economies for which data are available. It seems unlikely to me that labor mobility and unions could be simultaneously on the decline in so many countries, or that employee noncompetes have become globally important.

On the other hand, tech progress and capitalism are clearly both global phenomena, as we saw in chapter 10. So to me the most plausible explanation is that as these two horsemen gallop around the world, they're causing differences across companies to grow in country after country, and the difference between superstar and zombie firms is leading to concentration (and hence inequality) in personal wealth and income.

A Tale of Three Economies

The debate and ongoing research about the causes of growing wealth and income inequality are important because we want to understand what's driving important social and economic phenomena. It seems to me, though, that much of the discussion at present begs the question of whether these types of concentration are bad. The assumption is widespread that rising wealth and income inequality across peoples and households is a major problem. I'm not sure about that; I think a bigger problem lies elsewhere.

To see why this is, consider three different scenarios for change in a hypothetical country:

1. There's strong economic growth. The rich get much richer, but middle class and poor households also do better. Because wealth and income gains are fastest at the top—because the rich get richer faster than the rest do—inequality increases, but all segments of society see growing incomes and wealth. Tech progress exists but is not highly disruptive; people continue to do the same kinds of jobs for the same kinds of companies in the same communities year after year. Important institutions such as the educational system and the courts remain stable and inclusive.
2. The elites capture the economy and the political system and turn inclusive institutions into extractive ones. They change the laws, pack the courts, demand bribes, assume control of the largest companies (publicly or behind the scenes), hire security services for themselves and let law and order decay for everyone else, and so on. The economy slows down because it's so badly managed, and all tech progress has to be imported. The elite get fantastically rich while everyone else suffers and becomes poorer. Wealth and income inequality skyrocket.

3. Economic growth is healthy and institutions remain inclusive, but tech progress is extraordinarily powerful—so much so that it disrupts industry after industry. This progress fuels many types of concentration; it allows more crops to be grown on less land, more consumption from fewer natural resources, more output from fewer factories, and more sales and profits from a smaller number of companies. The people at the top of these superstar companies see huge wealth and income gains. Gains for those in the middle, however, slow down considerably. And some segments of the labor force face particularly tough challenges; the factories and farms that used to employ them close, and new ones don't open. Job opportunities concentrate in cities and in service industries. Wealth and income inequality rise a great deal.

Most readers, I believe, wouldn't find the society described in the first scenario above to be unfair or unjust, or one that they wouldn't want to live in. People at all levels of affluence are doing better, after all, and institutions remain inclusive. Few people, though, would want to live within the second scenario. The country has clearly been hijacked, and most people within it are getting a bad deal.

The third scenario is the most interesting because it's the most ambiguous. An observer could easily argue that nothing unfair has happened. Institutions haven't been captured by the elite, and tech progress yields all kinds of new goods and services (such as cheap smartphones that deliver unlimited amounts of knowledge, entertainment, and communication). Yet many people in this scenario face serious challenges. Not only their jobs have disappeared, but their communities and ways of life are also fading. These people would be justified in feeling that the bargain they signed up for—"If I acquire skills and am willing to show up and work diligently, I'll get economic and social stability and upward mobility"—isn't at all what they're receiving. No matter how good their smartphones are.

Thinking through these scenarios leads, I believe, to two conclusions. First, rising inequality itself isn't the problem; unfairness is. As Nobel Prize winner Angus Deaton put it in 2017, "Inequality is not the same thing as unfairness; and, to my mind, it is the latter that has incited so much political turmoil in the rich world today. Some of the processes that generate inequality are widely seen as fair. But others are deeply and obviously unfair, and have become a legitimate source of anger and disaffection." Psychologists Christina Starmans, Mark Sheskin, and Paul Bloom found widespread agreement with Deaton's viewpoint. They write, "There is no evidence that people are bothered by economic inequality itself. . . . Drawing upon laboratory studies, cross-cultural research, and experiments with babies and young children, we argue that humans naturally favor fair distributions, not equal ones, and that when fairness and equality clash, people prefer fair inequality over unfair equality."

The second conclusion is that it's not only objective unfairness and injustice inflicted by one group (as in scenario 2) that cause problems. Perceptions also matter a great deal. Scenario 3 has no bad actors, but a lot of people still feel that what's happening to them isn't fair. We'll look more deeply at the phenomenon of perceived unfairness in the next chapter. Let's conclude this one by noting how widespread concentration is, and how it's remaking economies and societies.

CHAPTER 13

Stressed Be the Tie That Binds: Disconnection

We must, indeed, all hang together, or assuredly we shall all hang separately.

—Attributed to Benjamin Franklin at the signing of
the American Declaration of Independence, 1776

Over his long career, US Marines general James Mattis built a reputation as both a fearsome fighter and a serious scholar, almost ascetic in his devotion to his country and its military. By the time he became secretary of defense in 2017, he was often referred to as a "warrior monk." So his reply when asked in 2018 what worried him most should carry some weight.

Mattis's answer didn't involve the rogue nuclear state of North Korea, the rise of China as an ambitious global power, the volatile Middle East, cyberattacks and other forms of digital and asymmetric warfare, or any of the other usual subjects of concern for a modern American general. Instead, he replied:

"The lack of a fundamental friendliness. It seems like an awful lot of people in America and around the world feel spiritually and personally alienated. . . . I think that, when you look at veterans coming out of the wars, they're more and more just slapped in the face by that isolation, and they're used to something better. They think it's PTSD—which it can be—but it's really about alienation.

If you lose any sense of being part of something bigger, then why should you care about your fellow man?"

A Capital under Attack

A social scientist would say that what Mattis has observed is a decline in *social capital* in the United States and elsewhere. That term, which has been in use since the turn of the twentieth century, is well defined by the sociologist Robert Putnam as "connections among individuals—social networks and the norms of reciprocity and trustworthiness that arise from them." Two things about this definition are important. First, at the heart of social capital are relationships between and among people (rather than, say, between citizens and governments or students and their school). Second, these relationships—rather than formal institutions such as courts—are the source of trust and reciprocity, or the practice of returning favors and good deeds.

Social capital is extremely valuable. It's a type of wealth, as important as money or physical capital such as machines and buildings. So if Mattis's observations are right and social capital is on the decline in America, it would truly be a decrease in the wealth of the nation. And a great deal of evidence indicates that this decline is both real and large. In the early 1970s, more than 60 percent of working-age Americans believed that "most people can be trusted." By 2012, only a bit more than 20 percent of the equivalent group believed so. The government has taken an even harder hit. Between 1958 and 2015, the Pew Research Center found that public trust in the federal government fell from about 73 percent to about 19 percent.

One of the things that most struck de Tocqueville when he toured the United States early in the Industrial Era was how much social capital existed in the young country. He found an "immense picture" of voluntary, nonpolitical groups and marveled, "Americans of all ages, all conditions, all minds constantly unite. Not only do they have commercial and industrial associations in which all take part but they also have a thousand other kinds: religious, moral, grave, futile, very general and very particular, immense and very small. . . . Everywhere that, at the head of a new undertaking, you see the government in France and a great lord in England, count on it that you will perceive an association in the United States."

Early in the Second Machine Age, however, Robert Putnam found something very different. He observed a decline in just about all forms of voluntary association, even recreational sports usually played in groups. As the title of his 2000 book put it, we were *Bowling Alone.*

Fatal Contraction

Because social capital is the product of connections among people, I and others use the term *disconnection* to refer to decreases in social capital. Disconnection is the weakening or severing of relationships; it's a contraction in the number of ties among people. This contraction is bad for the health of the economy since so much business depends on trust and reciprocity.* Recently, it's also become clear how bad it is for the health of people themselves.

In 2015 economists Anne Case and Angus Deaton uncovered a startling and dire trend within the data on American mortality rates. As we saw in chapter 11, most mortality trends around the world are moving in the right direction; people are living longer, so death rates for just about all demographic groups have been

---

* Even if courts work well, you don't want to have to sue people so they'll hold up their part of a deal. You'd much rather just be able to trust them.

going down. But Case and Deaton found an exception to this progress: mortality rates for middle-aged white Americans were on the rise.

This wasn't true for all people in this group or for all causes of death. Just about all the mortality increase was attributable to the least educated white middle-aged Americans, and to three causes of death: suicide, drug overdose, and chronic liver disease such as cirrhosis (which is often caused by alcoholism). People in this group were killing themselves, quickly and slowly, in numbers high enough to reverse the previous trend of decreasing overall mortality. Case and Deaton gave this phenomenon the label "deaths of despair."

These deaths continue to rise. The US suicide rate rose by 14 percent between 2009 and 2016, when it reached a level not previously seen since the end of World War II. Overdose deaths have climbed even more quickly. They almost doubled between 2008 and 2017, when more than 72,000 people lost their lives to an overdose. This is far more than the 58,220 American military deaths recorded throughout the Vietnam War.

The sharp and sustained rise in deaths of despair is a public health emergency for the United States. According to the Centers for Disease Control, in 2016, 197,000 deaths were related to suicide, alcohol, and drug abuse. This was more than four times the 44,674 people who died from HIV/AIDS at the peak of its epidemic in 1994.* It's also something of a puzzle because most of the rise occurred not during the Great Recession (which officially ended in June 2009), but instead during the steady economic expansion that followed it. In January 2019 the US economy had added jobs for one hundred months in a row (the longest such streak on record), was more than 22 percent bigger than it had been at the end of the

---

* By 2015, fewer than eight thousand Americans died annually from HIV/AIDS.

Great Recession, and had a headline unemployment rate of just 4 percent.

It's true that, as we saw in the last chapter, the wealth and income gains achieved during this expansion have been concentrated, with most going to already affluent people and households. But relatively few are worse off financially than they were at the start of the expansion, especially after assistance from the government and employer-provided benefits such as health care are taken into account. And extreme economic hardship has clearly decreased; researcher Scott Winship finds, for example, "Deep child poverty was as low in 2014 as it had been since at least 1979."

The last time the US suicide rate was as high as in 2016 was during and immediately after the Great Depression, a decade of grinding poverty and hardship when the annual unemployment rate peaked at almost 25 percent, with essentially no government-supplied safety net. So why are deaths of despair growing now, even as the economy does?

For a lot of reasons, not all of which are well understood. Saying that the recent rise in suicides and overdoses is due largely to economic hardship or any other single factor is sure to be wrong. These are complex phenomena, arising out of a combination of factors. The huge increase in overdoses, for example, has certainly been facilitated by increased availability of a range of powerful drugs.* One important factor common to both suicides and overdoses, though, is disconnection. Fewer ties among people mean more deaths of despair.

This fatal relationship has been understood for a long time. Émile Durkheim, a French polymath known as the father of sociology, published his book *Suicide* in 1897. In it, he argues that suicide is

---

* These drugs include prescription opioids, black tar heroin, and fentanyl and other synthetic opioids.

primarily a social phenomenon, rather than one rooted in individuals' personalities or mental illnesses. Suicides rise as people lose close ties to their extended family, their spouse (through divorce), or their place of work (through unemployment). Durkheim was adamant that "dropping out of society" (to use an appropriate but unscientific expression) was a primary cause of suicide, and more than a century of accumulated evidence and research provide a great deal of support for this view. In 2018, the World Health Organization found that "a sense of isolation" was strongly associated with suicide risk around the world.

Overdoses, too, appear to happen more often as relationships, communities, and social ties fray. People become addicted and overdose not only because the drugs they take are powerful but also because the lives they lead are marked by trauma and isolation. As Johann Hari, a writer and researcher on the global "war on drugs" puts it, "The opposite of addiction isn't sobriety, it's connection." Researchers Michael Zoorob and Jason Salemi might well agree with that statement. In a 2017 study covering all US counties they found a strong and negative relationship between social capital and overdose deaths: the less social capital, all other things being equal, the higher the fatality rate. The researchers concluded that Americans were "bowling alone, dying together."

Things Fall Apart

So deaths of despair stem in part from disconnection—from declining social capital. Yet mounting evidence suggests that some people just don't *want* more social capital, at least not of the kind that's being offered. As we saw in chapter 10, most countries are becoming significantly more pluralistic—they're seeing more ethnic diversity and immigration, gender equality, support for gay marriage and other nontraditional lifestyles, and related changes that enhance diversity.

A fascinating stream of recent research finds that a large percentage of people in all countries studied have an innate intolerance for this greater diversity. Instead, they want things to be the same everywhere. They value uniformity of beliefs, values, practices, and so on (as long, of course, as this uniformity reflects their own beliefs, values, and practices). The political scientist Karen Stenner labels people with this personality type "authoritarians" because they typically want a strong central authority to enforce obedience and conformity. Recent election results across countries as dissimilar as the United States, Poland, Turkey, Hungary, the Philippines, and Brazil indicate a global growing desire for authoritarian leaders.

Stenner documents how authoritarianism rises—how it changes from a latent personality trait into an active one. As she says, "The classic conditions that typically activate and aggravate authoritarians—rendering them more racially, morally, and politically intolerant—tend to be perceived loss of respect for/ confidence in/obedience to leaders, authorities and institutions, or perceived value conflict and loss of societal consensus/shared beliefs, and/or erosion of racial/cultural/group identity. This is sometimes expressed as a loss of 'who we are'/'our way of life . . .' These threatening/reassuring conditions can be real and/or perceived. They can reflect actual changes in political/social conditions, and/or be a product of media coverage/political manipulation."

Note how heavily Stenner's explanation stresses perceptions. Authoritarianism is triggered by how people *feel*, at least as much as by economic, political, and social realities. We'll come back to these perceptions later in this chapter.

Authoritarianism is bad for social capital because it offers trust and reciprocity only under the conditions of obedience and conformity. Those conditions are clearly unacceptable to those who value diversity, so ties don't form between pluralists and authoritarians.

As authoritarianism moves from latent to active in more people, existing ties break and social capital erodes.

The Pulitzer Prize–winning author Anne Applebaum experienced this type of disconnection firsthand in the years after she and her husband, the politician Radosław Sikorski, threw a 1999 New Year's Eve party in the Polish countryside. Their guests ushered in the twenty-first century with a sense of solidarity and optimism as the Iron Curtain faded into history. In the years after 2000, however, many of Applebaum's friends and colleagues became openly authoritarian. Applebaum wrote in 2018 about the resulting deep disconnection: "Nearly two decades later, I would now cross the street to avoid some of the people who were at my New Year's Eve party. They, in turn, would not only refuse to enter my house, they would be embarrassed to admit they had ever been there. In fact, about half the people who were at that party would no longer speak to the other half."

Left Behind by the Horsemen

What roles do the four horsemen play in all of this? How do they contribute to declining social capital and increasing disconnection and authoritarianism? I see the first two horsemen—capitalism and tech progress—contributing in two ways: one direct, one indirect.

As we saw in the previous chapter, economies are becoming more geographically concentrated as the first two horsemen gallop around the world. As an economy concentrates, many social ties are inevitably broken as companies, jobs, and work disappear from regions. This disappearing can happen even during extended economic expansions. America's GDP has grown by almost a quarter since the end of the Great Recession ended in mid-2009, but over 20 percent of the country's approximately three thousand counties experienced the opposite of growth: they saw a decline in their total output between 2010 and 2017.

Economic activity, as it brings people together to produce and exchange, builds bonds and social capital. So as economic activity declines, so does social capital. As factories close and farms go fallow in a county it's not just output that decreases; the number of relationships does, too. After all, it's a lot harder for assembly-line workers to maintain all their bonds after the line shuts down. The relationship between economic activity and social capital is a strong one.

Durkheim realized this. In *Suicide*, he maintained that companies were important institutions for maintaining social capital during the upheavals of the Industrial Era: "The corporation has everything needed to give the individual a setting, to draw him out of his state of moral isolation." As concentration continues in the Second Machine Age and establishments and jobs in industries such as manufacturing decrease, such settings become fewer. It's not surprising that suicides would increase as "moral isolation" does.

The importance of industrial jobs was also stressed by the writer Andrew Sullivan in his 2018 essay on drug overdoses. Sullivan makes a point that might help explain why European countries haven't seen fatal overdoses rise anywhere near as much as the United States has. As he writes, "Unlike in Europe, where cities and towns existed long before industrialization, much of America's heartland has no remaining preindustrial history, given the destruction of Native American societies. The gutting of that industrial backbone—especially as globalization intensified in a country where market forces are least restrained—has been not just an economic fact but a cultural, even spiritual devastation." In Sullivan's view, that devastation is now costing many lives.

Deaths of despair reveal disconnection. I think it's absolutely not a coincidence that they're increasing just as geographic concentration of the economy is, and in many of the areas that are getting left behind as capitalism and tech progress race ahead. As we've seen, these two horsemen are directly contributing to dematerialization, and to many fundamental improvements in both the state of nature and the human condition. But they're also contributing directly to disconnection by concentrating economic activity, and thereby eliminating bonds formed over work in many communities.

As Case and Deaton put it, "What our data show is that the patterns of mortality and morbidity for [non-Hispanic whites] without a college degree . . . move in tandem with other social dysfunctions, including the decline of marriage, social isolation, and detachment from the labor force." Whites without a college degree make up the bulk of the large American middle class that formed in the postwar decades. As capitalism and tech progress concentrated the economy, many former members of this middle class gave in to despair.

Perceived Unfairness: The Elephant in the Room

Capitalism and tech progress also contribute *indirectly* to disconnection by affecting how people feel about what's going on around them—about the trends in the communities, societies, and economies they're part of. As we saw earlier in this chapter, perceptions matter at least as much as objective facts for phenomena such as the rise of authoritarianism. The third scenario presented at the end of the previous chapter—in which capitalism and tech progress are powerful enough to disrupt many companies, jobs, and communities—could easily lead to widespread perceptions of unfairness and broken promises, even though the economy hasn't been hijacked by bad actors and even though institutions remain inclusive.

Have capitalism and tech progress in fact been changing how people feel? The two have clearly been increasing wealth and income inequality, but have they also been contributing to a rise in perceived unfairness?

In 2016 the sociologist Arlie Russell Hochschild published a book summarizing her research on the beliefs and views of Tea Party supporters in Louisiana.* Also that year another American sociologist, Kathy Cramer, published a similar book focusing on rural voters in Wisconsin. I find the titles chosen by these two authors fascinating. Hochschild's is *Strangers in Their Own Land*, and Cramer's is *The Politics of Resentment*.

Both titles, and the contents of both books, emphasize that the people depicted feel they've been treated unfairly. Hochschild uses the imagery of their standing patiently in line to reach the American Dream of prosperity and gives voice to their perceptions: "Blacks, women, immigrants, refugees, brown pelicans—all have cut ahead of you in line. But it's people like you who have made this country great. You feel uneasy. It has to be said: the line cutters irritate you. They are violating rules of fairness. You resent them, and you feel it's right that you do."†

Both of these books, and many other recent investigations, have focused on middle-class to lower-middle-class households and communities. The famous Elephant Graph, drawn by economists Branko Milanovic and Christoph Lakner, helps us understand why this segment of society might be feeling so much alienation and resentment.

Milanovic and Lakner had the great idea to essentially line up all the people in the world from poorest to richest, then see how much their incomes changed between 1988 and 2008. The resulting

---

* The Tea Party is a right-wing American political movement launched in the early years of the twenty-first century. It takes its name from the Boston Tea Party, a 1773 protest against taxation in which tea chests were thrown off ships into Boston Harbor.

† The brown pelican symbolizes environmental concerns.

graph looked to many like a drawing of an elephant with its trunk in the air.

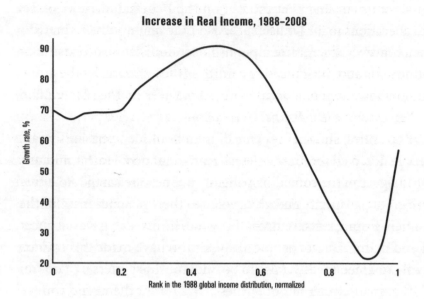

Increase in Real Income, 1988–2008

Growth rate, %

Rank in the 1988 global income distribution, normalized

The graph shows that over this twenty-year period real incomes improved substantially, often by more than 50 percent, for almost everyone around the world (keep in mind that, as we saw in chapter 1, it took *eight centuries* for real incomes to grow by 50 percent across the world prior to the start of the Industrial Era). The Elephant Graph thus supports the claims made in chapter 11 about large and widespread income gains around the world. The one big exception to this positive trend is obvious on the graph: it's the low point between the elephant's head and its trunk. This point on the spectrum of world incomes corresponds to the middle class of the richest countries. As Milanovic put it, "The people who gained the least were almost entirely from the 'mature economies' . . . the old conventional rich world. . . . Those around the median of the German income distribution have gained only 7 percent in real terms over 20 years; those in the US, 26 percent."

The Elephant Graph sparked a great deal of debate, both about the details of its construction and its implications, and many revisions and alterations to it have been proposed.* In all the versions of it I've seen, however, the middle class in the United States and other rich countries is at or near the lowest point of the elephant. It's the group with the lowest income gains in the world over the past generation.

Versions of the Elephant Graph drawn for earlier periods don't have the same shape. They don't look much like elephants at all. They're much closer to flat lines, showing that people all around the world saw their incomes growing at roughly the same rate. Only within the past three decades have we seen the appearance of the elephant's head, representing most of humanity, the upraised trunk representing the world's most affluent, and the trough between them occupied by the rich world's middle class.

The first decades after the end of World War II were a time of large and sustained income gains for this middle class. Recently, though, the gains for this group have slowed. While this was happening, gains for just about everyone else—from Chinese assembly-line workers to Indian call-center employees to bankers in New York and venture capitalists in Silicon Valley—increased as never before.

Is it any wonder, then, that many within the rich world's middle classes feel that they've been treated unfairly? Or that these feelings appear to be intensifying as we move deeper into the Second Machine Age and the two horsemen of capitalism and tech progress continue to gallop around the world? Disconnection is rising in part because the tectonic and impersonal forces of capitalism and

---

* The version of the Elephant Graph drawn here calculates how incomes changed for people within each country, then aggregates across all countries to show income changes across the entire world.

tech progress are contributing to feelings of anger, resentment, and alienation instead of trust, reciprocity, and, as Mattis puts it, "any sense of being part of something bigger."

Capitalism and tech progress contribute both directly and indirectly to the phenomenon of disconnection. What about the other two of our four horsemen of the optimist: responsive government and public awareness? What's their relationship to the declines in social capital we're experiencing?

We the People. Not You.

As we saw in the last chapter, both the economy and the population of the United States are concentrating geographically: the country is experiencing a "close gathering" of economic activity, and hence jobs and people, in a smaller area of land. Cities and states near the coasts have often seen the fastest growth in their economies and populations, while traditional agricultural and industrial regions have seen much lower growth and, in some cases, absolute declines. So has this increase in concentration affected how responsive the US government is?

Not really. It's true that the gaps between the most and least populous US states have gotten larger in recent years. But they've always been large, and important political bodies such as the Senate and electoral college were designed, in whole or in part, to be *unresponsive* to population concentration. These bodies don't seem to be greatly less representative today than earlier in the country's history. As the political analyst Philip Bump points out, "Census data stretching back to 1790 . . . shows that the most-populous states making up half of the country's population have always been represented by only about a fifth of the available Senate seats. That includes 2016." While both Al Gore in 2000 and Hillary Clinton in 2016 won the popular vote but didn't win a majority of electoral college votes (and so did not become president), this outcome also occurred three times in the nineteenth century. It's not clear that geographic concentration has caused American national politics to become much less responsive than in the past to the will of the country's people.

However, strong evidence suggests that politics, at least in the United States, has become more polarized, with elected officials working across party lines less often now than in the past. America's two-party system and requirement that federal legislation be approved by both houses of Congress and the president* have combined in recent years with political polarization to decrease the government's responsiveness to the will of the people. In polls, a majority of Americans consistently support tighter gun control, a path to citizenship for undocumented immigrants, access to abortion services, and action on global warming. However, the leadership of the Republican Party, which has moved steadily to the right since the early 1980s, supports none of these.†

Around the world, responsive government has met other setbacks in recent years. In 1867 the German statesman Otto von Bismarck famously observed, "Politics is the art of the possible." A century and a half later, as the Industrial Era rapidly gives way to the Second Machine Age, disconnection, authoritarianism, and polarization seem to be reducing the possibilities for effective government.

We Hold These Untruths to Be Self-Evident

Authoritarians and pluralists disconnect from one another because of deep differences in their values and morals. As this disconnection

---

* Congress can override a presidential veto with a two-thirds majority in both houses, but this does not happen often. Throughout US history, fewer than 10 percent of presidential vetoes have been overturned.

† America's Democrats haven't moved nearly as sharply to the left.

persists and combines with other phenomena such as greater geographic concentration, political polarization, and declining social capital and trust in institutions, another serious problem appears: people increasingly believe less in facts and more in false news, conspiracy theories, and other departures from the truth. Public awareness of objective reality can easily suffer as a result of disconnection.

Most of us think that we believe the things we believe because they're true. In many cases, though, we believe many things because the people around us believe them. There appear to be a couple of reasons for this. One is simply that the pressure to conform with the beliefs of others nearby can be strong. This phenomenon was demonstrated in a series of famous experiments conducted in the 1950s by the psychologist Solomon Asch. In these, people gave obviously incorrect answers to straightforward questions just because most others in the room (all of whom were "confederates" in the experiment) were also giving the wrong answers.

Another reason is that we humans outsource a lot of knowledge to other people, often without even realizing that we're doing so. As Steven Sloman and Philip Fernbach explain in their book, *The Knowledge Illusion*, many people believe that they have a good idea how a flush toilet works, but few can actually explain the mechanisms by which that device carries away waste and refills with water. This "illusion of explanatory depth" is widespread, covering everything from how a can opener operates to how a cap-and-trade system for reducing pollution is put into practice.

It makes great sense to outsource to other people most of the knowledge we rely on. The modern world is staggeringly complex; not even a supergenius can understand more than a tiny portion of how it all works. So knowledge has to be specialized and divided up across all the brains that make up a society and economy.

The problem arises when many brains in a social group come to believe something that is both wrong and harmful—that, for example, modern vaccines are so risky that small children are better off left unvaccinated. This false belief is widespread in some American communities, even as childhood vaccination has become a public health triumph around the world.

Globally, approximately 90 percent of children are vaccinated against pertussis, a highly infectious coughing disease that's especially dangerous to infants.* In some Los Angeles preschools, however, more than half of students are exempt from this vaccination because of paperwork filed by their parents. These schools' communities, which are usually affluent and well educated, appear to have immunization rates similar to those of Chad and South Sudan. And pertussis has returned as a public health risk in America after almost being vanquished. As recently as 1995, the United States had only six total deaths from the disease. In 2017, there were thirteen.†

As this case shows, objectively wrong and bad ideas can take hold in a social group once enough people believe them, since we humans rely so heavily on others to hold knowledge for us. In another example of disconnection, more and more people are choosing to have fewer ties to people with dissimilar values and beliefs, opting instead to spend more time among the like-minded. The journalist Bill Bishop calls this phenomenon "the big sort." He writes, "As people seek out the social settings they prefer—as they choose the group that makes them feel the most comfortable—the nation grows more politically segregated—and the benefit that ought to come with having a variety of opinions is lost to the righteousness that is the special entitlement of homogeneous groups."

* The coughing associated with pertussis can be so severe and constant that it's difficult for victims to even breathe. The disease is sometimes called whooping cough because of the noise people make as they try to quickly take in air before they have to cough again.

† The anti-vaccination movement is not confined to America. Europe had more than eighty thousand measles cases in 2018, a fifteenfold increase over 2016. These cases led to seventy-two deaths.

One other important factor hampers widespread public awareness of accepted facts: we're particularly reluctant to change our
opinions on topics that are close to our most deeply held values
and beliefs. As the psychologist Jonathan Haidt has demonstrated,
we humans all have a moral foundation, but we don't all have the
same moral foundation. Some of us believe that capitalism is the
best system humans have come up with to ensure individual liberty,
while others fundamentally believe that it's a system of oppression.
Some of us believe deeply in a benevolent and omniscient god,
while others are equally devout atheists. Some of us are certain
that fairness means equality (everybody receives the same), while
others are adamant that it means proportionality (everyone receives
in relation to his or her contributions).

If you've sorted yourself into a community with a shared belief
that global warming is a hoax perpetrated on American capitalism
by its enemies,* you're unlikely to be talked out of this belief no
matter how sound the science on climate change is, or to support
aggressive policies to reduce greenhouse gas emissions. If your
community believes that GMOs violate the sanctity and purity of
nature and must therefore be unsafe,† you'll tenaciously oppose
their use in agriculture.

As these examples show, disconnection can hamper shared
public awareness of important realities. This makes effective action
much more difficult, especially when actions depend on broad
agreement—at the national level or higher—about what the state
of the world is and what needs to be done.

As we saw in chapter 9, we had such an agreement around
CFCs and the hole in the ozone layer in the 1980s and '90s. Since
then, however, social capital (the network of relationships among

* It's not.

† They're not.

people) has decreased. We shouldn't be too surprised that shared public awareness has as well.

We'll come back to the topic of disconnection in chapter 15 when we look at what we should be doing differently to improve both the human condition and the state of nature. Before that, though, let's try to look into the future and see if we should expect to keep getting more from less. Should we be confident that dematerialization and related phenomena will continue?

CHAPTER 14

Looking Ahead:
The World Cleanses Itself This Way

This is my long-run forecast in brief: the material conditions of life will continue to get better for most people, in most countries, most of the time, indefinitely.

—Julian Simon, *WIRED*, 1997*

The decreases in resource use, pollution, and other exploitations of the earth cataloged in the preceding chapters are great news. But are they going to last? It could be that we're just living in a pleasant interlude between the Industrial Era and another rapacious period during which we massively increase our footprint on our planet and eventually cause a giant Malthusian crash.

It could be, but I don't think so. Instead, I think we're going to take better care of our planet from now on. I'm confident that the Second Machine Age will mark the time in our history when we started to progressively and permanently tread more lightly on the earth, taking less from it and generally caring for it better, even as we humans continue to become more numerous and prosperous. The work of Paul Romer, who shared the 2018 Nobel Prize in economics, is one of the sources of this confidence.

---

* Simon immediately added, "I also speculate, however, that many people will continue to think and say that the conditions of life are getting worse."

Growth Mindset

Romer's largest contribution to economics was to show that it's best not to think of new technologies as something that companies buy and bring in from the outside, but instead as something they create themselves (the title of his most famous paper, published in 1990, is "Endogenous Technological Change"). These technologies are like designs or recipes; as Romer put it, they're "the instructions that we follow for combining raw materials." This is close to the definitions of technology presented in chapter 7.

Why do companies invent and improve technologies? Simply, to generate profits. They come up with instructions, recipes, and blueprints that will let them grow revenues or shrink costs. As we saw repeatedly in chapter 7, capitalism provides ample incentive for this kind of tech progress.

So far, all this seems like a pretty standard argument for how the first two horsemen work together. Romer's brilliance was to highlight the importance of two key attributes of the technological ideas companies come up with as they pursue profits. The first is that they're *nonrival*, meaning that they can be used by more than one person or company at a time, and that they don't get used up. This is obviously not the case for most resources made out of atoms—I can't also use the pound of steel that you've just incorporated into the engine of a car—but it is the case for ideas and instructions. The Pythagorean theorem, a design for a steam engine, and a recipe for delicious chocolate chip cookies aren't ever going to get "used up" no matter how much they're used.

The second important aspect of corporate technologies is that they're *partially excludable*. This means that companies can kind of prevent others from using them. They do this by keeping the technologies secret (such as the exact recipe for Coca-Cola), filing for patents and other intellectual-property protection, and so on. However, none of these measures is perfect (hence the words *partially* and *kind of*). Trade secrets leak. Patents expire, and even before they expire, they must describe the invention they're claiming and so let others study it.

Partial excludability is a beautiful thing. It provides strong incentives for companies to create useful, profit-enhancing new technologies that they alone can benefit from for a time, yet it also ensures that the new techs will eventually "spill over"—that with time they'll diffuse and get adopted by more and more companies, even if that's not what their originators want.

Romer equated tech progress to the production by companies of nonrivalrous, partially excludable ideas and showed that these ideas cause an economy to grow. What's more, he also demonstrated that this idea-fueled growth doesn't have to slow down with time. It's not constrained by the size of the labor force, the amount of natural resources, or other such factors. Instead, economic growth is limited only by the idea-generating capacity of the people within a market. Romer called this capacity "human capital" and said at the end of his 1990 paper, "The most interesting positive implication of the model is that an economy with a larger total stock of human capital will experience faster growth."

This notion, which has come to be called "increasing returns to scale," is as powerful as it is counterintuitive. Most formal models of economic growth, as well as the informal mental ones most of us walk around with, feature decreasing returns—growth slows down as the overall economy gets bigger. This makes intuitive sense; it just feels like it would be easier to experience 5 percent growth in a $1 billion economy than a $1 trillion one. But Romer showed that as long as that economy continued to add to its human capital—the overall ability of its people to come up with new technologies and put them to use—it could actually grow faster even as it grew bigger. This is because the stock of useful, nonrivalrous, nonexcludable ideas would keep growing. As Romer convincingly showed, economies run and grow on ideas.

The Machinery of Prosperity

Romer's ideas should leave us optimistic about the planetary benefits of digital tools—hardware, software, and networks—for three main reasons. First, countless examples show us how good these tools are at fulfilling the central role of technology, which is to provide "instructions that we follow for combining raw materials." Since raw materials cost money, profit-maximizing companies are particularly keen to find ways to use fewer of them. So they use digital tools to come up with beer cans that use less aluminum, car engines that use less steel and less gas, mapping software that removes the need for paper atlases, and so on and so on. None of this is done solely for the good of the earth—it's done for the pursuit of profit that's at the heart of capitalism—yet it benefits the planet by, as we've seen, causing us to take less from it.

Digital tools are technologies for creating technologies, the most prolific and versatile ones we've ever come up with. They're machines for coming up with ideas. Lots of them. The same piece of computer-aided design software can be used to create a thinner aluminum can or a lighter and more fuel-efficient engine. A drone can be used to scan farmland to see if more irrigation is needed, or to substitute for a helicopter when filming a movie. A smartphone can be used to read the news, listen to music, and pay for things, all without consuming a single extra molecule.

In the Second Machine Age, the global stock of digital tools is increasing much more quickly than ever before. It's being used in countless ways by profit-hungry companies to combine raw materials in ways that use fewer of them. In advanced economies such as America's, the cumulative impact of this combination of capitalism and tech progress is clear: absolute dematerialization of the economy and society, and thus a smaller footprint on our planet.

The second way Romer's ideas about technology and growth are showing up at present is via decreased excludability. Pervasive digital tools are making it much easier for good designs and recipes to spread around the world. While this is often not what a company wants—it wants to exclude others from its great cost-saving idea—excludability is not as easy as it used to be.

This isn't because of weaker patent protection, but instead because of stronger digital tools. Once one company shows what's possible, others use hardware, software, and networks to catch up to the leader. Even if they can't copy exactly because of intellectual-property restrictions, they can use digital tools to explore other means to the same end. So, many farmers learn to get higher yields while using less water and fertilizer, even though they combine these raw materials in different ways. Steve Jobs would certainly have preferred for Apple to be the only provider of smartphones after it developed the iPhone, but he couldn't maintain the monopoly no matter how many patents and lawsuits he filed. Other companies found ways to combine processors, memory, sensors, a touch screen, and software into phones that satisfied billions of customers around the world.

The operating system that powers most non-Apple smartphones is Android, which is both free to use and freely modifiable. Google's parent company, Alphabet, developed and released Android without even trying to make it excludable; the explicit goal was to make it as widely imitable as possible. This is an example of the broad trend across digital industries of giving away valuable technologies for free.

The Linux operating system, of which Android is a descendant, is probably the best-known example of free and open-source software, but there are many others. The online software repository

GitHub maintains that it's "the largest open source community in the world" and hosts millions of projects. The Arduino community does something similar for electronic hardware, and the Instructables website contains detailed instructions for making equipment ranging from air-particle counters to machine tools, all with no intellectual-property protection. Contributors to efforts such as these have a range of motivations (Alphabet's goals with Android were far from purely altruistic—among other things, the parent of Google wanted to achieve a quantum leap in mobile phone users around the world, who would avail themselves of Google Search and services such as YouTube), but they're all part of the trend of technology without excludability, which is great news for growth.

As we saw in chapter 10, smartphone use and access to the Internet are increasing quickly across the planet. This means that people no longer need to be near a decent library or school to gain knowledge and improve their abilities. Globally, people are taking advantage of the skill-building opportunities of new technologies. This is the third reason that the spread of digital tools should make us optimistic about future growth: these tools are helping human capital grow quickly.

The free Duolingo app, for example, is now the world's most popular way to learn a second language. Of the nearly 15 billion Wikipedia page views during July of 2018, half were in languages other than English. Google's chief economist, Hal Varian, points out that hundreds of millions of how-to videos are viewed every day on YouTube, saying, "We never had a technology before that could educate such a broad group of people anytime on an as-needed basis for free."

Romer's work leaves me hopeful because it shows that it's our ability to build human capital, rather than chop down forests, dig mines, or burn fossil fuels that drives growth and prosperity. His model of how economies grow also reinforces how well capitalism and tech progress work together, which is a central point of this book. The surest way to boost profits is to cut costs, and modern technologies, especially digital ones, offer unlimited ways to combine and recombine materials—to swap, slim, optimize, and evaporate—in cost-reducing ways. There's no reason to expect that the two horsemen of capitalism and tech progress will stop riding together anytime soon. Quite the contrary. Romer's insights reveal that they're likely to gallop faster and farther as economies grow.

Our Brighter, Lighter Future

The world still has billions of desperately poor people, but they won't remain that way. All available evidence strongly suggests that most will become much wealthier in the years and decades ahead. As they earn more and consume more, what will be the impact on the planet?

The history and economics of the Industrial Era lead to pessimism on this important question. Resource use increased in lockstep with economic growth throughout the two centuries between James Watt's demonstration of his steam engine and the first Earth Day. Malthus and Jevons seemed to be right, and it was just a question of when, not if, we'd run up against the hard planetary limits to growth.

But in America and other rich countries something strange, unexpected, and wonderful happened: we started getting more from less. We decoupled population and economic growth from resource consumption, pollution, and other environmental harms. Malthus's and Jevons's ideas gave way to Romer's, and the world will never be the same.

This means that instead of worrying about the world's poor becoming richer, we should instead be helping them upgrade economically as much and as quickly as possible. Not only is it the morally correct thing to do, it's also the smart move for our planet.

As today's poor countries get richer, their institutions will improve and most will eventually go through what Ricardo Hausmann calls "the capitalist makeover of production." This makeover doesn't enslave people, nor does it befoul the earth.

As today's poor get richer, they'll consume more, but they'll also consume much differently from earlier generations. They won't read physical newspapers and magazines. They'll get a great deal of their power from renewables and (one hopes) nuclear because these energy sources will be the cheapest. They'll live in cities, as we saw in chapter 12; in fact, they already are. They'll be less likely to own cars because a variety of transportation options will be only a few taps away. Most important, they'll come up with ideas that keep the growth going, and that benefit both humanity and the planet we live on.

Predicting exactly how technological progress will unfold is much like predicting the weather: feasible in the short term, but impossible over a longer time. Great uncertainty and complexity prevent precise forecasts about, for example, the computing devices we'll be using thirty years from now or the dominant types of artificial intelligence in 2050 and beyond.

But even though we can't predict the weather long term, we can accurately forecast the climate. We know how much warmer and sunnier it will be on average in August than in January, for example, and we know that global average temperatures will rise as we keep adding greenhouse gases to the atmosphere. Similarly, we can predict the "climate" of future technological progress by starting from the knowledge that it will be heavily applied in the areas where it can affect capitalism the most. As we've seen over and over, tech progress supplies opportunities to trim costs (and improve performance) via dematerialization, and capitalism provides the motive to do so.

As a result, the Second Enlightenment will continue as we move deeper into the twenty-first century. I'm confident that it will accelerate as digital technologies continue to improve and multiply and global competition continues to increase. We'll see some of the most striking examples of slim, swap, evaporate, and optimize in exactly the places where the opportunities are biggest. Here are a few broad predictions, spanning humanity's biggest industries.

Manufacturing. Complex parts will be made not by the techniques developed during the Industrial Era, but instead by three-dimensional printing. This is already the case for some rocket engines and other extremely expensive items. As 3-D printing improves and becomes cheaper, it will spread to automobile engine blocks, manifolds and other complicated arrangements of pipes, airplane struts and wings, and countless other parts. Because 3-D printing generates virtually no waste and doesn't require massive molds, it accelerates dematerialization.

We'll also be building things out of very different materials from what we're using today. We're rapidly improving our ability to use machine learning and massive amounts of computing power to screen the huge number of molecules available in the world. We'll use this ability to determine which substances would be best for making flexible solar panels, more efficient batteries, and other important equipment. Our search for the right materials to use has so far been slow and laborious. That's about to change.

So is our ability to understand nature's proteins, and to generate new ones. All living things are made out of the large biomolecules known as proteins, as are wondrous materials such as spiders' silk. The cells in our bodies are assembly lines for proteins, but we currently understand little about how these assembly lines work—how they fold a two-dimensional string of amino acids into a complicated 3-D protein. But thanks to digital tools, we're learning quickly. In 2018, as part of a contest, the AlphaFold software developed by Google DeepMind correctly guessed the structure of twenty-five

out of forty-three proteins it was shown; the second-place fin-
isher guessed correctly three times. DeepMind cofounder Demis
Hassabis says, "We [haven't] solved the protein-folding problem,
this is just a first step . . . but we have a good system and we have
a ton of ideas we haven't implemented yet." As these good ideas
accumulate, they might well let us make spider-strength materials.

Energy. One of humanity's most urgent tasks in the twenty-first
century is to reduce greenhouse gas emissions. Two ways to do
this are to become more efficient in using energy and, when generating it, to shift away from carbon-emitting fossil fuels. Digital
tools will help greatly with both.

Several groups have recently shown that they can combine
machine learning and other techniques to increase the energy
efficiency of data centers by as much as 30 percent. This large
improvement matters for two reasons. First, data centers are heavy
users of energy, accounting for about 1 percent of global electricity
demand. So efficiencies in these facilities help. Second, and more
important, these gains indicate how much the energy use of all
our other complicated infrastructures—everything from electricity
grids to chemical plants to steel mills—can be trimmed. All are a
great deal less energy efficient than they could be. We have both
ample opportunity and ample incentive now to improve them.

Both wind and solar power are becoming much cheaper, so
much so that in many parts of the world they're now the most
cost-effective options, even without government subsidies, for
new electrical generators. These energy sources use virtually no
resources once they're up and running and generate no greenhouse
gases; they're among the world champions of dematerialization.

In the decades to come they might well be joined by nuclear
fusion, the astonishingly powerful process that takes place inside
the sun and other stars. Harnessing fusion has been tantalizingly

out of reach for more than half a century—the old joke is that it's twenty years away and always will be. A big part of the problem is that it's hard to control the fusion reaction inside any human-made vessel, but massive improvements in sensors and computing power are boosting hope that fusion power might truly be only a generation away.

Transportation. Our current transportation systems are chronically inefficient. Most vehicles aren't used much of the time, and even when they're in use, they're not nearly full. Now that we have technologies that let us know where every driver, passenger, piece of cargo, and vehicle is at all times, we can greatly increase the utilization and efficiency of every element of transportation.

Renting instead of owning transportation is a likely consequence of this shift. Instead of owning cars, which typically sit idle more than 90 percent of the time, more people will choose to access transportation as needed. We're already seeing this with car-hailing companies such as Uber and Lyft. These services are quickly spreading around the world, and expanding to cover more modes of transportation, from motorbikes to bicycles to electric scooters. They're also moving into commercial applications such as long- and short-haul trucking. As this shift continues, we'll need fewer tons of steel, aluminum, plastic, gasoline, and other resources to move the world's people and goods around.

We might also experience less congestion and gridlock as we try to get around. Bikes and scooters take up little space compared to cars, so streets can accommodate many more of them. Technology also gives us the ability to implement many forms of "congestion pricing," which has been shown to reduce gridlock by making car access to busy streets expensive enough that people use other options. The most intriguing future transportation platform of all might be the sky. The same technologies that power today's small drones can be scaled up to build "air taxis" with as many as eight propellers and no pilot. Such contraptions sound like science fiction today, but they might be carrying us around by midcentury.

Agriculture. As we saw in chapter 5, leading farms have demonstrated an ability to increase their tonnage of output year after year while decreasing their use of inputs such as land, water, and fertilizer. This trend toward optimization will continue thanks to a set of innovations under the label *precision agriculture*. The precision comes from many sources, including better sensors of plant and animal health, soil quality and moisture, and so on; the ability to deliver fertilizer, pesticides, and water just where they're needed; and machinery that adapts itself to each plant or animal. All these varieties of precision will combine to allow traditional farms to generate more from less.

So will changes to the genomes of plants and animals. DNA modifications will increase disease and drought tolerance, expand where crops can be grown, and allow us to get more of what we want from each crop or herd. As we saw in chapter 9, they'll also allow us to take better care of vulnerable populations such as infants in poor countries by creating golden rice and other nutrition enhancers. We'll also be able to make much more precise and targeted genetic modifications thanks to a new crop of gene-editing tools that are large improvements over their more scattershot predecessors. Opposition to genetically modified organisms is fierce in some quarters, but isn't based on reason or science. This opposition will, one hopes, fade.

Throughout human history, just about all farming has been done in fields. For some crops, this is now changing. Agriculture has moved indoors, where parameters such as light, humidity, fertilizer, and even the composition of the atmosphere can be precisely monitored and controlled. In everything from urban buildings to shipping containers, crops are now being grown with progressively less labor and fewer material inputs. These completely contained farms will spread and help reduce the planetary footprint of our agriculture.

These examples aren't intended to be comprehensive, and I don't have precise estimates of how likely each innovation is, or when it's most likely to occur. I offer them only to indicate how broad and exciting are the possibilities offered by the two horsemen of capitalism and technological progress, and how they'll continue to dematerialize our consumption and let us increase our prosperity while treading more lightly on our planet.

Healing a Hotter World

But what if we're overheating the earth so drastically that all of our planet-sparing technologies and other innovations won't matter much? Does global warming overshadow all the good news about dematerialization, pollution reduction, and other benefits brought by the four horsemen?

No, it absolutely doesn't. In the next chapter we'll discuss how bad for the planet climate change will be over the twenty-first century (for now, a short answer is that it'll most likely be somewhere between bad and catastrophically bad), and the most effective steps we can take to reduce its risks and harms. A critical point, though, is that these harms will appear over many decades.

The battle against global warming isn't the only battle we need to fight and win during these decades. We also need to fight against pollution of the air, water, and land so that we and the rest of life on Earth can be healthier. We need to reduce our planetary footprint and give land back to nature so that forests can regrow and animals can move back in. We should leave fewer scars on the land from mines, wells, and clear-cut timberland. We should learn to use less energy if generating that energy also generates greenhouse gases and other pollutants. And we need to continue to lift people out of poverty, reduce mortality rates and disease burdens, ensure clean water and sanitation, give more people more education, increase economic opportunities, and improve the human condition in countless other ways.

None of these things become any less important in the face of global warming. So our recent victories in dematerializing our consumption and improving both the human condition and the state of nature matter a great deal. As will our future victories in these same areas.

How confident am I in these future victories? Confident enough to bet on them.

Betting the Planet, Round 2

Like Julian Simon in 1980, I'm willing to make monetary bets. Simon believed that prices for natural resources would decline and was willing to put his money behind his predictions. My bets are about quantities rather than prices. I believe that America's total consumption of most natural resources will go down in the years ahead, and I am willing to put money on it. I'll also wager that greenhouse gas emissions will decrease in the United States, and that the country's environmental footprint will shrink in other ways as well.

These bets are unconditional. In other words, I'm wagering that American resource consumption and pollution will go down no matter what else happens—no matter how quickly the economy and population grow, no matter who gets elected, and no matter what happens elsewhere in the world. I'll offer the bets over the same ten-year horizon that Julian Simon and Paul Ehrlich settled on.

Simon offered his bet specifically to Ehrlich. I'm offering mine to any and all takers. If you believe my predictions are wrong, put up some money and let's see who wins. The winners, though, don't get to keep the money. Instead, they get to designate a charity to receive the money put up by both parties. You can think of this as a way to, if you win, make a charitable contribution to a cause you support and get me to match that contribution. If you lose, you double my contribution to a cause I support.

Here are the even-money bets I'm offering:

Compared to 2019, in 2029 the United States will consume in total

- Fewer metals
- Fewer "industrial materials" (diamonds, mica, etc.)
- Less timber
- Less paper
- Less fertilizer
- Less water for agriculture
- Less energy

Compared to 2019, in 2029 the US will

- Use less cropland
- Have lower greenhouse gas emissions

Details about these bets—what data they draw on, how quantities are calculated, how payouts will be handled, and so on—are available at the Long Bets website (longbets.org). This site is also where you can sign up for one or more bets if you're interested, and confident enough that these predictions are wrong. Each bet can be between $50 and $1,000. I'm putting up $100,000 of my own money.

These bets are about the United States for four reasons. First, it's a country where I believe the four horsemen of the optimist—

capitalism, tech progress, responsive government, and public awareness—are pretty firmly in place (certainly not perfectly, but firmly) and will continue to be for at least the next decade. So it's where my confidence about future trends is high and I'm willing to make bets. Second, it's a country that matters simply because of the size of its economy; America generates about 25 percent of total global output. Third, it matters also because I believe that demateri-alization trends in America are leading indicators of global trends, so it's important to watch what happens in that country. And fourth, data about resource use, pollution, and other relevant indicators are collected regularly and with high quality in the United States.

Of course, having confidence that the human condition and the state of nature will continue to improve in the future isn't the same as saying that they're improving quickly enough now. They're certainly not. We can and should be doing more to let the four horsemen gallop faster and farther around the world. So in the next and final chapter, let's look at what changes by governments, companies, philanthropies and nonprofits, and families and individuals would be most helpful at this point in the Second Machine Age.

CHAPTER 15

Interventions: How to Be Good

*Never doubt that a small group of thoughtful, committed citizens
can change the world. Indeed, it is the only thing that ever has.*

—Attributed to Margaret Mead (1901–78)

A s I've tried to show throughout this book, our current path is
encouraging but far from perfect. The four horsemen of capitalism, technological progress, public awareness, and responsive
government are galloping around the world and improving it in
most of the ways that matter most. Both the human condition and
the state of nature are generally getting better. I predict that these
positive trends will continue into the future. As we saw in the previous chapter, I'm literally willing to bet on it.

But we still face serious challenges—ones that demand our
attention and effort. If we continue along our current trajectory,
we're likely to harmfully heat up our planet over the twenty-first
century. Businesses will also pollute and exploit animal species if
they're not prevented from doing so. And unless we make changes,
we'll also probably see continued increases in deaths of despair
in America and other symptoms of disconnection and declining
social capital around the world. We have our work cut out for us
to prevent, or at least minimize, these harms.

Our goals should be to continue and to accelerate the dematerialization of our economies and the many increases in prosperity
we've seen, while dealing both with negative externalities such as

pollution and with declining social capital. Another way to say this
is that we should keep enabling the first two horsemen of capitalism
and tech progress to carry us deeper into a Second Enlightenment
while using the second pair of horsemen—public awareness and
responsive government—to constrain capitalism appropriately and
deal with other harms caused by rapid change.

These simple guidelines point to a range of smart actions and
interventions for governments, businesses, philanthropies and
other nonprofits, and individuals and families. Let's look at each
of these four actors in turn.

Statecraft

Markets don't deal well with externalities, pollution is the classic
externality, and greenhouse gases are the type of pollution that
most threatens the long-term health of our planet (and therefore
ourselves). So the most important task for responsive governments,
now and into the future, is to bring about reductions in the carbon
intensity of our economic activities.

How bad will global warming be? Answering this question is
complicated because there's so much uncertainty about how much
warming we'll experience, and how bad any given level of warming
will be for us and the rest of life on the planet. Economist William
Nordhaus uses the image of a "climate casino" to convey the uncertainty about the future trajectory of climate change.

Nordhaus stresses, though, that we're sure that the planet is
warming as never before in our history: "No climate changes of the
speed and scope we are currently witnessing have occurred through
the course of human civilization . . . The best guess is that the rate
of global climate change people will face over the next century will
be about ten times as rapid as any change experienced by humanity
during the last five millennia." The scientific consensus is strong that

this warming will cause more and more variable precipitation, ocean acidification, droughts in some regions, and other deep changes.

Nordhaus continues, "We also are likely to encounter surprises, and some of them will be nasty. Perhaps winters in the Northern Hemisphere will become much snowier. Perhaps hurricanes will intensify greatly and change their storm tracks. Perhaps the giant Greenland Ice Sheet will begin to melt rapidly. Perhaps the West Antarctic Ice Sheet, which sits on the seabed, might disintegrate rapidly and slide into the ocean." We don't want to gamble in the climate casino. So what should we do to stay out of it as much as possible?

Nordhaus won the 2018 Nobel Prize in economics (sharing it with Paul Romer, whose work we discussed in the last chapter) in large part because of his research to quantify the risks of global warming and identify sound strategies for combating it. The strategies promoted by Nordhaus and others are familiar ones: they use well-understood techniques to handle the externality of greenhouse gas pollution. CFCs were simply phased out by the Montreal Protocol, and SO2 and other forms of particulate pollution were greatly reduced by cap-and-trade programs in the United States and elsewhere.

A tax on carbon, which is one of Nordhaus's main proposals, is even more straightforward than a cap-and-trade program. Such a tax would make products and energy sources that generate a lot of carbon more expensive and so cause many buyers to shift to lower-carbon alternatives such as wind-, solar-, and nuclear-generated electricity. Increasing the tax gradually over time would give buyers ever-stronger incentives to shun carbon-heavy producers and also allow these producers time to clean up their acts.

A "revenue-neutral" carbon tax is an interesting variant on the basic idea. Under it, money collected from carbon producers goes not to the government, but directly to people. Nordhaus worked with the government of the Canadian province of British Columbia on a revenue-neutral carbon tax that went into effect in 2008; it established an initial tax of ten Canadian dollars per ton of carbon dioxide and returned the money to BC residents in the form of tax credits and income tax reductions. In January of 2019, an all-star collection of American economists (featuring Nobel Prize winners, Fed chairs, treasury secretaries, and others) signed an open letter advocating that the United States adopt a revenue-neutral carbon tax.

More and more carbon taxes have been put in place in recent years, including in Chile, Mexico, South Africa, and Ireland. More and more, but still not nearly enough. China and America, the two nations responsible for approximately 45 percent of total global emissions, still don't have them at the national level. And the EU's cap-and-trade program for carbon hasn't yet succeeded in sharply reducing emissions, in part because the cap is so high that carbon producers haven't needed to change much.

A big obstacle to the carbon-taxation approach is that taxes aren't popular—even if they're in the service of a laudable goal such as reducing global warming. French president Emmanuel Macron found this out in late 2018 when mass protests occurred throughout France in response to an increase in the gasoline tax. As these demonstrations grew and turned violent, the government backed down, announcing a (perhaps indefinite) delay in imposing the tax.

France's neighbor Germany is also running into problems as it works to combat global warming, and its troubles highlight an important failure at the intersection of public awareness and responsive government. Germany has embarked on an ambitious *Energiewende*—literally, a national "energy transition"—away from fossil fuels and toward renewables. However, the results to date have been unimpressive: electricity prices for consumers have doubled since 2000, and carbon emissions have been flat or increasing in recent years (after decreasing substantially for more than a decade after 1990).

Why is this? In part because while Germany has invested heavily in expensive wind and solar power, the country has also been steadily moving away from nuclear power, decommissioning existing plants and not building new ones.* As nuclear capacity decreases, the country must rely on high-carbon coal plants to generate electricity when winds aren't high or the sun isn't shining (and Germany is not a sunny place).

Nuclear power is deeply unpopular among Germans, and they're not alone. A 2011 poll found that solid majorities of citizens in twenty-four countries surveyed oppose the use of nuclear energy. It's not hard to see why. Radiation poisoning is a terrifying prospect, and the accidents at Three Mile Island in the United States, Chernobyl in Ukraine, and Fukushima in Japan seem to provide all the evidence one could need that nuclear power plants can't be operated safely.

As the environmental policy analyst and self-described "ecomodernist" Michael Shellenberger highlights, however, the evidence is strong that nuclear is actually the *safest* source of reliable energy. A study published in the *Lancet* in 2007 found that over the previous fifteen years death rates from pollution were generally hundreds of times lower for nuclear power than for coal, gas, or oil, and that accident rates were also comparatively low for nuclear.† As Shellenberger points out, "Nobody died from radiation at Three Mile Island or Fukushima,‡ and fewer than fifty died from Chernobyl in the thirty years since the accident."§

---

* Germany's booming manufacturing and transportation sectors have also generated more carbon in recent years.

† The only exception was that occupational death rates in gas plants were lower than for nuclear facilities.

‡ In September 2018 a worker who had participated in the Fukushima cleanup died from lung cancer. The Japanese government attributed his death to the accident.

§ A 2016 report from the Chernobyl Forum, the United Nations, and the World Health Organization concluded that radiation from Chernobyl would be responsible for an estimated total four thousand additional deaths from cancer, but noted, "As about a quarter of people die from spontaneous cancer not caused by Chernobyl radiation, the radiation-induced increase of only about 3% will be difficult to observe."

Nuclear power doesn't deserve its bad reputation. As is the case with vaccines, glyphosate, and GMOs, public awareness around nuclear power is broadly out of step with reality. Getting power from nuclear fission has its challenges, including safely handling its waste and modernizing and standardizing reactor designs, but operators have demonstrated that this energy is constant, clean, safe, scalable, and reliable.

It's the only energy source we have at present with all these characteristics. So along with a carbon tax, it should be a primary weapon for fighting global warming. But instead, many governments around the world are yielding to public sentiment rather than acting on sound science and evidence. This is understandable, but it's also unfortunate. The good news is that public opinion is changing in some countries and becoming more pro-nuclear. In 2017 a citizen commission in Korea recommended restarting construction on two reactors in that country, and in a referendum held in late 2018 Taiwanese voters overturned a plan to phase out nuclear power there by 2025.

Governments should obviously also continue to make other kinds of pollution (besides greenhouse gases) so costly that businesses decide not to pollute. We're not there yet. As we saw in chapter 9 oceanic plastic trash is a serious problem, caused largely by heavy pollution from rivers in Africa and Asia. Rich countries in general do a much better job of controlling pollution than developing ones do, but even in wealthy countries there is cause for concern. For example, in the United States the Trump administration has undertaken what one former EPA official calls "the quiet dismantling of the regulatory framework" for pollution. This dismantling includes rule changes to reduce oil and gas companies' responsibilities to monitor their equipment for methane leaks, challenges to restrictions on mercury emissions from coal plants, a reinterpretation of the Clean Water Act that excludes some types of streams and wetlands, and many other similar efforts. These are transparent cases of putting profits ahead of people and the planet.

In addition to fighting greenhouse gases and other pollution, governments should continue to put vulnerable territory and wildlife outside the reach of the capitalist system. As we saw in chapter 11, the trends here are encouraging, with both land and marine parks expanding around the world. Restrictions on where, when, and whether animals can be hunted—and on trade in products made from them—have been highly effective, bringing many species back from the brink of extinction.

We continue to see heartening examples of governments responding appropriately to public concerns over animal welfare. In October 2018 China's State Council announced a relaxation of the "three strict bans" in place since 1993 on the import, sale, and use of tiger and rhino products. This move prompted sharp and sustained protests from many quarters. The outcry worked. In November, State Council executive deputy secretary-general Ding Xuedong announced, "The 'three strict bans' will continue to be enforced."

As they take some animals out of the market, governments should also work to put many ideas into it. As we saw in the last chapter, economies grow based on the total stock of ideas available. Profit-seeking companies generate a lot of these ideas and technologies, but they tend to underinvest in areas where commercialization seems too unlikely or too far out. As a result, most economists agree that the government has a role to play in funding early-stage and more speculative research, especially in domains where success would yield large benefits for our well-being. Batteries, solar and nuclear power, and many other energy technologies are clearly in this category and so are excellent candidates for increased research support.

The economics playbook for encouraging growth and dealing with negative externalities is quite well developed. Unfortunately, the same is not true of the playbook for dealing with disconnection and declines in social capital. This is a serious problem because, as we saw in chapter 13, disconnection is on the rise in America and other rich countries. Political polarization is increasing, demagogues and populists are winning elections, people are separating into antagonistic tribes of pluralists and authoritarians, and deaths of despair are sharply on the rise in the United States.

One of the factors contributing to increasing disconnection is greater geographic concentration. As we get more and more output from fewer and fewer farms, factories, and regions, more and more workers and communities face disruption. As certain jobs migrate elsewhere or disappear entirely, many people are left behind.

It's not at all clear how to reverse this trend. The two horsemen of capitalism and tech progress are taking us into a more concentrated world, not a more evenly distributed one. This is an improvement in some ways—for example, we can satisfy our total demand for food on a smaller footprint of land and return the rest to nature—but it's also a challenge. It's far from obvious how to bring back good jobs and social capital to communities where the factories have closed and the farms have gone fallow.

This is partly because we don't have much experience with successful interventions aimed at particular regions. As economists Benjamin Austin, Ed Glaeser, and Larry Summers wrote in 2018, "Traditionally, economists have been skeptical about [place-based] policies because of a conviction that relief is best targeted toward poor people rather than poor places, [and] because incomes in poor areas were converging toward incomes in rich areas anyway."

However, this convergence has in recent years turned into a divergence, so perhaps it's time to experiment more with place-based policies. These could include tax credits for companies that create jobs in distressed areas, wage subsidies for workers there, and "entrepreneur visas" for immigrants who are willing to bring their expertise and capital to specified regions. How well will these work? We just don't know yet. Glaeser is forthcoming that economists, who as a rule are a pretty confident bunch, are unsure how to deal with disconnection and shrinking social capital: "Our call for a wage subsidy is us saying, 'We can't figure this out, and we hope the private sector will.' "

Good Company

I think that disconnection is the most worrying short-term problem we face, at least in America and other rich countries. Glaeser's quote highlights that it won't be solved by government action alone. Jobs create a great deal of social capital, and most jobs come from the private sector instead of the state. Place-based policies will hopefully encourage companies to show up, invest, and create jobs in communities that have been left behind as capitalism and tech progress have raced ahead.

To do this, companies will have to reverse course. They'll have to move against the current of concentration—of over time generating more and more of their output from a smaller and smaller geographic footprint—and, instead, start spreading out their work. Smart policies can encourage this "rediffusion" of economic activity. So, too, can the realization that even the places that are getting left behind have a huge amount of human capital. As the social entrepreneur Leila Janah puts it, "Talent is equally distributed; opportunity is not."

This fact presents a great opportunity for companies to do well by doing good—to help themselves by building and tapping into the human capital that exists in disconnected communities. A number of intriguing efforts are underway to harness both the power of markets and the great global thirst for talent to create opportunity in places where it's currently lacking. Samasource, founded by Janah in 2008, trains people to do entry-level technology work (such as

data entry and image labeling) and connects them with employers. Online education companies such as Udacity, Coursera, and
Lambda aim to provide higher-level online training. I like these
efforts because they often train people for jobs that can be done
wherever there's an Internet connection. Not every coder or data
scientist wants to live in a big city, or to have to move to one to
acquire new skills. I'm encouraged to see that promising alternatives
are now appearing.

I'm also encouraged to see that business leaders are taking seriously the issue of disconnection and working on efforts to bring back
economic opportunity to communities in danger of being left behind
as globalization and tech progress race ahead. AOL cofounder Steve
Case has launched the Rise of the Rest venture-capital fund, which
will make early investments in tech companies founded outside
Northern California, New York, and Boston (three regions that
together receive about 75 percent of all US venture-capital funding). As Case and JPMorgan Chase CEO Jamie Dimon write, "By
investing in underserved entrepreneurs, we can create inclusive
growth that benefits everyone and ensures all communities are
part of America's future."

I'm not sure that the overall trend toward economic concentration can be reversed, but I'm sure that it's too early to give up
on non-superstar regions. I hope we'll see more efforts from leaders in the private sector to help talent, no matter where it is, find
opportunities.

The most worrying longer-term problem that we face is clearly
global warming. Companies are obviously huge contributors to
this problem. Are they also contributing meaningfully to solutions?

In some sectors, they are. The software company Salesforce
is buying enough carbon offsets to make up for all the CO_2 produced by its data centers around the world. Because of this, all of
Salesforce's cloud computing customers can now say that their

interactions with the company are carbon neutral. Salesforce has also announced its intentions to move away entirely from fossil fuel energy sources by 2022. Other large technology companies, including Apple, Facebook, and Microsoft, have similar plans. In 2017 Google reached 100 percent renewable energy for all global operations including both their data centers and offices, becoming the world's largest corporate buyer of renewable power.

Why are these companies doing this if there's no meaningful carbon tax in place in their largest markets? I've talked with some of their leaders, and I believe they're sincere in their desire to fight global warming. But another important reason is public awareness, and how it affects companies' activities. Around the world, large majorities of people believe in the reality of global warming and want to fight against it. It's therefore good for the reputation and brand (and thus the value) of companies to be seen as joining in that fight, and combating climate change rather than contributing to it.

A litany of examples from the transportation industry shows the breadth and depth of efforts to reduce greenhouse gas emissions. Because transportation currently relies so heavily on burning fossil fuels, it's a major contributor to global warming. But many companies are making efforts to improve the situation. United Airlines has committed to cutting its greenhouse gas emissions in half by 2050. Shipping giant A.P. Møller-Maersk has gone further, pledging carbon neutrality across its fleet by the middle of the century. This is a particularly ambitious goal because, as the company dryly notes, a "vessel carrying thousands of [containers] sailing from Panama to Rotterdam [travels] around 8,800 km. With short battery durability and no charging points along the route, innovative developments are imperative." Maersk has called for collaborators in its efforts to create carbon-neutral transoceanic cargo vessels by 2030. Major automobile companies including Toyota, Ford, BMW, General Motors, and VW have announced plans to stop producing internal combustion engines within the next few decades. These carmakers were almost certainly motivated by announcements from such countries as Norway, France, and the United Kingdom that they'll ban internal combustion engines by or before 2050.

How much weight should we give these announcements? It's difficult to say. CEO speeches and press releases are very different from ironclad commitments. But it does feel as if a large wave of public sentiment is building to encourage companies to fight global warming, and perhaps to do less business with firms that are perceived as being part of the problem instead of the solution.

If so, this is an important development. In the absence of widespread and effective carbon taxes or other government-imposed methods for dealing with greenhouse gas pollution, we have to rely more on public awareness and public pressure to constrain capitalism appropriately. Signs are encouraging that this is happening. For example, smelters that make aluminum using zero-carbon energy sources now appear to be able to charge a premium since, as Reuters puts it, even "industrial customers [are] under pressure to reduce their carbon footprints."

What else should companies be doing differently to improve the state of the world and the human condition? What changes would be helpful? Companies that are dumping pollution into the air, land, and water or killing endangered animals should stop. I don't want to spend any more time on such obvious recommendations. Not because they're not important, but because I can't imagine any CEO reading this chapter and saying, "Hey, everyone, I've been convinced by this book. Let's stop doing these bad things we've been doing."

My point is that scolding companies for their misdeeds makes the scolder feel virtuous (it's a form of rebuke often labeled "virtue signaling"), but rarely accomplishes much beyond that. Other forces are necessary. One of this book's major themes is that the second pair of horses—public awareness and responsive government—are a powerful and necessary combination for stopping companies' bad behavior. So organizing boycotts and other protests against bad corporate actors, shining a light on their misdeeds (as the American Supreme Court justice Louis Brandeis put it, "Sunlight is the best disinfectant"), and voting for candidates who take seriously government's responsibility to fight pollution and to protect endangered species are all more effective and important than scolding CEOs.

CEOs and other members of the business community don't need to be encouraged to keep pursuing dematerialization. They're going to do this anyway. Especially when so many exciting technologies are available, and so much capital around the world is looking for a return. Under these conditions, a lot of wild ideas—from commercial nuclear fusion to synthetic spider silk to electricity-powered autonomous air taxis—will get a chance to prove themselves. Some will succeed. Even the ones that don't will increase our knowledge. As a result, I'm confident that the first two horsemen of capitalism and tech progress will keep doing what they've been doing for a while now, which is to progressively dematerialize our total consumption.

The Nonprofit Vector

If capitalism and tech progress are sufficient to bring about dematerialization, and governments are the appropriate entities to deal with negative externalities such as pollution, then where do philanthropies and other nonprofits fit in? What's their role in lightening our footprint on our planet? We've seen them do important work both to help the horsemen ride faster and to provide substitutes for them.

Carbon offsets are an ingenious substitute for carbon taxes and other steps that governments should be taking against greenhouse gas pollution. When a business or person buys one of these offsets, they are buying a set amount (usually a metric ton) of greenhouse gas reduction somewhere in the world. This reduction can occur in many ways: trees get planted that absorb carbon, people are supplied with cookstoves that are more energy efficient than wood fires, and so on. What all projects that are supported by carbon offsets have in common is that they cause less carbon to enter the atmosphere than would have happened without the project.

Since greenhouse gases are global pollutants, carbon offsets benefit the whole planet. Nonprofits such as Cool Effects and Carbonfund.org certify that the carbon-reducing projects receiving their money are actually causing reductions that wouldn't happen otherwise, a property called *additionality* (even though the trees in my backyard absorb carbon, Cool Effects won't pay me for them because I'm not bringing about any additional reductions beyond what nature is already accomplishing).

As we saw in chapter 11, governments have protected animals by setting up parks in which hunting is illegal. Philanthropies and nonprofits have frequently done something similar by buying up land and either giving it to governments or otherwise conserving it. The Jackson Hole National Monument in Wyoming, which eventually became part of Grand Teton National Park, consisted of land bought by John D. Rockefeller Jr. in the 1920s and donated to the federal government. In 2018, Chile expanded its total parkland by 40 percent when it added 9 million acres to the 1 million donated by the conservationist couple Kristine McDivitt Tompkins and Douglas Tompkins and created the Patagonia National Park system in the southern part of the country. Around the world, countless conservation groups have bought up land and assigned it to preservation trusts and other legal structures designed to protect it from development, hunting, and other exploitations.

Other nonprofits focus on animals instead of land. The comprehensive African Great Elephant Census discussed in chapter 9 was funded by Microsoft cofounder Paul Allen, and China's 2018 effort to roll back its ban on tiger and rhino products was vigorously protested by the World Wildlife Fund, WildAid, and many other conservation groups. That China soon changed its position and maintained the ban highlights an important truth: without conservationists' vigilance, research, and public outreach efforts, many animal species would be in much worse shape than they are today.

Oddly enough, nonprofits established by hunters and those who fish have also helped many species. These groups have a strong interest in maintaining large and healthy populations of the animals they're interested in and can play a large role in protecting species (even as their members kill individual animals). Ducks Unlimited, for example, has since its establishment in 1937 conserved 14 million acres in North America, an area as big as West Virginia. Waterfowl populations across the North American prairie have increased by 37 million birds since 1990, and "one of the reasons waterfowl are faring pretty well is because hunters, [Ducks Unlimited] included, have done a fantastic job recognizing the needs of those organisms and implementing successful conservation programs," according to conservation scientist Ron Rohrbaugh. Trout Unlimited, Salmon Unlimited, Pheasants Forever, and many other groups are similarly dedicated to preserving the species they go after for sport and food.

One of the most important and encouraging things we've learned since the first Earth Day is that economic growth is not the enemy of the environment. America and other rich countries have already moved post-peak in their exploitations of our planet. This isn't despite these nations' steady and sustained growth; it's because of it. So increasing economic growth around the world is an essential element of taking better care of it.

Thanks to the work of Paul Romer and many others, we now have a much better idea of the playbook for fostering economic growth. As we saw in the last chapter, two important elements of this playbook are lots of human capital (people with the skills required for innovation) and nonexcludable technologies (ones

that aren't withheld from general use by patents or other intellectual-property protection).

We've seen philanthropies and nonprofits make important contributions in both of these areas. Khan Academy got its start in 2006
when Sal Khan began posting videos of the online tutorials he was
offering his cousins. It has expanded to become a worldwide force
in educating people of all ages. Khan Academy is funded by a wide
range of corporate and family philanthropies. Another of my favorite
examples of new approaches to human capital formation is 42, a
technology academy founded by the French entrepreneur Xavier
Niel.* All courses at 42 are free and in person rather than online.
The school has no professional teachers or discrete courses; it relies
entirely on peer learning and project-based learning. Admission is
based not on prospective students' backgrounds or credentials, but
instead only on their performance on a set of reasoning tests and an
initial short course. Admitted students are expected to take about
three years to complete all the projects that make up the curriculum
at 42. The school has campuses in Paris and Silicon Valley and is
advising similar organizations in South Africa, Morocco, Romania,
Bulgaria, and other countries.

As discussed in chapter 2, the efforts by Norman Borlaug and
others to improve wheat and rice were so important that they really
do deserve to be called a Green Revolution. This work was supported
over many years by the Rockefeller and Ford Foundations, which
also ensured that the improved crop varieties were made available
to farmers around the world for no fee. These innovations have
always been completely nonexcludable.

This practice continues for new technologies such as golden
rice, which has the potential to greatly improve the health of young

---

* In Douglas Adams's iconic science fiction novel *The Hitchhiker's Guide to the Galaxy*, 42 is
the answer to "the Ultimate Question of Life, the Universe, and Everything."

children in Africa and Asia (if people and governments can get over their unfounded fears of GMOs). The Golden Rice Project, which is supported by the Rockefeller Foundation, gives free humanitarian licenses to plant-breeding organizations in the developing world. The project is an example of a successful public-private collaboration, since the Swiss biotech company Syngenta was instrumental both in advancing research on golden rice and in acquiring relevant patents and then donating them to the nonprofit.

One other interesting type of nonprofit attempts to fight disconnection and declines in social capital by preserving traditional jobs. An example is the Martha's Vineyard Fishermen's Preservation Trust, which has created a "permit bank"—a collection of licenses to fish for different types of seafood in the waters around the Massachusetts island of Martha's Vineyard.

These permits have increased in value so much that many local fishers can no longer afford them. The Fishermen's Preservation Trust uses its funds to buy permits on the open market. It then leases the associated fishing rights at below-market rates to islanders, many of whom come from families that have been fishing for generations. Organizations such as the trust show us that in addition to conserving land and animals, it might also be possible to conserve jobs and the communities built up around them.

Enlightened Citizenry

Many readers probably have the impression that I believe capitalism and tech progress to be the most important forces bringing us into a healthier relationship with our planet. After all, I've spent a lot of this book documenting how they've caused the wonderful and surprising phenomenon of dematerialization.

But I think something else is even more important. I believe we the people are the key. Why? Because so much flows from the choices and desires of the people in a society. Governments, if they're at all responsive, listen to their citizens. As we've seen, even autocratic China has followed the will of its inhabitants and greatly reduced air pollution. And of course companies want to sell to people and maintain their reputations and brands.

So the public—not government or business or technology—is the most important force shaping the health of our planet. This places a heavy obligation on us: the obligation not just to act, but to act in accordance with the facts. I believe that by far the most important thing we can do for the planet is inform ourselves, and to use the best available information to guide our actions and decisions. This sounds like such weak and obvious advice that it's not even worth writing down. But it's actually radical advice because it's so far from current practice.

Most people (including myself before I started researching this book) base their beliefs and practices related to humanity's relationship with the earth not on the best available evidence, but instead on very different foundations. We base our views on theories and projections that seemed quite plausible at the time of the first Earth Day in 1970 but have since been shown to be badly wrong. We base them on fear about the immense power of nuclear reactions that was born with the explosions at Hiroshima and Nagasaki and has metastasized around the world since then. Or on the commonsense notion that because our planet is finite, the danger is real that we'll exhaust its resources and bounty, especially if we humans keep becoming more numerous and prosperous.

We believe things because the people around us believe them, or members of our political tribe do, or members of the opposite political tribe believe the opposite. Many of us believe things because we have an inherently zero-sum perspective: if someone is doing better, it must be because someone else is doing worse. Most of us are more likely to believe things if we hear them enough times, since we have a glitch in our mental hardware to mistake familiarity for truth. Similarly, we believe a lot of things because our innate negativity bias is reinforced by a constant stream of dire headlines, expert predictions of decline and doom, and vivid images of things going wrong.

None of this serves us well, especially in making decisions and taking action on something as important as our relationship with our planet. So I've tried to do two things with this book. First, I've presented a lot of evidence about the human condition, the state of nature, and the relationship between the two. Second, I've put all this evidence in a theory—a story about what causes what, and why, and under what circumstances, as the management guru Clay Christensen puts it.

My story is basic economic theory, phrased in the language of the four horsemen of the optimist: capitalism, tech progress, responsive government, and public awareness. The story is that in recent years capitalism and tech progress have combined not only to increase human prosperity but also to bring us post-peak in resource consumption in America and other rich countries and finally allow us to get more from less. This happened because resources cost money, profit-seeking competitors don't want to spend that money if they don't have to, and tech progress now offers them many ways to slim, swap, evaporate, and optimize their way out of using resources. As a result we continue to consume more, but our consumption is now dematerializing. We are entering a Second Enlightenment.

But that's not the end of the story. Capitalism and tech progress won't by themselves deal with the negative externality of pollution and won't isolate vulnerable ecosystems and animals from market forces. To accomplish these critical goals, we need both responsive government and public awareness. This awareness is twofold: it's awareness both of the challenges that need to be addressed (as opposed to the false challenges that don't) and of the best ways to meet them.

This awareness is too important to be left to tribalism, cognitive biases, stale theories, intuitions and superstitions, unreasonable fears, and the misinformation campaigns of parties with vested interests. We have to do better than that. The stakes are too high. We have to follow the best available evidence and go where it leads us, even if that's far from where we started.

Families and people who are aware of the evidence, and who want to do right by their fellow humans and the planet we all live on, will do a few things. One of the most important is that they'll influence their governments by voting and persuading others to vote, contacting elected officials, speaking in public, coming together at rallies and in peaceful protests, and using all the other tools of engaged citizens. As they do this, I recommend that they focus on seven issues:

1. **Reducing pollution.** Pollution is not a necessary cost of doing business; it's a negative externality that causes great harm to people and the environment. However, efforts are now underway in America and other countries to roll back restrictions on pollution to reduce businesses' costs. But better health is much more important than higher profits.

2. **Reducing greenhouse gases.** Greenhouse gases deserve to be called out separately from other forms of pollution because of the long-term harm they can cause across the planet, and because they're not yet being controlled with regulations, taxes, and the many other tools we have for dealing with externalities.

3. **Promoting nuclear energy.** We currently have only one power source that doesn't emit greenhouse gases and is scalable, safe, reliable, and widely available. We should be working to drive down the cost of nuclear power, and to overcome barriers to adopting it.

4. **Preserving species and habitats.** Even though capitalism is now shrinking its geographic footprint in many countries, it still has a great thirst for attractive pieces of real estate, and for many animals. Conserving land, limiting hunting, and banning trade in products made from threatened species are highly effective interventions.

5. **Promoting genetically modified organisms.** GMOs have been extensively studied and found to be safe. They also have the potential to greatly improve crop yields, reduce pesticide use, and improve nutrition. Yet they are strenuously resisted in many parts of the world. This needs to change.

6. **Funding basic research.** Private businesses spend money on research and development, but they tend not to invest much in areas and ideas that won't become products anytime soon. This means that governments have an important role to play in supporting more fundamental scientific and technical research as well as research into social phenomena such as disconnection.

7. **Promoting markets, competition, and work.** Capitalism is widely unpopular at present, and socialist ideas are making a comeback. Yet markets, competition, and innovation have brought us previously unimaginable prosperity. As we've seen, they've also finally enabled us to take less from the earth. So we need to not turn away from them now. Instead, we need to focus them on finding meaningful opportunities for people at risk of disconnecting from society.

I'm highlighting these seven areas for two reasons. First, they're important. Progress in each of them will greatly improve the human condition and the state of nature, while reversals will hurt us and our planet. Second, they're battlegrounds. In each case influential groups are opposing the things I'm recommending. The opponents include governments, business lobbies, and advocacy groups, and they change with each issue. In all cases, though, I think they're on the wrong side of good ideas and clear evidence. Hence my call here for public awareness and support.

In addition to interacting with governments to make them more responsive to good ideas, individuals and families have two other levers for bringing about change: their spending and their personal activities. As we saw earlier in this chapter, businesses are increasingly sensitive about their contributions to global warming. In the future we'll see more companies launch efforts to reduce their greenhouse gas emissions. In addition, households will have more ways to determine which of these efforts are most sincere and effective. This will allow them to reward decarbonizers by buying their goods and services.

Strong evidence suggests that efforts to highlight good corporate behavior and socially responsible business practices work. Economists Raluca Dragusanu and Nathan Nunn studied the effects of Fair Trade certification on coffee growers in Costa Rica from 1999 to 2014. The Fair Trade label certifies (among other things) that producers are treating their workers according to a set of standards and that the companies that buy from them are paying above-market prices that can never fall below a minimum level. The researchers found that even though their coffee cost more, Fair Trade Certified growers enjoyed higher sales. The study also found that the certification "is associated with higher incomes for all families, but especially for those working in the coffee sector."

One of this book's main themes is that companies within a capitalist system are exquisitely sensitive to price changes, so making pollution expensive via taxes or cap-and-trade programs is a sure way to reduce it. This is why carbon taxes are such a great idea for reducing greenhouse gases. But companies are also sensitive to their reputations, for many reasons. Perhaps the most straightforward is that people tend to buy more from companies with excellent reputations, and to shun those with a lousy public image. So a well-constructed "carbon reducing" certification might well have two positive effects: reducing greenhouse gas emissions and increasing sales for certified companies.

Another way households can harness the power of the market is by buying clean-energy products. It's difficult for a family to buy its own nuclear reactor (as it probably should be), but easy to buy solar panels and batteries. Even if this purchase is more of an experiment than a complete home-energy makeover, it serves an important purpose: it signals demand for clean-tech products. As we've seen over and over, markets respond to this demand signal by increasing supply and boosting investment and R&D.

Increased demand also causes more competition, which drives down prices. The prices of battery and solar energy products have been dropping rapidly. The surest way to sustain and accelerate these huge price declines is to keep increasing demand for clean-energy products. By buying and using these products, households can keep demand strong.

What other things can households do to benefit the planet? Excellent personal guides to helping fight climate change have been written by Chris Goodall, whose work to uncover the dematerialization of the UK economy we saw in chapter 5, and by Mark Lynas, whose defense of glyphosate was highlighted in chapter 9. Goodall's *How to Live a Low-Carbon Life* and Lynas's *Carbon Counter* both stress that housing and transportation combine to account for nearly half of the typical person's carbon footprint. So turning down heating and air-conditioning, using insulation and LED light bulbs to make homes more energy efficient, driving fewer miles, and taking fewer flights are all effective steps.

So is adopting a vegan diet, though few seem willing to abandon altogether foods made from animals: in 2018, only 3 percent of Americans identified as vegan. Short of this extreme step, eating less beef and dairy would help reduce greenhouse gases. As Linus Blomqvist of the ecomodernist think tank Breakthrough Institute puts it, "A diet including chicken and pork, but no dairy or beef, has lower greenhouse gas emissions than a vegetarian diet that includes milk and cheese, and almost gets within spitting distance of a vegan diet." For the greenhouse-gas-generating activities that households can't avoid (or choose not to), they can buy carbon offsets against them.

One other important thing individuals can do is work to reverse the increasing disconnection we're experiencing in many societies and communities. This is hard to do because of our innate tribalism and desire to associate with like-minded people. But it's also easy to do. Social capital can be increased and disconnection decreased in lots of ways. Joining a grassroots political or advocacy movement; volunteering to help vulnerable populations such as disabled veterans, refugees, or elderly people living alone; attending religious services and related activities; and teaching others your skills are all good ways to build links among people.

It's important to do these things with members of other tribes— people who we know feel differently from us about important things. And it's particularly important not to try to win arguments with them. For many of us, the strong tendency when we interact with people who have different beliefs and moral foundations is to quickly try to show them why they're wrong—why their logic is flawed, their evidence is fake news, and their beliefs are unsupportable. This almost never works. It usually just makes other people dig in their heels and hold on to their existing beliefs even more strongly. A lot of debate and discussion increases disconnection.

A better way is to start by finding common ground. The psychologist Jonathan Haidt, whose work has been mentioned in prior pages several times already, highlights that people with both liberal and conservative moral foundations believe deeply that we have a responsibility to care. This applies both to other humans and to the rest of the natural world. Few of us are unmoved by the sight of a sick child, a starving animal, or a pile of trash on a beach. So a good way to start building relationships with others, especially with members of distant tribes, is to find out which aspects of the human condition and the state of the world they care most about, then go from there. Doing so can't hurt and might lead to more connection.

Our Next Planet

We've sent robotic probes to every planet in this solar system. Earth is BY FAR the best one.

—Jeff Bezos, Twitter, 2018

Imagine that a genius invents time travel and uses the capability to offer nature lovers tours around the world of two hundred thousand years ago, before we *Homo sapiens* burst out from our African homeland and began to swarm all over the earth.*

What would these travelers see?

The oceans would contain animals that don't exist anymore. Of these, the largest was probably Steller's sea cow. This gentle, bewhiskered kelp eater weighed more than ten tons and grew as long as a school bus. Naturalist Georg Wilhelm Steller sighted it among the Bering Strait's islands in 1741. The first time he and his shipmates tried to kill one, they failed because its hide was too thick to pierce. Harpoons and determination solved this problem and gave sailors access to the animal's meat, fat, and hides. But only for a short time. By 1768, they'd killed all the sea cows.

Our appetite for massive creatures didn't stop at the shoreline; we went after them on land as well. There's intriguing evidence that, as we spread around the planet, we wiped out the biggest ani-

---

* Some fossils indicate that we *Homo sapiens* may have left Africa as much as 180,000 years ago, so 200,000 years seems like enough distance between us and our earliest non-African ancestors.

mals first in each new region (which makes sense, since the largest animals provided the most meat per kill). So time travelers to the land before our time would see ground sloths in Chile, wombats in Australia, and armadillo-like glyptodonts in Brazil—all at least the size of cars.

There were mastodons in New Jersey and mammoths in London. These hairy pachyderms roamed all throughout the higher latitudes of the Northern Hemisphere. They were so numerous that they were likely what kept the grasslands grassy. Once they went extinct about ten thousand years ago much of the land they'd inhabited turned into forest, since there were no longer enough heavy beasts around to trample young trees before they could grow. (Because grasslands keep the planet cooler than forests do,* our current lack of mammoths and mastodons is bad news for climate change.)

The Irish elk had antlers twelve feet across. It was hunted by actual dire wolves. There were marsupial lions in Tasmania as large and fierce as those in Africa today. The biggest moa—flightless birds native to New Zealand—stood more than ten feet tall and weighed over five hundred pounds.†

They are all gone.

When our nature-loving time travelers came back to today, can you imagine their grief? They would be as inconsolable as Eurydice forced to return to the underworld.

They would despair over the devastation we have caused, for the species we turned into skeletons. Most of our extinctions were inadvertent and perhaps this makes them more forgivable, but it

---

* Compared to forests, grasslands keep the earth cooler in two ways: they reflect more sunlight back into space, and they insulate the ground less, leading to longer and deeper winter freezes.

† Because New Zealand had never had any large mammalian predators, many of its birds evolved away working wings—there was nothing they needed to fly away from—and some became huge.

doesn't make them any less bitter. We impoverished our planet beyond measure as we spread across it and turned it to our purposes.

Before and during the Industrial Era countless people took seriously a command from the God of the Hebrew Bible. The book of Genesis declares that immediately after creating human beings, "God blessed them, and God said unto them, Be fruitful, and multiply, and replenish the earth, and subdue it: and have dominion over the fish of the sea, and over the fowl of the air, and over every living thing that moveth upon the earth."

We were fruitful. We multiplied. And we subdued so much, so thoroughly, that it's easy to believe our dominion was ordained from on high. But we failed miserably at our duty to *replenish*. It's as if we didn't hear that crucial divine word.

We now have the opportunity to atone for that mistake. We have the tools, the ideas, and the institutions we need to withdraw from most of the world. To get all the food we need from a small amount of land, and to give the rest back to nature. To stop pumping fast and slow poisons into the sky and oceans. To dig fewer mines, clear fewer forests, and decapitate fewer mountains. To spend time in the world's wide places not to strip their treasures but, instead, because they "announce our place in the family of things," to use the poet Mary Oliver's beautiful phrase.

Amazingly enough, doing all this won't require radical course changes in our economies or societies. We just need to let the four horsemen of the optimist—capitalism, technological progress, public awareness, and responsive government—do more of what they do. Which is, as we've seen, to let us *and* our planet flourish. Jesse Ausubel, the first great scholar of dematerialization, counsels that "we must make Nature worthless." He means, of course, that we should be working to make it *economically* worthless, so that it's safe from the voracious attention of capitalism. Then we can enjoy its true worth.

In the parts of the world where the four horsemen have galloped the farthest, they've finally let us get more from less and brought us post-peak in our exploitations of the earth and injuries to it. Not quickly enough, certainly, or deeply enough yet. But we're finally past the peak and are now getting more from less in more and more places all the time. Thanks to the work of the many people discussed in this book, we now know how that glad milestone was achieved, and how to keep the momentum going—how to lead more prosperous and healthy lives while living on a more whole earth.

As our creators and children look at this turning point, they will see that it was good.

Acknowledgments

It's absurd that there's only one name on the front cover of this book. At every step, from inception to production, many others were involved. They helped make this book, and definitely made it much better. I take full credit only for the errors here; for all the rest, a lot of people were involved.

As I mentioned in the introduction, Jesse Ausubel's essay "The Return of Nature," published in the *Breakthrough Journal*, got me started down the path of investigating how we were able to turn the corner and start getting more from less. Jesse provided advice and encouragement, and answered many questions, as did his collaborators at Rockefeller University, Iddo Wernick and Alan Curry. At the Breakthrough Institute Ted Nordhaus, Alex Trembath, Linus Blomquist, and Rachel Pritzker were beyond welcoming.

Back home at MIT my colleagues at the Initiative on the Digital Economy created an ideal environment for this work and lots of other research. David Verrill and Christie Ko kept the place running smoothly, Adjovi Koene took a lot of tasks off my plate, and Seth Benzel and Daniel Rock were great sounding boards for the work as it progressed. By this point it should go without saying that Erik Brynjolfsson, my frequent coauthor and collaborator, sharpened my thinking with every conversation.

The research team that spun up around *More from Less* included three generations of MIT Sloan MBA students. Atad Peled led off, then passed the shared folders to Aya Suchi. She advanced the cause greatly, then handed off to the team of Maor Zeevi and Gal Schwartz, who worked with me to get things over the finish line before they graduated. Throughout all of this, Jonathan Ruane worked on the project with his unique combination of intelligence, tenacity, and good cheer. Erez Yoeli and I both spoke at TEDxCambridge in 2018, and my many conversations with him about dematerialization are reflected in these pages. Dmitri Gunn, who organizes TEDxCambridge, thought enough of the ideas found here to give them their first public airing.

Once I had some pages written I needed some people to read them and give me feedback. The global group that sprang up to do this included Ed Fine, Leslie Fine, Nils Gilman, Maika Hemphill, and Marty Manley in California (on top of everything else, the Fines also gave me a place to stay and the warmth of a family when I came to San Francisco); Bo Cutter in New York; Jérôme de Castries in Paris; Ruth Luscombe on the Sunshine Coast of Australia; and Vyda Bielkus, Jim Pallotta, and Amy Shepherd in Boston. They helped show me where the manuscript was losing its way, confusing the reader, or just plain wrong. On energy Mike Shellenberger and Ramez Naam helped me be much less incorrect than I would have been otherwise; Allan Adams provided the same service around global warming.

Alexander Rose and Andrew Warner listened to the bets I wanted to make about humanity's future planetary footprint, and agreed to host them on the Long Bets site, which is part of the Long Now Foundation. Long Now was cofounded by Stewart Brand, whose *Whole Earth Catalog* I devoured when it was reproduced as a coffee-table book sometime around 1980. Some of it clearly stuck with me. Like so many others, I'm grateful to Stewart for helping us think different.

My agent, *consigliere*, and friend, Rafe Sagalyn, not only helped me think through the book at every stage but also arranged for

Scribner to publish it. At that house, my editor, Rick Horgan, made the book better at every level from word to chapter to manuscript. Publisher Nan Graham helped it find its voice, its title, and its cover. Brian Belfiglio, Kate Lloyd, and Ashley Gilliam worked to give it its best possible launch into the marketplace of ideas; Allison McLean and Elizabeth Hazelton of Amplify Partners were also essential in this effort.

Throughout all of this time Joan Powell helped me manage an active speaking schedule, and Esther Simmons kept me on track and made sure I showed up in the right place at the right time, every time. I don't know how she does it.

I want to end this book where it began—with my mom, Nancy Haller. I feel like she and my dad, David McAfee, gave me the whole earth. All I had to do was look at it properly.

Notes

Introduction: README

4 **Jesse Ausubel's amazing essay:** Jesse Ausubel, "The Return of Nature: How Technology Liberates the Environment," *Breakthrough Journal* 5 (Summer 2015), https://thebreakthrough.org/journal/issue-5/the-return -of-nature.

Chapter 1: All the Malthusian Millennia

8 **"the passion between the sexes is less ardent":** Thomas Malthus, *An Essay on the Principle of Population, as it Affects the Future Improvement of Society with Remarks on the Speculations of Mr. Godwin, M. Condorcet, and Other Writers* (1798; repr., Electronic Scholarly Publishing Project, http://www.esp.org, 1998), 12, http://www.esp.org/books/_althus/popu lation/_althus.pdf.

8 **"That in all old states some such vibration does exist":** Ibid., 10.

9 **"Population, when unchecked, increases":** Ibid., 4–5.

11 **Population and Prosperity in England, 1200–1800:** Data from Gregory Clark, "The Condition of the Working Class in England, 1209–2004," *Journal of Political Economy* 113, no. 6 (2005): 1307–40. Data, calculation details, and sources are available at morefromlessbook.com/data.

11 **"confirmation of one of the basic tenets of the Malthusian model":** Gregory Clark, "The Long March of History: Farm Wages, Population and Economic Growth, England 1209–1869" (Working Paper 05-40, University of California–Davis, Department of Economics, 2005), 28, http://hdl.handle.net/10419/31320.

12 **Malthusian vibrations . . . over the same period:** Rodney Edvinsson, "Pre-industrial Population and Economic Growth: Was There a Mal-

thusian Mechanism in Sweden?" (Working Paper 17, Stockholm Papers in Economic History, Stockholm University, Department of Economic History, 2015), http://www.historia.se/SPEH17.pdf.

12 we *Homo sapiens* left our African cradle: Chris Stringer and Julia Galway-Witham, "When Did Modern Humans Leave Africa?," *Science* 359 (January 2018): 389–90, https://doi:10.1126/science.aas8954.

12 Tenochtitlán . . . spread out over five square miles: Susan Toby Evans, *Ancient Mexico and Central America: Archaeology and Culture History* (New York: Thames & Hudson, 2013), 549.

12 London's population exceeded half a million: Clive Emsley, Tim Hitchcock, and Robert Shoemaker, "A Population History of London," Old Bailey Proceedings Online, www.oldbaileyonline.org, version 7.0, accessed February 28, 2019, https://www.oldbaileyonline.org/static/Population-history-of-london.jsp.

13 about 5 million people were on the planet: Max Roser and Esteban Ortiz-Ospina, "World Population Growth," Our World in Data, last updated April 2017, https://ourworldindata.org/world-population-growth.

13 "about 28.5 years in 1800": James C. Riley, "Estimates of Regional and Global Life Expectancy, 1800–2001," *Population and Development Review* 31 (September 2005): 537, http://www.jstor.org/stable/3401478.

13 "The advance in per-capita income was a slow crawl": Angus Maddison, *Growth and Interaction in the World Economy: The Roots of Modernity* (Washington, DC: AEI Press, 2005), 5.

Chapter 2: Power over the Earth: The Industrial Era

16 twice as much useful energy per bushel of coal: John Enys, "Remarks on the Duty of the Steam Engines Employed in the Mines of Cornwall at Different Periods," *Transactions of the Institution of Civil Engineers* vol. 3 (London: Institution of Civil Engineers, 1842), 457.

16 *The Most Powerful Idea in the World*: William Rosen, *The Most Powerful Idea in the World: A Story of Steam, Industry, and Invention* (New York: Random House, 2010).

17 William Wheelwright founded a company: Roland E. Duncan, "Chilean Coal and British Steamers: The Origin of a South American Industry," Society for Nautical Research, August 1975, https://snr.org.uk/chilean-coal-and-british-steamers-the-origin-of-a-south-american-industry/.

17 taken place only fifteen years earlier: James Croil, *Steam Navigation: And*

Its Relation to the Commerce of Canada and the United States (Toronto: William Briggs, 1898), 57, https://books.google.com/books?id=Xv2ovQEA CAAJ&printsec=frontcover#v=onepage&q&f=false.

18 **discovered in huge deposits in Southeast England:** Bernard O'Connor, "The Origins and Development of the British Coprolite Industry," *Mining History: The Bulletin of the Peak District Mines Historical Society* 14, no. 5 (2001): 46–57.

18 **the Corn Laws:** David Ross, ed., "The Corn Laws," *Britain Express*, accessed February 28, 2019, https://www.britainexpress.com/History/victorian /corn-laws.htm.

19 **Samuelson tells the story:** Paul A. Samuelson, "The Way of an Economist," in *International Economic Relations: Proceedings of the Third Congress of the International Economic Association*, ed. Paul Samuelson (London: Macmillan, 1969), 1–11.

19 **8 percent of Europe's iron . . . 60 percent:** Stephen Broadberry, Rainer Fremdling, and Peter Solar, "Chapter 7: Industry, 1700–1870" (unpublished manuscript, n.d.), 34–35, table 7.6, fig. 7.2.

19 **two-thirds of the world's coal:** Gregory Clark, "The British Industrial Revolution, 1760–1860" (unpublished manuscript, Course Readings ECN 110B, Spring 2005), 1.

19 **six thousand miles of track:** Ibid., 36.

19 **patents . . . rose twentyfold in the United Kingdom:** Ibid., 38–39, fig. 10.

20 **Population and Prosperity in England, 1200–2000:** Data on wages from 1200 to 2000 and population from 1200–1860 from Clark, "Condition of the Working Class," 1307–40. Data for population in later years from GB Historical GIS, University of Portsmouth, England Dep., Population Statistics, Total Population, A Vision of Britain through Time, and the UK Office for National Statistics. Data, calculation details, and sources are available at morefromlessbook.com/data.

21 **"as capital accumulates, the situation of the worker":** Karl Marx, *Capital: A Critique of Political Economy*, vol. 1, pt. 1, *The Process of Capitalist Production*, ed. Friedrich Engels, trans. Ernest Untermann (1867; repr., New York: Cosimo, 2007), 708–9.

21 **"oiled with the blood of the workers":** George Meyer, Sam Simon, John Swartzwelder, and Jon Vitti, "The Crepes of Wrath," *The Simpsons*, season 1, episode 11, April 15, 1990.

22 **cities in many ways became more healthy:** Jeffrey G. Williamson, "Was the Industrial Revolution Worth It? Disamenities and Death in 19th Century British Towns," *Explorations in Economic History* 19, no. 3 (July 1982): 221–45, https://doi:10.1016/0014-4983(82)90039-0.

22 **home in the Ganges River delta**: "Cholera," World Health Organization Fact Sheets, updated January 17, 2019, https://www.who.int/en/news-room/fact-sheets/detail/cholera.

22 **two major outbreaks killed more than fifteen thousand**: Jacqueline Banerjee, "Cholera," Victorian Web: Literature, History, & Culture in the Age of Victoria, last modified January 19, 2017, http://www.victorianweb.org/science/health/cholera/cholera.html.

22 **plotted all London cholera cases on a map**: Simon Rogers, "John Snow's Data Journalism: The Cholera Map That Changed the World," *Guardian Datablog*, March 15, 2013, https://www.theguardian.com/news/datablog/2013/mar/15/john-snow-cholera-map.

23 **something like an Engels Pause**: C.W., "Did Living Standards Improve during the Industrial Revolution?," *Economist*, Economics: Free Exchange, September 13, 2013, https://www.economist.com/free-exchange/2013/09/13/did-living-standards-improve-during-the-industrial-revolution.

23 **Urban infant mortality**: Williamson, "Was the Industrial Revolution Worth It?," passim.

23 **around 100 to 200 deaths per 1,000**: Williamson, "Was the Industrial Revolution Worth It?," 227, table 1.26.

23 **3.8 infant deaths per 1,000 births**: "Child and Infant Mortality in England and Wales: 2016," Office for National Statistics, accessed March 1, 2019, https://www.ons.gov.uk/peoplepopulationandcommunity/birthsdeathsandmarriages/deaths/bulletins/childhoodinfantandperinatalmortalityinenglandandwales/2016.

23 **among the world's tallest people**: Gregori Galofré-Vilà, Andrew Hinde, and Aravinda Guntupalli, "Heights across the Last 2,000 Years in England," Discussion Papers in Economic and Social History, no. 151 (Oxford: University of Oxford, January 2017).

23 **improvements to their nutrition and diets**: Felipe Fernández-Armesto, *Near a Thousand Tables: A History of Food* (New York: Free Press, 2002), Kindle, location 3886.

24 **"afford yourself an old hen or cock"**: Charles Elmé Francatelli, *A Plain Cookery Book for the Working Classes* (1852; repr., Stroud, Gloustershire: History Press, 2010), "No. 15. Cocky Leeky," https://books.google.com/books?id=5ikTDQAAQBAJ&printsec=frontcover&source=&cad=0#v=onepage&q&f=false.

24 **working classes in York were eating much the same diets**: B. S. Rowntree, *Poverty and Progress: A Second Social Survey of York* (London: Longmans, Green, 1941), 172–97.

24 exported from the Canary Islands: June Young Choi, "The Introduction of Tropical Flavours into British Cuisine, 1850–1950" (unpublished paper for AP European History class, Korean Minjok Leadership Academy, Fall 2009).

24 quantifies the level of social development in a civilization: Ian Morris, *The Measure of Civilization: How Social Development Decides the Fate of Nations* (Princeton, NJ: Princeton University Press, 2013).

25 "The transformation beggared belief": Ian Morris, *Why the West Rules— for Now: The Patterns of History, and What They Reveal About the Future* (New York: Farrar, Straus & Giroux, 2010), Kindle, location 8098.

25 Western Social Development, 2000 BCE–1900 CE: Ibid. Data, calculation details, and sources are available at morefromlessbook.com/data.

26 Western and Eastern Social Development, 2000 BCE–2000 CE: Ibid. Data, calculation details, and sources are available at morefromlessbook .com/data.

27 Davenport received a US patent: Dylan Tweney, "Feb. 25, 1837: Davenport Electric Motor Gets Plugged In," *WIRED*, February 25, 2010, https://www .wired.com/2010/02/0225davenport-electric-motor-patent/.

27 "look upon electricity as an enormously powerful": Warren D. Devine, "From Shafts to Wires: Historical Perspective on Electrification," *Journal of Economic History* 43, no. 2 (June 1983): 356.

28 America's fifth largest industry: Andrew C. Isenberg, *The Destruction of the Bison: An Environmental History, 1750–1920*, Studies in Environment and History (Cambridge, UK: Cambridge University Press, 2000), Kindle, location 3660.

28 an idea that had seemed ludicrous: Devine, "From Shafts to Wires," 359.

28 clean water explains fully half: David M. Cutler and Grant Miller, "The Role of Public Health Improvements in Health Advances: The Twentieth Century United States," *Demography* 42, no. 1 (February 2005): 1–22.

29 "most important public health intervention": Harvey Green, *Fit for America: Health, Fitness, Sport, and American Society* (New York: Pantheon Books, 1986), 108.

29 'My back got bent': Robert A. Caro, *The Path to Power: The Years of Lyndon Johnson* (New York: Knopf, 1982), 505.

29 "to have electricity in your house": Edmund Lindop, *America in the 1930s*, Decades of Twentieth-Century America Series (Minneapolis: Twenty-First Century Books, 2010), 57.

30 a global "general scarcity" of wheat: Charles C. Mann, *The Wizard and*

the Prophet: Two Remarkable Scientists and Their Dueling Visions to Shape Tomorrow's World (New York: Knopf, 2018), Kindle, location 167.

30 **"win bread from air"**: Ibid., 170.

30 **necessary for fundamental things such as proteins**: Anne Bernhard, "The Nitrogen Cycle: Processes, Players, and Human Impact," Nature Education Knowledge Project, accessed March 15, 2019, https://www.nature.com /scitable/knowledge/library/the-nitrogen-cycle-processesplayers-and -human-15644632.

31 **Haber's work got a big boost**: Mann, *Wizard and the Prophet*, 168–72 passim.

31 **1 percent of the world's industrial energy**: Ibid., 171–72.

31 **"the prevailing diets of 45 percent"**: Ibid, 170.

31 **"More than three billion"**: Ibid., 171.

32 **global population of *Homo sapiens***: Roser and Ortiz-Ospina, "World Population Growth."

32 **life expectancy more than doubled**: Max Roser, "Life Expectancy," *Our World in Data*, accessed March 15, 2019, https://ourworldindata.org /life-expectancy.

32 **real GDP per capita increased**: Max Roser, "Average Real GDP Per Capita across Countries and Regions," Our World in Data, accessed March 15, 2019, https://ourworldindata.org/grapher/average-real-gdp-per-capita -across-countries-and-regions.

32 **weighs 4.7 trillion times more than all of us**: Michael Marshall, "Humanity Weighs in at 287 Million Tonnes," *New Scientist*, June 18, 2012, https://www .newscientist.com/article/dn21945-humanity-weighs-in-at-287-million -tonnes/.

Chapter 3: Industrial Errors

37 **"the universal capacity of a person"**: Steven Pinker, *Enlightenment Now: The Case for Reason, Science, Humanism, and Progress* (New York: Penguin, 2018), Kindle, location 408.

37 **"sometimes called the Humanitarian Revolution"**: Ibid., preview location 4117.

37 **"if slavery is not wrong, nothing is wrong"**: Abraham Lincoln, letter to Albert G. Hodges, April 14, 1864, Abraham Lincoln Online: Speeches & Writings, accessed March 18, 2019, http://www.abrahamlincolnonline .org/lincoln/speeches/hodges.htm.

38 **the bloodiest in the country's history**: "Civil War Casualties," American

Battlefield Trust, accessed March 18, 2019, https://www.battlefields.org
/learn/articles/civil-war-casualties.

38 **children . . . were given no choice**: Lawrence W. Reed, "Child Labor
and the British Industrial Revolution," Foundation for Economic Education, last updated October 23, 2009, https://fee.org/articles/child
-labor-and-the-british-industrial-revolution/.

38 **two-thirds . . . were children**: Douglas A. Galbi, "Child Labor and the
Division of Labor in the Early English Cotton Mills," *Journal of Population
Economics* 10 (1997): 357–75.

38 **a succession of laws**: Emma Griffin, "Child Labour," Discovering Literature: Romantics & Victorians, last updated May 15, 2014, https://www
.bl.uk/romantics-and-victorians/articles/child-labour#.

40 **"The pretext upon which the Spanish invaded"**: Bartolomé de las Casas,
A Short Account of the Destruction of the Indies, trans. Nigel Griffen (1542,
published 1552; repr., Harmondsworth, UK: Penguin, 1992), 52–53, http://
www.columbia.edu/~daviss/work/files/presentations/casshort/.

40 **"The most modern pretense for colonial conquest"**: "Colonialism,"
Wikiquote, last revised September 5, 2018, https://en.wikiquote.org/wiki
/Colonialism.

40 **By 2018 the United Nations recognized**: "Non-Self-Governing Territories," United Nations and Decolonization, accessed March 19, 2019, http://
www.un.org/en/decolonization/nonselfgovterritories.shtml.

40 **"dark Satanic Mills"**: William Blake, "Jerusalem," Poetry Foundation,
accessed March 20, 2019, https://www.poetryfoundation.org/poems/54684
/jerusalem-and-did-those-feet-in-ancient-time.

41 **air-pollution levels weren't monitored until the twentieth century**:
Department for Environment, Food & Rural Affairs, "Chapter 7: What
Are the Main Trends in Particulate Matter in the UK?," GOV.UK, https://
uk-air.defra.gov.uk/assets/documents/reports/aqeg/ch7.pdf.

41 **"Industrial coal use explains roughly one-third"**: Brian Beach and
W. Walker Hanlon, "Coal Smoke and Mortality in an Early Industrial
Economy," *Economic Journal* 128 (November 2018): 2652–75.

41 **a full inch shorter**: Tim Hatton, "Air Pollution in Victorian-Era Britain—
Its Effects on Health Now Revealed," *The Conversation*, November 14,
2017.

41 **town of Donora, Pennsylvania**: Sean D. Hamill, "Unveiling a Museum, a
Pennsylvania Town Remembers the Smog That Killed 20," *New York Times*,
November 1, 2008, https://www.nytimes.com/2008/11/02/us/02smog.html.

41 **couldn't cut through it even in daylight**: Ibid.

42 **early 1900s . . . portmanteau of** *smoke* **and** *fog*: Tom Skilling, "Ask Tom: Is 'Smog' a Combination of 'Smoke' and 'Fog'?," *Chicago Tribune*, August 30, 2017, https://www.chicagotribune.com/news/weather/ct-wea-asktom -0831-20170830-column.html.

42 **"A rare wild rhinoceros on the brink of extinction"**: "Yuval Noah Harari," *Wikiquote*, last revised December 21, 2018, https://en.wikiquote.org/wiki /Yuval_Noah_Harari.

43 **telegraph system communicated**: Carl Zimmer, "Century After Extinction, Passenger Pigeons Remain Iconic—and Scientists Hope to Bring Them Back," *National Geographic*, August 30, 2014, https://news.nationalgeo graphic.com/news/2014/08/140831-passenger-pigeon-martha-deextinc tion-dna-animals-species/.

43 **A sea otter has many more hairs**: Jaymi Heimbuch, "How Many Hairs Does a Sea Otter Have in Just One Square Inch of Coat?," MNN, August 9, 2018, https://www.mnn.com/earth-matters/animals/blogs/how-many -hairs-does-a-sea-otter-have-in-just-one-square-inch-of-coat.

43 **the total number of pelts available**: Roland M. Nowak, *Walker's Mammals of the World*, vol. 2, 5th ed. (Baltimore and London: Johns Hopkins University Press, 1991), 1141–43.

43 **"a single colony of five beavers"**: Jim Sterba, *Nature Wars: The Incredible Story of How Wildlife Comebacks Turned Backyards into Battlegrounds* (New York: Broadway Books, 2013), Kindle, location 73.

44 **"annually bringing to the steamboats over 100,000 bison robes"**: Isenberg, *Destruction of the Bison*, Kindle, location 2735.

45 **"dead, solitary putrid desert"**: Ibid., Kindle, location 3763.

46 **The Vikings and Basques were the first people to pursue whales**: "Whales and Hunting," New Bedford Whaling Museum, accessed March 25, 2019, https://www.whalingmuseum.org/learn/research-topics/overview-of -north-american-whaling/whales-hunting.

46 **at least one fatality per voyage**: Ibid.

46 **severely depleted the world's populations of sperm, bowhead, and right whales**: J. R. McNeill, *Something New Under the Sun: An Environmental History of the Twentieth-Century World*, Global Century Series (New York: W. W. Norton, 2000), Kindle, location 3748

47 **By 1989, about five hundred**: Ibid., Kindle, location 3793.

48 **"No chemical or mechanical operation, perhaps, is quite impossible to us"**: William Stanley Jevons, *The Coal Question: An Enquiry Concerning the Progress of the Nation, and the Probable Exhaustion of Our Coal-Mines* (Macmillan, 1865), 171.

48 **"will before long render our consumption of coal comparable with the
total supply"**: Ibid., 177.

50 **"Human wants and desires are countless in number and very various
in kind"**: Alfred Marshall, *Principles of Economics*, vol. 1 (Macmillan,
1890), 150.

Chapter 4: Earth Day and Its Debates

53 **"the birth of the modern environmental movement"**: "The History of
Earth Day," Earth Day Network, accessed March 25, 2019, https://www
.earthday.org/about/the-history-of-earth-day/.

54 **"flipped from what it meant for space to what it means for Earth"**: John
Noble Wilford, "On Hand for Space History, as Superpowers Spar," *New
York Times*, July 13, 2009, https://www.nytimes.com/2009/07/14/science
/space/14mission.html?auth=login-smartlock.

54 **"brothers on that bright loveliness in the eternal cold"**: Archibald
MacLeish, "A Reflection: Riders on Earth Together, Brothers in Eternal Cold," *New York Times*, December 25, 1968, https://www.nytimes
.com/1968/12/25/archives/a-reflection-riders-on-earth-together-brothers
-in-eternal-cold.html.

54 **actually a file photo from a fire . . . in 1952**: Michael Rotman, "Cuyahoga
River Fire," *Cleveland Historical*, accessed March 25, 2019, https://cleve
landhistorical.org/items/show/63.

55 **more than doubled between 1900 and 1970 in the United States**: Gerhard
Gschwandtner, Karin Gschwandtner, Kevin Eldridge, Charles Mann, and
David Mobley, "Historic Emissions of Sulfur and Nitrogen Oxides in
the United States from 1900 to 1980," *Journal of the Air Pollution Control
Association* 36, no. 2 (1986): 139–49, https://doi.org:10.1080/00022470.19
86.10466052.

55 **"We have to get over the idea that smog is just a nuisance"**: Patrick Allitt,
A Climate of Crisis, Penguin History American Life (New York: Penguin,
2014), Kindle, location 43.

55 **"can actually cause acute disabling diseases"**: Ibid.

55 **"The battle to feed all of humanity is over"**: Paul R. Ehrlich, *The Population Bomb* (New York: Ballantine Books, 1968), 11.

56 **The Paddocks divided developing countries into three categories**: William Paddock and Paul Paddock, *Famine 1975! America's Decision: Who
Will Survive?* (Boston: Little, Brown, 1967).

56 **"the possibility of massive famines"**: "Implications of Worldwide Popu-

lation Growth for U.S. Security and Overseas Interests" ("The Kissinger Report"), National Security Study Memorandum NSSM 200, December 10, 1974, https://pdf.usaid.gov/pdf_docs/Pcaab500.pdf.

57　**US GDP and Resource Consumption, 1900–1970**: US GDP from Louis Johnston and Samuel H. Williamson, "What Was the U.S. GDP Then?," MeasuringWorth, 2019, https://www.measuringworth.com/datasets /usgdp/. Resource consumption from the US Geological Survey. Data, calculation details, and sources are available at morefromlessbook.com /data.

57　**known global reserves . . . would all be exhausted within fifty-five years**: Donella Meadows, Dennis Meadows, Jørgen Randers, and William Behrens III, *The Limits to Growth* (New York: Universe Books, 1972), 56–58.

58　**The ecologist Kenneth Watt predicted in 1970**: Ronald Bailey, "Earth Day, Then and Now," *Reason*, May 1, 2000, http://reason.com /archives/2000/05/01/earth-day-then-and-now.

58　**"abundant electrical energy in the power-starved areas of the world"**: "Atoms for Peace Speech," IAEA, July 16, 2014, https://www.iaea.org /about/history/atoms-for-peace-speech.

58　**"It'd be little short of disastrous . . . because of what we would do with it"**: "Amory Lovins: Energy Analyst and Environmentalist," *Mother Earth News*, November/December 1977, https://www.motherearthnews.com /renewable-energy/amory-lovins-energy-analyst-zmaz77ndzgoe.

59　**"exploit every last bit of the planet"**: FAS Public Interest Report, May– June 1975, https://fas.org/faspir/archive/1970-1981/May-June1975.pdf.

59　**US Real GDP and Total Energy Consumption, 1800–1970**: US GDP from Johnston and Williamson, "What Was the U.S. GDP Then?" Resource consumption from the US Energy Information Administration. Data, calculation details, and sources are available at morefromlessbook.com /data.

60　**"Flow of Energy in an Industrial Society"**: Earl Cook, "The Flow of Energy in an Industrial Society," *Scientific American* 225, no. 3 (September 1971): 134–47.

61　**"Dr. S. Dillon Ripley, secretary of the Smithsonian Institution"**: Walter E. Williams, "Environmentalists Are Dead Wrong," *Creators*, April 26, 2017, https://www.creators.com/read/walter-williams/04/17/environmen talists-are-dead-wrong.

61　**"Demographers agree almost unanimously on the following grim timetable"**: Bailey, "Earth Day."

61　**"Scientists have solid experimental and theoretical evidence"**: Matt

Ridley, "Apocalypse Not: Here's Why You Shouldn't Worry About End Times," *WIRED*, August 17, 2012, https://www.wired.com/2012/08/ff -apocalypsenot/.

61 **"civilization will end within 15 or 30 years"**: Bailey, "Earth Day."

61 **"We are prospecting for the very last of our resources"**: Ibid.

62 **"tend[ed] to be slow, costly, and insufficient in scale"**: Paul R. Ehrlich and John P. Holdren, "Impact of Population Growth," *Science* 171 (1971): 1212–17, https://www.agro.uba.ar/users/fernande/EhrlichHoldren1971 impactPopulation.pdf.

62 **"mathematical propaganda"**: N. Koblitz, "Mathematics as Propaganda," in *Mathematics Tomorrow*, ed. Lynn Steen (New York: Springer-Verlag, 1981), 111–20.

63 **"Is the earth's balance . . . compatible with the survival of the capitalist system?"**: "A History of Degrowth," *Degrowth*, accessed March 25, 2019, https://www.degrowth.info/en/a-history-of-degrowth/.

64 **"there is no other way of conserving the available reserves for future generations"**: André Gorz, *Ecology as Politics*, trans. Patsy Vigderman and Jonathan Cloud (Boston: South End Press, 1980), 13.

64 **"The present system of production is self-destructive [and] . . . suicidal"**: Barry Commoner, *The Closing Circle* (New York: Bantam Books, 1974), 294–95.

64 **"man must find his place in a cyclical . . . continuous reproduction of material form"**: Kenneth E. Boulding, "The Economics of the Coming Spaceship Earth," in *Environmental Quality in a Growing Economy*, ed. H. Jarrett (Baltimore: Resources for the Future/Johns Hopkins University Press, 1966), 3–14.

65 **By 1995, approximately 25 percent of all municipal solid waste in the United States was being recycled**: Gregory Scruggs, "A Brief Timeline of Modern Municipal Recycling," *Next City*, February 12, 2015, https:// nextcity.org/daily/entry/history-city-recycling-pickup-modern.

65 **"We must rapidly bring the world population under control"**: Ehrlich, *Population Bomb*, 127.

66 **"Such policies as reducing the birth"**: Meadows, Meadows, Randers, and Behrens, *Limits to Growth*, 167–68.

66 **The Clean Air Act was substantially amended and strengthened in 1970**: Holly Hartman, "Milestones in Environmental Protection," *Infoplease*, accessed March 25, 2019, https://www.infoplease.com/spot/milestones -environmental-protection.

66 **representative Paul Rogers recalled in 1990**: "EPA History: The Clean

Air Act of 1970," US EPA web archive, October 4, 2016, https://archive
.epa.gov/epa/aboutepa/epa-history-clean-air-act-1970.html.

68 **won a National Book Award in the Contemporary Affairs category:**
"Stewart Brand and His Five Pounds of Ideas for the '80s," *Christian Science Monitor*, January 15, 1981, https://www.csmonitor.com/1981/0115/011
556.html.

68 **The first Foxfire book sold more than 9 million copies:** Tove Danovich,
"The Foxfire Book Series That Preserved Appalachian Foodways," NPR,
March 17, 2017, https://www.npr.org/sections/thesalt/2017/03/17/520038859
/the-foxfire-book-series-that-preserved-appalachian-foodways.

69 **"Are we now 'entering an age of scarcity'?":** Julian Simon, *The Ultimate Resource* (Princeton, NJ: Princeton University Press, 1981), 3.

70 **"I made many calculations":** R. Buckminster Fuller, *Utopia or Oblivion*
(Zurich: Lars Müller, 1969), 293.

71 **"Ephemeralization . . . is the number one economic surprise of world
man":** Ibid., 297.

72 **The real price of all five metals had fallen by late September of 1990:**
Ed Regis, "The Doomslayer," *WIRED*, December 15, 2017, https://www
.wired.com/1997/02/the-doomslayer-2/.

72 **"smart but lucky":** Paul Kedrosky, "Taking Another Look at Simon vs.
Ehrlich on Commodity Prices," *Seeking Alpha*, February 19, 2010, https://
seekingalpha.com/article/189539-taking-another-look-at-simon-vs-ehrlich
-on-commodity-prices?page=2.

73 **"technological improvement has not resulted in 'automatic' dematerialization":** Christopher L. Magee and Tessaleno C. Devezas, "A Simple
Extension of Dematerialization Theory: Incorporation of Technical Progress and the Rebound Effect," *Technological Forecasting and Social Change*
117 (April 2017): 196–205, https://doi.org/10.1016/j.techfore.2016.12.001.

Chapter 5: The Dematerialization Surprise

75 **website *Quote Investigator* found no reference earlier than Samuelson's:**
"When the Facts Change, I Change My Mind. What Do You Do, Sir?,"
Quote Investigator, July 7, 2011, https://quoteinvestigator.com/2011/07/22
/keynes-change-mind/.

75 **As Ausubel remembers it:** Personal communication, May 10, 2018.

75 **"forces drive society toward materialization or dematerialization":** Robert
Herman, Siamak A. Ardekani, and Jesse H. Ausubel, "Dematerialization,"
Technological Forecasting and Social Change 37, no. 4 (1990): 333–48.

76 "The reversal in use of some of the materials so surprised me": Ausubel, "Return of Nature."

76 as the *Guardian* put it: Duncan Clark, "Why Is Our Consumption Falling?," *Guardian*, October 31, 2011, https://www.theguardian.com/environment/2011/oct/31/consumption-of-goods-falling.

76 in a 2011 paper titled "'Peak Stuff'": Chris Goodall, "'Peak Stuff': Did the UK Reach a Maximum Use of Material Resources in the Early Part of the Last Decade?," research paper, October 13, 2011, http://static .squarespace.com/static/545e40d0e4b054a6f8622bc9/t/54720c6ae4b 06f326a8502f9/1416760426697/Peak_Stuff_17.10.11.pdf.

79 US Consumption of Metals, 1900–2015: Data from the US Geological Survey. Data, calculation details, and sources are available at morefrom lessbook.com/data.

80 US GDP and Consumption of Metals, 1900–2015: US GDP from Johnston and Williamson, "What Was the U.S. GDP Then?" Metal consumption from the US Geological Survey. Data, calculation details, and sources are available at morefromlessbook.com/data.

81 US Crop Tonnage and Consumption of Agricultural Inputs, 1955–2015: Crop tonnage from https://www.usda.gov/topics/farming/crop-production. Fertilizer from https://www.usgs.gov/centers/nmic/historical-statistics mineral-and-material-commodities-united-states. Water from https:// waterdata.usgs.gov/nwis/water_use?format=html_table&rdb_compres sion=file&wu_ycar=ALL&wu_category=ALL. Cropland from https:// www.ers.usda.gov/data-products/major-land-uses/major-land-uses. Data, calculation details, and sources are available at morefromlessbook.com /data.

82 US GDP and Consumption of Building and Wood Products, 1900–2015: US GDP from Johnston and Williamson, "What Was the U.S. GDP Then?" Wood consumption from https://www.fpl.fs.fed.us/documnts/fplrp /fpl_rp679.pdf, table 5a. Paper consumption from https://pubs.er.usgs .gov/publication/fs20173062. Building products consumption from the US Geological Survey. Data, calculation details, and sources are available at morefromlessbook.com/data.

83 calculated by the Global Carbon Project: Data from Noah Smith, "China Is the Climate-Change Battleground," *Bloomberg* Opinion, October 14, 2018, https://www.bloomberg.com/opinion/articles/2018-10-14/china-is -the-climate-change-battleground.

84 US Real GDP and Total Energy Consumption, 1800–2017: US GDP from Johnston and Williamson, "What Was the U.S. GDP Then?" Resource

consumption from the US Energy Information Administration. Data, calculation details, and sources are available at morefromlessbook.com /data.

84 **natural gas produces 50–60 percent less carbon per kilowatt hour:** "Environmental Impacts of Natural Gas," Union of Concerned Scientists, accessed March 25, 2019, https://www.ucsusa.org/clean-energy/coal-and -other-fossil-fuels/environmental-impacts-of-natural-gas#.Wvc1_9MvzUI.

Chapter 6: CRIB Notes

88 **change in the real GDP of the United States:** "Real Gross Domestic Product," FRED, February 28, 2019, https://fred.stlouisfed.org/series /A191RL1A225NBEA.

88 **Population growth also slowed down:** "Population," FRED, February 28, 2019, https://fred.stlouisfed.org/series/B230RC0A052NBEA.

88 **US personal consumption of services has risen:** "Shares of Gross Domestic Product: Personal Consumption Expenditures: Services," FRED, February 28, 2019, https://fred.stlouisfed.org/series/DSERRE1Q156NBEA.

88 **the United States has not recently shifted away from "heavy" manufacturing:** Joseph J. Shapiro and Reed Walker, "Why Is Pollution from U.S. Manufacturing Declining? The Roles of Trade, Regulation, Productivity, and Preferences" (January 1, 2015), US Census Bureau Center for Economic Studies Paper no. CES-WP-15-03, https://ssrn.com/abstract=2573747 or https://dx.doi.org/10.2139/ssrn.2573747.

89 **US GDP, Industrial Production, and Consumption of Metals, 1900–2015:** US GDP from Johnston and Williamson, "What Was the U.S. GDP Then?" Industrial production from https://fred.stlouisfed.org/series/INDPRO. Metals consumption from the US Geological Survey. Data, calculation details, and sources are available at morefromlessbook.com/data.

90 **"attending to life's little comforts":** Alexis de Tocqueville, *Democracy in America: A New Translation by Arthur Goldhammer* (New York: Library of America, 2004), 617.

90 **47 percent, 33 percent, 68 percent, and 49 percent of all the tonnage:** John F. Papp, *2015 Minerals Yearbook: Recycling—Metals* (advance release), US Department of the Interior, US Geological Survey, May 2017, https:// minerals.usgs.gov/minerals/pubs/commodity/recycle/myb1-2015-recyc .pdf.

90 **almost 65 percent of paper products came from recycled newspapers:** "Paper and Paperboard: Material-Specific Data," US EPA, July 17, 2018,

https://www.epa.gov/facts-and-figures-about-materials-waste-and-recy
cling/paper-and-paperboard-material-specific-data.

91 **as many as 1 million North American back-to-the-landers:** Jeffrey Jacob,
*New Pioneers: The Back-to-the-Land Movement and the Search for a
Sustainable Future* (University Park, PA: Penn State University Press,
2010), 22.

91 **number of American city dwellers increased by more than 17 million:**
"Population and Housing Unit Costs," US Census Bureau, Table 4: Population: 1790 to 1900, https://www.census.gov/population/censusdata
/table-4.pdf.

92 **Farms of less than one hundred acres, for example:** Nigel Key, "Farm Size
and Productivity Growth in the United States Corn Belt" (presentation
at Farm Size and Productivity Conference, Washington, DC, February
2–3, 2017), https://www.farmfoundation.org/wp-content/uploads/attach
ments/1942-Session%201_Key_US.pdf.

92 **Between 1982 and 2012 farms under one hundred acres grew:** Ibid.

92 **"The best thing that we can do for the planet is build more skyscrapers":**
Edward L. Glaeser, Matthew Kahn, Manhattan Institute, and UCLA,
"Green Cities, Brown Suburbs," *City Journal*, January 27, 2016, https://
www.city-journal.org/html/green-cities-brown-suburbs-13143.html.

92 **Poland, for example, today has . . . thirty-three of the Continent's fifty
most polluted cities:** Maciek Nabrdalik and Marc Santora, "Smoth-
ered by Smog, Polish Cities Rank Among Europe's Dirtiest," *New York
Times*, April 22, 2018, https://www.nytimes.com/2018/04/22/world/europe
/poland-pollution.html.

93 **cut down such a huge percentage of their trees:** John U. Nef, "An Early
Energy Crisis and Its Consequences," *Scientific American*, November
1977, 140–50.

93 **A comprehensive review published in Nature Sustainability in 2018:**
Andrew Balmford et al., "The Environmental Costs and Benefits of High-
Yield Farming," *Nature Sustainability* 1 (September 2018): 477–85, https://
www-nature-com.libproxy.mit.edu/articles/s41893-018-0138-5.pdf.

93 **the missile scientist Song Jian came to believe:** Matt Ridley, "The Western
Environmental Movement's Role in China's One-Child Policy," *Rational
Optimist* (blog), November 7, 2015, http://www.rationaloptimist.com
/blog/one-child-policy/.

94 **journalist Barbara Demick wrote its unflattering obituary:** Barbara
Demick, "Judging China's One-Child Policy," *New Yorker*, June 19, 2017,
https://www.newyorker.com/news/news-desk/chinas-new-two-child-policy.

94 **"The additional contribution of coercion"**: Amartya Sen, "Population: Delusion and Reality," *New York Review of Books*, September 22, 1994.

94 **"How Will History Judge China's One-Child Policy?"**: Wang Feng, Yong Cai, and Baochang Gu, "Population, Policy, and Politics: How Will History Judge China's One-Child Policy?," in *Population and Public Policy: Essays in Honor of Paul Demeny*, suppl., *Population and Development Review* 38 (2012): 115–29.

94 **Paul Ehrlich responded with a tweet**: https://twitter.com/paulrehrlich /status/659814941633986560.

95 **total emissions of six principal air pollutants decreased by 65 percent**: "History of Reducing Air Pollution from Transportation in the United States," US EPA, April 19, 2018, https://www.epa.gov/transportation-air -pollution-and-climate-change/accomplishments-and-success-air-pol lution-transportation.

95 **American children in 1999 had IQs that were on average 2.2 to 4.7 points higher**: Scott D. Grosse, Thomas D. Matte, Joel Schwartz, and Richard J. Jackson, "Economic Gains Resulting from the Reduction in Children's Exposure to Lead in the United States," *Environmental Health Perspectives*, June 2002, https://www.ncbi.nlm.nih.gov/pmc/articles/PMC1240871/.

96 **As he said during debate on the bill**: Barry Yeoman, "Why the Passenger Pigeon Went Extinct," *Audubon*, May–June 2014, http://www.audubon .org/magazine/may-june-2014/why-passenger-pigeon-went-extinct.

96 **the snowy egret, which was ruthlessly hunted for its gorgeous plumes**: William Souder, "How Two Women Ended the Deadly Feather Trade," *Smithsonian*, March 2013, https://www.smithsonianmag.com/science-nature /how-two-women-ended-the-deadly-feather-trade-23187277/.

96 **North America now has more than half a million bison**: "Basic Facts about Bison," *Defenders of Wildlife*, January 10, 2019, https://defenders .org/bison/basic-facts.

96 **over three thousand sea otters live off the coast of Northern California**: "Basic Facts about Sea Otters," *Defenders of Wildlife*, January 10, 2019, https://defenders.org/sea-otter/basic-facts.

Chapter 7: What Causes Dematerialization? Markets and Marvels

100 **total cropland in the country stood at approximately 380 million acres**: "Major Land Uses," USDA ERS—Major Land Uses, accessed March 25, 2019, https://www.ers.usda.gov/data-products/major-land-uses/.

100 **an amount of cropland equal in size to the state of Washington**: "Rank-

ing of States by Total Acres," *Beef2Live*, accessed March 25, 2019, https://beef2live.com/story-ranking-states-total-acres-0-108930.

100 **The average milk cow's productivity thus improved by over 330 percent**: https://twitter.com/HumanProgress/status/1068596289485586432.

101 **"A decade later steel cans were on the way out"**: Vaclav Smil, *Making the Modern World: Materials and Dematerialization* (Hoboken, NJ: John Wiley & Sons, 2014), 123.

102 **Cichon noticed something striking about the ad**: Steve Cichon, "Everything from This 1991 Radio Shack Ad I Now Do with My Phone," *Huffington Post*, December 7, 2017, https://www.huffingtonpost.com/steve-cichon/radio-shack-ad_b_4612973.html.

102 **A November 2007 cover story in Forbes magazine**: "Forbes in 2007: Can Anyone Catch Nokia?," Nokiamob.net, November 12, 2017, http://nokiamob.net/2017/11/12/forbes-in-2007-can-anyone-catch-nokia/.

102 **CEO Stephen Elop said at the time of the deal**: Walt Mossberg et al., "Elop in July: It's 'Hard to Understand the Rationale' for Selling Nokia's Devices Business," *All Things D*, accessed March 25, 2019, http://allthingsd.com/20130903/elop-in-july-its-hard-to-understand-the-rationale-for-selling-nokias-devices-business.

102 **Microsoft sold what remained of Nokia's mobile phone business**: Arjun Kharpal, "Nokia Phones Are Back as Microsoft Sells Mobile Assets to Foxconn," CNBC, May 18, 2016, https://www.cnbc.com/2016/05/18/nokia-phones-are-back-after-microsoft-sells-mobile-assets-for-350-million-to-foxconn-hmd.html.

102 **Radio Shack filed for bankruptcy in 2015, and again in 2017**: "RadioShack Files for Bankruptcy, Again, Placing Future in Doubt," *CNN Money*, March 3, 2017, http://money.cnn.com/2017/03/09/news/companies/radioshack-bankruptcy/index.html.

102 **In 2007 US coal consumption reached a new high**: "Annual Coal Report 2007," US Energy Information Administration, February 2009, https://www.eia.gov/coal/annual/archive/05842007.pdf.

102 **Total coal use had increased by more than 35 percent since 1990**: "Independent Statistics and Analysis—Coal," US Energy Information Administration, accessed March 25, 2019, https://www.eia.gov/coal/review/coal_consumption.php.

103 **forecast further growth of up to 65 percent by 2030**: "Annual Energy Outlook 2007," US Energy Information Administration, https://www.eia.gov/outlooks/aeo/.

103 **published a report with an admirably explanatory title**: "Crude

Oil: Uncertainty about Future Oil Supply Makes It Important to Develop a Strategy for Addressing a Peak and Decline in Oil Production," US Government Accountability Office, https://www.gao.gov/assets/260/257064.pdf.

104 **In 2000 fracking accounted for just 2 percent of US oil production:** "Fracking Now Fuels Half of U.S. Oil Output," *CNN Money*, March 24, 2016, http://money.cnn.com/2016/03/24/investing/fracking-shale-oil-boom/index.html.

104 **By September of 2018 America had surpassed Saudi Arabia:** "America Unseats Russia, Saudi Arabia, as No. 1 Oil Producer," *CNN Money*, September 12, 2018, https://money.cnn.com/2018/09/12/investing/us-oil-production-russia-saudi-arabia/index.html.

104 **American natural gas production . . . jumped by nearly 43 percent:** "U.S. Natural Gas Marketed Production (Million Cubic Feet)," US Energy Information Administration, accessed March 25, 2019, https://www.eia.gov/dnav/ng/hist/n9050us2A.htm.

104 **By 2017 total US coal consumption was down 36 percent from its 2007 high point:** "Independent Statistics and Analysis—Coal Data Browser," US Energy Information Administration, accessed March 25, 2019, https://www.eia.gov/coal/data/browser/#/topic/20?agg=0,2,1&geo=vvvvvvvvvvvvo&freq=A&start=2001&end=2016&ctype=map<ype=pin&rtype=s&maptype=0&rse=0&pin=.

104 **As a 2017 *Bloomberg* headline put it, "Remember Peak Oil?":** Javíer Blas, "Remember Peak Oil? Demand May Top Out Before Supply Does," *Bloomberg*, July 11, 2017, https://www.bloomberg.com/news/articles/2017-07-11/remember-peak-oil-demand-may-top-out-before-supply-does.

104 **as a 2018 article in Fortune about the future of oil hypothesized:** Jeffrey Ball, "Inside Oil Giant Shell's Race to Remake Itself for a Low-Price World," *Fortune*, January 1, 2018, http://fortune.com/2018/01/24/royal-dutch-shell-lower-oil-prices/.

105 **My friend Bo Cutter started his career:** Personal communication, January 2019.

106 **companies started putting radio-frequency identification tags:** "How Real-Time Railroad Data Keeps Trains Running," RTInsights.com, December 10, 2015, https://www.rtinsights.com/how-real-time-railroad-data-keeps-trains-running/.

106 **At present over 5 million messages:** "Technical Information," *Railinc*, accessed March 25, 2019, https://www.railinc.com/rportal/technical-information.

106 **China responded by imposing an embargo**: Keith Bradsher, "Amid Tension, China Blocks Vital Exports to Japan," *New York Times*, September 22, 2010, https://www.nytimes.com/2010/09/23/business/global/23rare.html.

106 **rare earths are "vitamins of chemistry"**: Sarah Zielinski, "Rare Earth Elements Not Rare, Just Playing Hard to Get," *Smithsonian*, November 18, 2010, https://www.smithsonianmag.com/science-nature/rare-earth -elements-not-rare-just-playing-hard-to-get-38812856/?no-ist=.

107 **A bundle of REE . . . soared to more than $42,000 by April of 2011**: "Rare Earths Crisis in Retrospect," Human Progress, accessed March 25, 2019, https://humanprogress.org/article.php?p=1268.

107 **cerium, is about as common in the earth's crust as copper**: Mark Tyrer and John P. Sykes, "The Statistics of the Rare Earths Industry," *Significance*, April 2013, 12–16, https://rss.onlinelibrary.wiley.com/doi/pdf/10.1111/j.1740 -9713.2013.00645.x.

107 **As Representative Brad Sherman put it during the congressional hearing**: Mark Strauss, "How China's 'Rare Earth' Weapon Went from Boom to Bust," *Io9* (blog), December 16, 2015, https://io9.gizmodo.com/how -chinas-rare-earth-weapon-went-from-boom-to-bust-1653638596.

107 **Eugene Gholz noted in a 2014 report on the "crisis"**: Eugene Gholz, "Rare Earth Elements and National Security," Council on Foreign Relations Energy Report, October 2014, https://cfrd8-files.cfr.org/sites/default /files/pdf/2014/10/Energy%20Report_Gholz.pdf.

109 **Central Appalachian coal prices declined by more than half**: "US Coal Prices by Region," *Quandl*, accessed March 25, 2019, https://www.quandl .com/data/EIA/COAL-US-Coal-Prices-by-Region.

109 **the 1980 Staggers Act removed government subsidies for freight-hauling railroads**: Arne Beck, Heiner Bente, and Martin Schilling, "Railway Efficiency—an Overview and a Look at Opportunities for Improvement," OECD International Transport Forum Discussion Paper #2013-12, https:// www.itf-oecd.org/sites/default/files/docs/dp201312.pdf.

110 **A kilogram of uranium-235 fuel contains approximately 2–3 million times as much energy**: Marion Brünglinghaus, "Fuel Comparison," www .euronucler.org, accessed March 25, 2019, https://www.euronuclear.org /info/encyclopedia/f/fuelcomparison.htm.

110 **the total amount of energy . . . could be supplied by just seven thousand tons of uranium fuel**: Ethan Siegel, "How Much Fuel Does It Take to Power the World?," *Forbes*, September 20, 2017, https://www.forbes.com /sites/startswithabang/2017/09/20/how-much-fuel-does-it-take-to-power -the-world/#114bc5f316d9.

111 **from 56 percent in 1971:** "Airline Capacity Discipline: A New Global Religion Delivers Better Margins—but for How Long?," CAPA—Centre for Aviation, February 8, 2013, https://centreforaviation.com/analysis /reports/airline-capacity-discipline-a-new-global-religion-delivers-better -margins-but-for-how-long-96762.

111 **more than 81 percent in 2018:** Michael Goldstein, "Meet the Most Crowded Airlines: Load Factor Hits All-Time High," *Forbes*, July 9, 2018, https:// www.forbes.com/sites/michaelgoldstein/2018/07/09/meet-the-most -crowded-airlines-load-factor-hits-all-time-high/#6d753fb454fb.

113 **Humanity as a whole probably hit peak paper in 2013:** "World Wood Production Up for Fourth Year; Paper Stagnant as Electronic Publishing Grows," UN Report, *UN News*, United Nations, accessed March 25, 2019, https://news.un.org/en/story/2014/12/486692-world-wood-production -fourth-year-paper-stagnant-electronic-publishing-grows-un#.Vq6bffFilI-.

114 **"the organization of knowledge for the achievement of practical purposes":** Adam Thierer, "Defining 'Technology,'" *The Technology Liberation Front*, July 5, 2017, https://techliberation.com/2014/04/29/defining-tech nology/.

114 **Ursula K. Le Guin . . . wrote, "Technology is the active human interface with the material world":** Ursula K. Le Guin, "A Rant About 'Technology,'" *Ursula K. Le Guin*, accessed March 25, 2019, http://www.ursula kleguin.com/Note-Technology.html.

115 **Jonathan Haidt has pointed out, some hear it:** Jonathan Haidt, "Two Stories about Capitalism, Which Explain Why Economists Don't Reach Agreement," *The Righteous Mind*, January 1, 2015, http://righteousmind .com/why-economists-dont-agree/.

118 **in 2017 it took less than six days to start a business in America, Denmark, Singapore:** "Doing Business 2017," World Bank *Doing Business* (blog), accessed March 25, 2019, http://www.doingbusiness.org/en/reports global-reports/doing-business-2017.

119 **"We can thus say with some confidence that":** Meadows, Meadows, Randers, and Behrens, *Limits to Growth*, 126.

120 **planet would run out of gold within twenty-nine years:** Ibid., 56–58.

121 **Lincoln's patent was for a flotation system that lifted riverboats:** Owen Edwards, "Abraham Lincoln Is the Only President Ever to Have a Patent," *Smithsonian*, October 1, 2006, https://www.smithsonianmag.com/history /abraham-lincoln-only-president-have-patent-131184751/#O9U5xwgQ iTQwhk4J.99.

121 **"added the fuel of interest to the fire of genius":** "Abraham Lincoln's

Second Lecture on Discoveries and Inventions," abrahamlincolnonline
.org, accessed March 25, 2019, http://www.abrahamlincolnonline.org
/lincoln/speeches/discoveries.htm.

122 **According to Mokyr, the Enlightenment created a "culture of growth":**
Joel Mokyr, *A Culture of Growth: The Origins of the Modern Economy*
(Princeton, NJ: Princeton University Press, 2016).

Chapter 8: Adam Smith Said That: A Few Words about Capitalism

125 **capitalism found majority support only among Americans over fifty:**
Ehrenfreund, "A Majority of Millennials Now Reject Capitalism, Poll
Shows," *Washington Post*, April 26, 2016, https://www.washingtonpost.com
/news/wonk/wp/2016/04/26/a-majority-of-millennials-now-reject-cap
italism-poll-shows/?utm_term=.aa4e85460054.

126 **his article "The Conference Handbook":** George Stigler, "The Conference
Handbook," *Journal of Political Economy* 85, no. 2 (1977), https://www
.journals.uchicago.edu/doi/pdfplus/10.1086/260576.

127 **"It is not from the benevolence":** Adam Smith, *An Inquiry into the Nature
and Causes of the Wealth of Nations*, 2 vols. (London: W. Strahan and T.
Cadell, 1776), vol. 1, chap. 2, p. 19.

127 **"people doubt the contributions of profit-seeking industry to societal
progress":** A. Bhattacharjee, J. Dana, and J. Baron, "Anti-profit Beliefs:
How People Neglect the Societal Benefits of Profit," *Journal of Personality
and Social Psychology* 113, no. 5 (2017): 671–96, http://dx.doi.org/10.1037
/pspa0000093.

127 **"Nobody but a beggar chooses to depend":** Smith, *Wealth of Nations*,
vol. 1, chap. 2, p. 15.

128 **"be necessary for promoting that of the consumer":** Ibid., book 4, chap. 8,
p. 49.

128 **"Wherever there is great property, there is great inequality":** Ibid.,
book 5, chap. 1, p. 770.

129 **"in the same obscurity as if shut up in his own hovel":** Adam Smith,
The Theory of Moral Sentiments (printed for Andrew Millar, in the Strand;
and Alexander Kincaid and J. Bell, in Edinburgh, 1759), chap. 2.

129 **"People of the same trade seldom meet together":** Adam Smith, *Wealth
of Nations*, book 1, chap. 10, p. 127.

129 **"The member of parliament who supports every proposal":** Ibid., book 4,
chap. 2.

130 **"little else is requisite . . . but peace, easy taxes, and a tolerable adminis-**

tration of justice": "Adam Smith on the Need for 'Peace, Easy Taxes, and a Tolerable Administration of Justice'" (1755), *Online Library of Liberty*, accessed March 25, 2019, http://oll.libertyfund.org/quote/436.

130 **"Taxes are what we pay for civilized society":** "Taxes Are What We Pay for Civilized Society," *Quote Investigator*, April 13, 2012, https://quote investigator.com/2012/04/13/taxes-civilize/.

132 **"I can drag it into the bathroom and drown it in the bathtub":** "Grover Norquist," *Wikiquote*, accessed January 6, 2018, https://en.wikiquote.org /wiki/Grover_Norquist.

134 **Hayek used this insight to shoot down the idea of socialism in 1977:** Interview with Thomas W. Hazlett, May 1977, in "The Road to Serfdom, Foreseeing the Fall," *Reason*, July 1992.

134 **South America's richest country as recently as 2001:** "Report for Selected Countries and Subjects," International Monetary Fund, accessed March 25, 2019, http://www.imf.org/external/pubs/ft/weo/2016/02/weodata /weorept.aspx?sy=2001&ey=2001&scsm=1&ssd=1&sort=country&ds= .&br=1&c=213,218,223,228,288,233,293,248,298,299&s=PPPPC&grp=0 &a=&pr.x=61&pr.y=10.

135 **They nationalized companies in industries:** "Factbox: Venezuela's Nationalizations under Chavez," *Reuters World News*, October 8, 2012, https:// www.reuters.com/article/us-venezuela-election-nationalizations-idus bre89701x20121008.

135 **ran *misiones* that provided meals and groceries:** José Orozco, "With 'Misiones,' Chavez Builds Support Among Venezuela's Poor," *World Politics Review*, December 10, 2006, https://www.worldpoliticsreview.com/arti cles/404/with-misiones-chavez-builds-support-among-venezuelas-poor.

135 **then sold it internally at subsidized prices (in other words, at a loss):** Mercy Benzaquen, "How Food in Venezuela Went from Subsidized to Scarce," *New York Times*, July 16, 2017, https://www.nytimes.com/inter active/2017/07/16/world/americas/venezuela-shortages.html.

135 **Currency controls were put in place for most businesses:** Emiliana Disilvestro and David Howden, "Venezuela's Bizarre System of Exchange Rates," *Mises Wire* (blog), Mises Institute, December 28, 2015, https:// mises.org/library/venezuelas-bizarre-system-exchange-rates.

135 **A set of "fair price" laws set not only prices:** Benzaquen, "How Food in Venezuela Went from Subsidized to Scarce."

135 **mainly because of the strength of its oil industry:** "Venezuela Facts and Figures," OPEC, accessed March 25, 2019, http://www.opec.org/opec_web /en/about_us/171.htm.

135 **Venezuela has the largest proven oil reserves in the world**: "List of Countries by Proven Oil Reserves," *Wikipedia*, March 4, 2019, https:// en.wikipedia.org/wiki/List_of_countries_by_proven_oil_reserves.

135 **oil prices that largely stayed above $100 per barrel**: "Crude Oil Prices—70 Year Historical Chart," Macrotrends.net, accessed March 25, 2019, http:// www.macrotrends.net/1369/crude-oil-price-history-chart.

136 **adults lost an average of nearly twenty pounds in a year**: "Venezuela Leaps towards Dictatorship," *Economist*, March 31, 2017, https://www.economist .com/the-americas/2017/03/31/venezuela-leaps-towards-dictatorship.

136 **"Children arrive with the same weight and height of a newborn"**: Isayen Herrera and Meridith Kohut, "As Venezuela Collapses, Children Are Dying of Hunger," *New York Times*, December 17, 2017, https://www.nytimes.com /interactive/2017/12/17/world/americas/venezuela-children-starving.html.

136 **a decline greater than that experienced by Iraq**: Anatoly Kurmanaev, "Venezuela's Oil Production Is Collapsing," *Wall Street Journal*, January 18, 2018, https://www.wsj.com/articles/venezuelas-oil-industry-takes-a -fall-1516271401.

136 **the IMF estimated that the country's GDP dropped 35 percent between 2013 and 2017**: "The Tragedy of Venezuela," *Michael Roberts Blog*, August 3, 2017, https://thenextrecession.wordpress.com/2017/08/03/the-tragedy -of-venezuela/.

136 **According to economist Ricardo Hausmann, this is the largest economic collapse ever**: Ricardo Hausmann, "Venezuela's Unprecedented Collapse," *Project Syndicate*, July 31, 2017, https://www.project-syndicate .org/commentary/venezuela-unprecedented-economic-collapse-by-ri cardo-hausmann-2017-07?referrer=/nvBcqfkklA&barrier=accesspaylog.

136 **By November of that year, the annual inflation rate was 1,290,000 percent**: Robert Valencia, "Venezuela's Inflation Rate Passes 1 Million Percent and It's Costing Lives Every Day. This Is What It Looks Like," *Newsweek*, December 14, 2018, https://www.newsweek.com/venezuela-million-hyper inflation-losing-lives-everyday-1256630.

137 **by 2016 Venezuela had the second-highest homicide rate in the world after El Salvador**: Juan Forero, Maolis Castro, and Fabiola Ferrero, "Venezuela's Brutal Crime Crackdown: Executions, Machetes and 8,292 Dead," *Wall Street Journal*, December 21, 2017, https://www.wsj.com /articles/venezuelas-brutal-crime-crackdown-executions-machetes-and -8-292-dead-1513792219.

137 **By early 2018 at least five thousand people a day were streaming into Colombia**: Gideon Long, "Venezuela's Imploding Economy Sparks Ref-

ugee Crisis," *Financial Times*, April 16, 2018, https://www.ft.com/content/a62038a4-3bdc-11e8-b9f9-de94fa33a81e.

137 **"All of them showed up with their degrees in hand"**: Jim Wyss, "In Venezuela, They Were Teachers and Doctors. To Buy Food, They Became Prostitutes," *Miami Herald*, September 25, 2017, http://www.miamiherald.com/news/nation-world/world/americas/venezuela/article174808061.html.

137 **put its infant mortality rate higher than that of Syria in 2016**: Sara Schaefer Muñoz, "Infant Mortality Soars in Venezuela," *Wall Street Journal*, October 17, 2016, https://www.wsj.com/articles/infant-mortality-soars-in-venezuela-1476716417.

138 **More than 80 percent of Venezuelans wanted him to resign**: Virginia López Glass, "Nothing Can Prepare You for Life with Hyperinflation," *New York Times*, February 12, 2019, https://www.nytimes.com/2019/02/12/opinion/venezuela-hyperinflation-food-shortages.html.

138 **"The trouble with socialism is that eventually you run out of other people's money"**: David Mikkelson, "Fact Check: Margaret Thatcher on Socialism," *Snopes*, accessed March 25, 2019, https://www.snopes.com/fact-check/other-peoples-money/.

138 **"The capitalist reorganization of production petered out in the developing world"**: Ricardo Hausmann, "Does Capitalism Cause Poverty?," *Project Syndicate*, August 21, 2015, https://www.project-syndicate.org/commentary/does-capitalism-cause-poverty-by-ricardo-hausmann-2015-08.

Chapter 9: What Else Is Needed? People and Policies

143 **an alliance of market-loving conservatives and liberal environmentalists**: Richard Conniff, "The Political History of Cap and Trade," *Smithsonian*, August 1, 2009, https://www.smithsonianmag.com/science-nature/the-political-history-of-cap-and-trade-34711212/.

143 **The cap-and-trade approach to reducing pollution has been a huge success**: Ibid.

146 **"I hope in the future we'll move to a foreign country"**: Edward Wong, "In China, Breathing Becomes a Childhood Risk," *New York Times*, April 22, 2013, https://www.nytimes.com/2013/04/23/world/asia/pollution-is-radically-changing-childhood-in-chinas-cities.html.

146 **"would also experience a reduction in its population of about 2.7 percent"**: "A Toxic Environment: Rapid Growth, Pollution and Migration," *VoxDev*, accessed March 25, 2019, https://voxdev.org/topic/labour

-markets-migration/toxic-environment-rapid-growth-pollution-and
-migration.

146 **The Communist Party censored attempts to highlight the air-pollution problem**: Anthony Kuhn, "For Some in China's Middle Class, Pollution Is Spurring Action," *Parallels* (blog), NPR, March 2, 2017, https://www .npr.org/sections/parallels/2017/03/02/518173670/for-some-in-chinas -middle-class-pollution-is-spurring-action.

146 **"We will resolutely declare war against pollution as we declared war against poverty"**: Michael Greenstone, "Four Years After Declaring War on Pollution, China Is Winning," *New York Times*, March 12, 2018, https:// www.nytimes.com/2018/03/12/upshot/china-pollution-environment -longer-lives.html.

147 **reductions in fine-particulate pollution of more than 30 percent**: Ibid.

147 **By 2018 the country had the fourteen most-polluted cities in the world**: Joe McCarthy, "India Has the World's 14 Most Polluted Cities, New Report Shows," *Global Citizen*, May 3, 2018, https://www.globalcitizen.org/en /content/india-has-worlds-most-polluted-cities/.

147 **"India has never been able to boss around its population like China does"**: Jeffrey Gettleman, Kai Schultz, and Hari Kumar, "Environmentalists Ask: Is India's Government Making Bad Air Worse?," *New York Times*, December 8, 2017, https://www.nytimes.com/2017/12/08/world /asia/india-pollution-modi.html.

148 **saw children vomiting out the windows of their school bus**: Kai Schultz, Hari Kumar, and Jeffrey Gettleman, "In India, Air So Dirty Your Head Hurts," *New York Times*, November 8, 2017, https://www.nytimes .com/2017/11/08/world/asia/india-air-pollution.html.

148 **slash-and-burn agriculture—is generally illegal in Indonesia**: Seth Mydans, "Southeast Asia Chokes on Indonesia's Forest Fires," *New York Times*, September 25, 1997, https://www.nytimes.com/1997/09/25/world /southeast-asia-chokes-on-indonesia-s-forest-fires.html.

148 **companies' desire not to pay lawsuit damages will have an effect on this pollution**: Vaidehi Shah, "5 Ways Singapore Is Dealing with the Haze," *Eco-Business*, October 7, 2015, http://www.eco-business.com/news/5 -ways-singapore-is-dealing-with-the-haze/.

148 **88–95 percent of all plastic garbage that flowed into the world's oceans from rivers**: Christian Schmidt, Tobias Krauth, and Stephan Wagner, "Export of Plastic Debris by Rivers into the Sea," *Environmental Science & Technology* 51, no. 21 (2017): 12246–53, https://doi.org:10.1021/acs.est.7b02368.

149 **contributes 28 percent of total oceanic plastic trash**: Shivali Best, "95%

of Plastic in Oceans Comes from Just Ten Rivers," *Daily Mail*, October 11, 2017, http://www.dailymail.co.uk/sciencetech/article-4970214/95-plastic -oceans-comes-just-TEN-rivers.html.

149 **consumers in several countries organized boycotts of CFC-containing spray cans**: Mario Molina and Durwood J. Zaelke, "A Climate Success Story to Build On," *New York Times*, September 25, 2012, https://www .nytimes.com/2012/09/26/opinion/montreal-protocol-a-climate-success -story-to-build-on.html.

149 **The Association of European Chemical Companies cautioned**: Kenneth S. Overway, *Environmental Chemistry: An Analytical Approach* (Hoboken, NJ: John Wiley & Sons, 2017), 154.

150 **twenty-four countries and the European Economic Community signed**: *The Ozone Hole*, accessed March 25, 2019, http://www.theozonehole.com /montreal.htm.

150 **a phaseout of existing chemicals gave them a great chance to profit**: James Maxwell and Forrest Briscoe, "There's Money in the Air: The CFC Ban and DuPont's Regulatory Strategy," *Business Strategy and the Environment* 6 (1997): 276–86.

150 **"Perhaps the single most successful international agreement to date"**: *The Ozone Hole*, http://www.theozonehole.com/montreal.htm.

150 **the hole in the ozone layer was closing more quickly than initially expected**: Eric Hand, "Ozone Layer on the Mend, Thanks to Chemical Ban," *Science*, June 30, 2016, http://www.sciencemag.org/news/2016/06 /ozone-layer-mend-thanks-chemical-ban.

151 **it's classified by the Canadian government as abundant**: "Harp Seal," Fisheries and Oceans Canada, Communications Branch, Government of Canada, November 25, 2016, http://www.dfo-mpo.gc.ca/species-especes /profiles-profils/harpseal-phoquegroenland-eng.html.

152 **in the late nineteenth century that prices for their pelts rose tenfold**: Nowak, *Walker's Mammals of the World*, 1141–43.

152 **In the 1890s buffalo heads sold for as much as $1,500**: Isenberg, *Destruction of the Bison*, Kindle, locations 4873–74.

153 **Africa had an estimated 26 million elephants**: "Conservation," Great Elephant Census, accessed March 25, 2019, http://www.greatelephant census.com/background-on-conservation/.

153 **Great Elephant Census . . . counted just over 350,000 animals across the continent**: "The Final Report," *Great Elephant Census*, accessed March 25, 2019, http://www.greatelephantcensus.com/final-report.

154 **Kenya, Zambia, and Botswana are effectively managing their herds**:

"Map Updates," *Great Elephant Census*, accessed March 25, 2019, http://www.greatelephantcensus.com/map-updates/.

154 **"many animals there are bigger than me"**: Simon Denyer, "Yao Ming Aims to Save Africa's Elephants by Persuading China to Give Up Ivory," *Washington Post*, September 4, 2014, https://www.washingtonpost.com/world/ex-rocket-yao-ming-aims-to-save-africas-elephants-with-china-campaign/2014/09/03/87ebbe2a-d3e1-4283-964e-8d87dea397d6_story.html?utm_term=.9027067b620a.

154 **wholesale prices in Chinese markets for new ivory had dropped more than 50 percent**: Lucy Vigne and Esmond Martin, "Decline in the Legal Ivory Trade in China in Anticipation of a Ban," *Save the Elephants*, 2017, https://www.savetheelephants.org/wp-content/uploads/2017/03/2017_Decline-in-legal-Ivory-trade-China.pdf.

154 **"a once-in-a-century herbicide"**: Stephen O. Duke and Stephen B. Powles, "Glyphosate: A Once-in-a-Century Herbicide," *Pest Management Science* 64, no. 4 (2008): 319–25.

154 **"herbicide does not pose a health risk to humans"**: Gary M. Williams, Robert Kroes, and Ian C. Munro, "Safety Evaluation and Risk Assessment of the Herbicide Roundup and Its Active Ingredient, Glyphosate, for Humans," *Regulatory Toxicology and Pharmacology* 31, no. 2 (2000): 117–65, https://www.ncbi.nlm.nih.gov/pubmed/10854122.

155 **"red meat, wood smoke . . . and even the occupation of being a hairdresser"**: "Europe Still Burns Witches—If They're Named Monsanto," *Alliance for Science* Cornell, accessed March 25, 2019, https://allianceforscience.cornell.edu/blog/2017/11/europe-still-burns-witches-if-theyre-named-monsanto/.

155 **"no immediate relation to anything in the real world"**: Sarah Zhang, "Does Monsanto's Roundup Herbicide Cause Cancer or Not? The Controversy Explained," *WIRED*, June 3, 2017, https://www.wired.com/2016/05/monsantos-roundup-herbicide-cause-cancer-not-controversy-explained/.

155 **By 2016 two-thirds of people . . . supported a ban on glyphosate**: Arthur Neslen, "Two-Thirds of Europeans Support Ban on Glyphosate—Poll," *Guardian*, April 11, 2016, https://www.theguardian.com/environment/2016/apr/11/two-thirds-of-europeans-support-ban-on-glyphosate-says-yougov-poll.

155 **continue to allow use of the herbicide within the EU**: Arthur Neslen, "Controversial Glyphosate Weedkiller Wins New Five-Year Lease in Europe," *Guardian*, November 27, 2017, https://www.theguardian.com

/environment/2017/nov/27/controversial-glyphosate-weedkiller-wins
-new-five-year-lease-in-europe.

155 **that France would ban glyphosate within three years:** "France Says
Farmers Exempt from Glyphosate Ban When No Alternative," *Reuters*,
January 25, 2018, https://www.reuters.com/article/us-eu-health-glypho
sate/france-says-farmers-exempt-from-glyphosate-ban-when-no-alter
native-idUSKBN1FE2C6.

156 **"safety from these [genetically engineered] foods than from their non-GE
counterparts":** National Academies of Sciences, Engineering, and Medicine, *Genetically Engineered Crops: Experiences and Prospects* (Washington,
DC: National Academies Press, 2016), https://www.nap.edu/catalog/23395
/genetically-engineered-crops-experiences-and-prospects.

156 **"GMOs, are not per se more risky than e.g. conventional plant-breeding
technologies":** "A Decade of EU-Funded GMO Research (2001–2010),"
European Commission Directorate-General for Research and Innovation, 2010, https://ec.europa.eu/research/biosociety/pdf/a_decade_of
_eu-funded_gmo_research.pdf.

156 **thirty-eight countries don't allow their farmers to grow GMO crops:**
"Where Are GMO Crops and Animals Approved and Banned?," GMO
FAQs, *Genetic Literacy Project*, accessed March 25, 2019, https://gmo
.geneticliteracyproject.org/FAQ/where-are-gmos-grown-and-banned/.

157 **the deficiency is thought to cause more than a million deaths annually:**
Jorge Mayer, "Why Golden Rice?," *Golden Rice Project*, accessed March
25, 2019, http://www.goldenrice.org/Content3-Why/why.php.

157 **It has been approved as safe by the US FDA:** "US FDA Approves GMO
Golden Rice as Safe to Eat," *Genetic Literacy Project*, May 28, 2018, https://
geneticliteracyproject.org/2018/05/29/us-fda-approves-gmo-golden-rice
-as-safe-to-eat/.

157 **free licenses are available to developing countries:** Jorge Mayer, "Golden
Rice and Intellectual Property," *Golden Rice Project*, accessed March 25,
2019, http://www.goldenrice.org/Content2-How/how9_IP.php.

157 **"environmentally irresponsible and could compromise food, nutrition and financial security":** "Special Report: Golden Rice," *Greenpeace
International*, accessed March 25, 2019, https://www.greenpeace.org
/archive-international/en/campaigns/agriculture/problem/Greenpeace
-and-Golden-Rice/.

157 **more than half of Americans believe they're as safe or safer than conventional crops:** "Public Opinion about Genetically Modified Foods and Trust
in Scientists," Pew Research Center Science & Society, December 1, 2016,

http://www.pewinternet.org/2016/12/01/public-opinion-about-genetically
-modified-foods-and-trust-in-scientists-connected-with-these-foods/.

158 **a majority of people supported the country's participation in the Paris Agreement**: "Majorities of Americans in Every State Support Participation in the Paris Agreement," Yale Program on Climate Change Communication, accessed March 25, 2019, http://climatecommunication.yale.edu /publications/paris_agreement_by_state/.

158 **as he tweeted in 2012**: Dylan Matthews, "Donald Trump Has Tweeted Climate Change Skepticism 115 Times. Here's All of It," *Vox*, June 1, 2017, https://www.vox.com/policy-and-politics/2017/6/1/15726472/trump -tweets-global-warming-paris-climate-agreement.

159 **"the humanly devised constraints that shape human interaction"**: Douglass North, *Institutions, Institutional Change and Economic Performance* (Cambridge, UK: Cambridge University Press, 1990), 3.

160 **"in which people can exchange and contract"**: Daron Acemoglu and James A. Robinson, *Why Nations Fail: The Origins of Power, Prosperity, and Poverty* (New York: Crown, 2013), 144.

161 **"new cars, SUVs and pickup trucks are roughly 99 percent cleaner for common pollutants"**: "History of Reducing Air Pollution from Transportation in the United States," US EPA, April 19, 2018, https://www .epa.gov/transportation-air-pollution-and-climate-change/accomplish ments-and-success-air-pollution-transportation.

161 **"A car today emits less pollution traveling at full speed"**: Matt Ridley, "17 Reasons to Be Cheerful," *Rational Optimist* (blog), September 23, 2015, http://www.rationaloptimist.com/blog/17-reasons-to-be-cheerful/.

162 **Average horsepower went down over this period**: Kyle Stock and David Ingold, "America's Cars Are Suddenly Getting Faster and More Efficient," *Bloomberg*, accessed May 17, 2017, https://www.bloomberg.com/news /features/2017-05-17/america-s-cars-are-all-fast-and-furious-these-days.

162 **"Combustion engines on America's roads are about 42 percent smaller"**: Ibid.

163 **The initial global quota under the treaty was sixteen thousand whales**: Gerald Elliot and Stuart M. Frank, "Whaling, 1937–1967: The International Control of Whale Stocks," monograph, Kendall Whaling Museum, 1997, https://www.whalingmuseum.org/sites/default/files/pdf/International%20 Control%20of%20Whale%20Stocks.pdf.

163 **Soviets actually killed 180,000 more whales than they reported**: Yulia V. Ivashchenko and Phillip J. Clapham, "Too Much Is Never Enough: The Cautionary Tale of Soviet Illegal Whaling," *Marine Fisheries Review* 76,

no. 1–2 (2014): 1–22, https://spo.nmfs.noaa.gov/sites/default/files/pdf-con tent/mfr761-21.pdf.

164 **"The plan—at any price!"**: Alfred A. Berzin, *The Truth About Soviet Whaling: A Memoir*, special issue, *Marine Fisheries Review* 70, no. 2 (2008): 4–59, https://spo.nmfs.noaa.gov/mfr702/mfr702opt.pdf.

164 *The Truth About Soviet Whaling*: Ibid.

165 **the USSR succeeded in keeping international monitors off its boats until 1972**: Charles Homans, "The Most Senseless Environmental Crime of the 20th Century," *Pacific Standard*, November 12, 2013, https://psmag .com/social-justice/the-senseless-environment-crime-of-the-20th-century -russia-whaling-67774.

Chapter 10: The Global Gallop of the Four Horsemen

168 **In 2016, more people in the world had a phone than a flush toilet**: "The World's Poorest Are More Likely to Have a Cellphone than a Toilet," *Fortune*, January 15, 2016, http://fortune.com/2016/01/15/cellphone-toilet/.

168 **or piped water**: Phoebe Parke, "More Africans Have Phone Service than Piped Water," CNN, January 19, 2016, https://www.cnn.com/2016/01/19 /africa/africa-afrobarometer-infrastructure-report/index.html.

168 **"many have to walk for miles to get a signal or recharge their phones' batteries"**: "In Much of Sub-Saharan Africa, Mobile Phones Are More Common than Access to Electricity," *Economist*, November 8, 2017, https:// www.economist.com/graphic-detail/2017/11/08/in-much-of-sub-saharan -africa-mobile-phones-are-more-common-than-access-to-electricity.

168 **the world had more mobile phone subscriptions than people on the planet**: "Mobile Cellular Subscriptions (per 100 People)," The World Bank Data, accessed March 25, 2019, https://data.worldbank.org /indicator/IT.CEL.SETS.P2?end=2016&start=1960&view=chart.

168 **1.5 billion smartphones were sold globally in 2017**: "Gartner Says World- wide Sales of Smartphones Recorded First Ever Decline During the Fourth Quarter of 2017," *Gartner*, accessed March 25, 2019, https://www.gartner .com/newsroom/id/3859963.

168 **450 million non-smartphones**: Aaron Pressman, "Why Feature Phone Sales Are Suddenly Growing Faster Than Smartphones," *Fortune*, March 12, 2018, http://fortune.com/2018/03/12/feature-phone-sales-facebook -google-nokia-jio-8110/.

168 **India's most popular smartphone in 2018 was the Lyf Jio F90M**: Jkielty,

"The Most Popular Smartphones in 2019," *DeviceAtlas*, January 18, 2019, https://deviceatlas.com/blog/most-popular-smartphones#india.

169 **512 MB RAM and internal storage of up to 128 GB**: Ansh Sharma, Jyotsna Joshi, Monu Sharma, and K. Rajeev, "Buy Jio Phone F90M, 2.4 Inch Display, Wireless FM, 512 MB RAM, 4 GB Internal Storage (Black, 512 MB RAM, 4 GB), Price in India (26 Mar 2019), Specification & Reviews," *Gadgets 360*, April 13, 2018, https://gadgets360.com/shop/jio-phone-f90m -black-363131302d3130353636.

169 **"has access to more information than the US president did just fifteen years ago"**: Peter Diamandis, "The Future Is Brighter Than You Think," CNN, May 6, 2012, https://www.cnn.com/2012/05/06/opinion/diamandis -abundance-innovation/index.html.

169 **The World Bank estimated that in 2016 more than 45 percent**: "Individuals Using the Internet (% of Population)," The World Bank Data, accessed March 25, 2019, https://data.worldbank.org/indicator/IT.NET .USER.ZS?end=2016&start=1960&view=chart.

170 **"There are no fundamental contradictions between socialism and a market economy"**: "Deng Xiaoping, Chinese Politician, Paramount Leader of China," *Wikiquote*, September 5, 2018, https://en.wikiquote.org/wiki /Deng_Xiaoping.

171 **the Russian-made felt pen Gorbachev tried to use didn't work**: Conor O'Clery, "Remembering the Last Day of the Soviet Union," *Irish Times*, December 24, 2016, https://www.irishtimes.com/news/world/europe /conor-o-clery-remembering-the-last-day-of-the-soviet-union-1.2916499.

171 **Soviet-style socialism ended . . . behind the Iron Curtain**: "Eastern Bloc," *Wikipedia*, March 25, 2019, https://en.wikipedia.org/wiki/Eastern _Bloc#Population.

171 **Singh proposed deep changes to the way his country's economy worked**: "One More Push," *Economist*, July 21, 2011, https://www.economist.com /leaders/2011/07/21/one-more-push.

172 **"1991 . . . deserves its spot in the annals of economic history"**: Ibid.

172 **about 40 percent of the world's 1990 population**: "Total Population of the World by Decade, 1950–2050," *Infoplease*, accessed March 25, 2019, https://www.infoplease.com/world/population-statistics/total-population -world-decade-1950-2050.

172 **Index of Economic Freedom for virtually all the world's countries**: "2019 Index of Economic Freedom," Heritage Foundation, accessed March 25, 2019, https://www.heritage.org/index/.

173 **Benedict Evans illustrates how well this partnership has worked in recent years:** "Telecoms and Competition," Twitter, accessed March 25, 2019, https://twitter.com/i/moments/782831197126660096.

173 **an estimated 45 percent of São Paulo's businesses didn't have a telephone line:** Kevin G. Hall, "Brazil Telecom Bid Takes Market by Surprise," *Journal of Commerce and Technology*, July 27, 1997, https://www.joc.com /brazil-telecom-bid-takes-market-surprise_19970727.html.

174 **Max Roser calculates that in 1988 41.4 percent of humanity:** Max Roser, "Democracy," *Our World in Data*, March 15, 2013, https://ourworldindata .org/democracy.

174 **most democracies are holding strong:** Bruce Jones and Michael O'Hanlon, "Democracy Is Far from Dead," *Wall Street Journal*, December 10, 2017, https://www.wsj.com/articles/democracy-is-far-from-dead-1512938275.

175 **the World Bank has maintained governance indicators:** "Worldwide Governance Indicators," *The World Bank* (newsletter), accessed March 25, 2019, http://info.worldbank.org/governance/wgi/#reports.

175 **developed a "human rights protection" score:** Keith E. Schnakenberg and Christopher J. Fariss, "Dynamic Patterns of Human Rights Practices," *Political Science Research and Methods* 2, no. 1 (2014): 1–31, https://ssrn .com/abstract=1534335 or http://dx.doi.org/10.2139/ssrn.1534335.

176 **"accepting our citizenship in the world":** Pinker, *Enlightenment Now*, Kindle, location 11.

176 **are embracing more and more of these values:** Christian Welzel, *Freedom Rising: Human Empowerment and the Quest for Emancipation* (Cambridge, UK: Cambridge University Press, 2013).

177 **"Young Muslims in the Middle East, the world's most conservative culture":** Pinker, *Enlightenment Now*, location 228.

177 **By 2014, the figure had dropped to less than 15 percent:** Max Roser and Esteban Ortiz-Ospina, "Global Rise of Education," *Our World in Data*, August 31, 2016, https://ourworldindata.org/global-rise-of-education.

Chapter 11: Getting So Much Better

179 **"But in online polls, in most countries, fewer than 10 percent of people knew this":** Hans Rosling, "Good News at Last: The World Isn't as Horrific as You Think," *Guardian*, April 11, 2018, https://www.theguardian.com /world/commentisfree/2018/apr/11/good-news-at-last-the-world-isnt-as -horrific-as-you-think.

180 **Across all countries surveyed in 2017, only 20 percent of people correctly**

answered: "Most of Us Are Wrong about How the World Has Changed (Especially Those Who Are Pessimistic about the Future)," *Our World in Data*, accessed March 25, 2019, https://ourworldindata.org/wrong-about -the-world.

180 **"is admired by a large class of persons as a sage":** "John Stuart Mill Quote," *LibQuotes*, accessed March 25, 2019, https://libquotes.com/john -stuart-mill/quote/lbn8u1p.

181 **"When things are improving we know we are on the right track":** Bjørn Lomborg, *The Skeptical Environmentalist: Measuring the Real State of the World* (Cambridge, UK: Cambridge University Press, 2001), 5.

182 **Stewart Brand explained how implausible this is:** Stewart Brand, "We Are Not Edging Up to a Mass Extinction," *Aeon*, accessed March 25, 2019, https://aeon.co/essays/we-are-not-edging-up-to-a-mass-extinction.

182 **documented extinctions are relatively rare . . . in the past fifty years:** Douglas J. McCauley, Malin L. Pinsky, Stephen R. Palumbi, James A. Estes, Francis H. Joyce, and Robert R. Warner, "Marine Defaunation: Animal Loss in the Global Ocean," *Science* 347, no. 6219 (2015), 1255641.

182 **Church and others to adapt an elephant:** Rachel Riederer, "The Woolly Mammoth Lumbers Back into View," *New Yorker*, December 27, 2018, https://www.newyorker.com/science/elements/the-wooly-mammoth -lumbers-back-into-view.

183 **"regions have increased numbers of species":** Richard Lea, "Scientist Chris D. Thomas: 'We Can Take a Much More Optimistic View of Conservation,'" *Guardian*, July 13, 2017, https://www.theguardian.com/books/2017 /jul/13/chris-d-thomas-conservation-inheritors-of-the-earth-interview.

183 **"Fish biomass . . . appears to be about one-tenth the level of the fish":** Ausubel, "Return of Nature."

183 **Elinor Ostrom . . . developed principles for managing commons successfully:** "Elinor Ostrom's 8 Principles for Managing a Commons," *On the Commons*, accessed March 25, 2019, http://www.onthecommons.org /magazine/elinor-ostroms-8-principles-managing-commmons#sthash .XO1DrTaX.dpbs.

184 **but by 2015, this figure had almost quadrupled, to 15.4 percent:** Brand, "We Are Not Edging Up."

184 **At the end of 2017, 5.3 percent of the earth's oceans were similarly protected:** "Goal 14," Sustainable Development Knowledge Platform, United Nations, accessed March 25, 2019, https://sustainabledevelopment.un.org /sdg14.

184 **the demilitarized zone between North and South Korea:** Jennifer Billock,

"How Korea's Demilitarized Zone Became an Accidental Wildlife Paradise," *Smithsonian*, February 12, 2018, https://www.smithsonianmag.com /travel/wildlife-thrives-dmz-korea-risk-location-180967842/.

184 **exclusion zone around the still-radioactive Chernobyl nuclear plant:** John Wendle, "Animals Rule Chernobyl Three Decades After Nuclear Disaster," *National Geographic*, April 25, 2017, https://news.nationalgeographic.com/2016/04/060418-chernobyl-wildlife-thirty-year-anniversary -science/.

184 **overall reforestation has become the norm:** "Trees Are Covering More of the Land in Rich Countries," *Economist*, November 30, 2017, https:// www.economist.com/international/2017/11/30/trees-are-covering-more -of-the-land-in-rich-countries.

185 **experienced a "recent reversal in loss of global terrestrial biomass":** Yi Y. Liu, Albert I. J. M. van Dijk, Richard A. M. de Jeu, Josep G. Canadell, Matthew F. McCabe, Jason P. Evans, and Guojie Wang, "Recent Reversal in Loss of Global Terrestrial Biomass," *Nature Climate Change* 5 (2015): 470–74.

185 **Sustainability scientist Kim Nicholas has beautifully summarized key points:** Kim Nicholas, "Climate Science 101," *Kim Nicholas* (blog), accessed March 25, 2019, http://www.kimnicholas.com/climate-science-101.html.

186 **(CO2) has increased . . . to 408 ppmv in 2018:** "Atmospheric Carbon Dioxide (CO2) Levels, 1800–Present," SeaLevel.info, accessed March 25, 2019, https://www.sealevel.info/co2.html.

186 **Worldwide, over 20 percent of greenhouse gas emissions come from industry:** "Global Greenhouse Gas Emissions Data," US EPA, April 13, 2017, https://www.epa.gov/ghgemissions/global-greenhouse-gas-emissions -data.

188 **the amount of carbon added by America one hundred years ago, in 1918:** Hannah Ritchie and Max Roser, "CO_2 and Other Greenhouse Gas Emissions," *Our World in Data*, May 11, 2017, https://ourworldindata.org /co2-and-other-greenhouse-gas-emissions.

189 **and years of life lost have fallen even more quickly:** Hannah Ritchie and Max Roser, "Air Pollution," *Our World in Data*, April 17, 2017, https:// ourworldindata.org/air-pollution.

189 **"Poverty is the biggest polluter":** Akash Kapur, "Pollution as Another Form of Poverty," *New York Times*, October 8, 2009, https://www.nytimes .com/2009/10/09/world/asia/09iht-letter.html.

190 **"the Clean Water Act . . . contributed to this decline":** David A. Keiser and Joseph S. Shapiro, "Consequences of the Clean Water Act and the

Demand for Water Quality," *Quarterly Journal of Economics* 134, no. 1 (2018): 349–96.

190 **The results of this intervention were impressive:** Zhenling Cui et al., "Pursuing Sustainable Productivity with Millions of Smallholder Farmers," *Nature* 555, no. 7696 (2018): 363.

191 **his conclusion was notably exuberant:** Noah Smith, "The Incredible Miracle in Poor Country Development," *Noahpinion* (blog), May 30, 2016, http://noahpinionblog.blogspot.com/2016/05/the-incredible-miracle -in-poor-country.html.

191 **World Population . . . Living in Extreme Poverty, 1820–2015:** *Our World in Data*, https://ourworldindata.org/extreme-poverty. Data, calculation details, and sources are available at morefromlessbook.com/data.

192 **the World Bank thinks this might be possible by 2030:** Linda Yueh, "Is It Possible to End Global Poverty?," BBC News, March 27, 2015, https:// www.bbc.com/news/business-32082968.

192 **Share of the Population Living in Extreme Poverty, by World Region:** Ibid.

193 **Food Supply by Region . . . 1970–2013:** *Our World in Data*, https://our worldindata.org/food-per-person. Data, calculation details, and sources are available at morefromlessbook.com/data.

193 **to permit an active adult male to maintain his body weight:** "What Should My Daily Intake of Calories Be?," *NHS Choices*, accessed March 25, 2019, https://www.nhs.uk/common-health-questions/food-and-diet /what-should-my-daily-intake-of-calories-be/.

194 **Share of the Population with Access to Improved Drinking Water:** *Our World in Data*, https://ourworldindata.org/water-use-sanitation#share-of -total-population-with-improved-water-sources. Data, calculation details, and sources are available at morefromlessbook.com/data.

194 **More than 90 percent of the world's people now have access to improved water:** Hannah Ritchie and Max Roser, "Water Use and Sanitation," *Our World in Data*, November 20, 2017, https://ourworldindata.org /water-use-sanitation#share-of-total-population-with-improved-water -sources.

194 **The situation is similar for sanitation:** Ritchie and Roser, "Water Use and Sanitation."

195 **Gross Enrollment Ratio in Secondary Education:** *Our World in Data*, https://ourworldindata.org/primary-and-secondary-education. Data, calculation details, and sources are available at morefromlessbook.com /data.

196 Life Expectancy: *Our World in Data*, https://ourworldindata.org/life-expectancy. Data, calculation details, and sources are available at more fromlessbook.com/data.

197 **Maternal and Child Mortality**; *Our World in Data*, https://our worldindata.org/child-mortality and https://ourworldindata.org /maternal-mortality. Data, calculation details, and sources are available at morefromlessbook.com/data.

Chapter 12: Powers of Concentration

199 **estimated that 55 percent of the world's population lived in urban areas**: "68% of the World Population Projected to Live in Urban Areas by 2050, Says UN," UN Department of Economic and Social Affairs, accessed March 25, 2019, https://www.un.org/development/desa/en /news/population/2018-revision-of-world-urbanization-prospects.html.

199 **"Everything you heard about urbanization is wrong"**: "Everything You Heard About Urbanization Is Wrong," *Open Learning Campus* (blog), accessed March 25, 2019, https://olc.worldbank.org/content/everything -you-heard-about-urbanization-wrong.

202 **2.5 million in 1982**: Mary Clare Jalonick, "Farm Numbers Decline, But Revenue Rises," *Boston Globe*, February 21, 2014, https://www.bostonglobe .com/news/nation/2014/02/21/number-farms-declines-farmers-getting -older/LNON4aXK6Avf6CkfiH4YIK/story.html.

202 **fewer than 2,050,000 in 2017**: "U.S. Farming: Total Number of Farms 2017," *Statista*, accessed March 25, 2019, https://www.statista.com/statistics /196103/number-of-farms-in-the-us-since-2000/.

202 **America's manufacturing output increased by more than 43 percent**: "Manufacturing Sector: Real Output," FRED, March 7, 2019, https://fred .stlouisfed.org/series/OUTMS.

202 **physical locations where manufacturing happens—decreased by almost 15 percent**: "Table 5. Number of Private Sector Establishments by Age: Manufacturing," US Bureau of Labor Statistics, accessed March 25, 2019, https://www.bls.gov/bdm/us_age_naics_31_table5.txt.

203 **Friedman obliged, but also wrote "down with" before the game's title**: Damon Darlin, "Monopoly, Milton Friedman's Way," *New York Times*, February 19, 2011, https://www.nytimes.com/2011/02/20/weekinreview /20monopoly.html.

203 **an event that has been called "Woodstock for central bankers"**: Greg Robb, "Yellen to Stress Patience on Rates at Jackson Hole," *MarketWatch*,

August 18, 2014, https://www.marketwatch.com/story/yellen-to-stress
-patience-on-rates-at-jackson-hole-2014-08-17.

203 **One of the main papers . . . by the economist John Van Reenen**: John
Van Reenen, "Increasing Differences between Firms: Market Power and
the Macro-Economy" (paper prepared for the 2018 Jackson Hole Conference), https://www.kansascityfed.org/~/media/files/publicat/sympos/2018
/papersandhandouts/jh%20john%20van%20reenen%20version%2020
.pdf?la=en.

206 **six of the eight highest public-market valuations ever recorded**: Jeff
Sommer and Karl Russell, "Apple Is the Most Valuable Public Company
Ever. But How Much of a Record Is That?," *New York Times*, December
21, 2017, https://www.nytimes.com/interactive/2017/12/05/your-money
/apple-market-share.html.

206 **Jeff Bezos, for example, became known as the "richest man in modern
history"**: Robert Frank, "Jeff Bezos Is Now the Richest Man in Modern
History," CNBC, July 16, 2018, https://www.cnbc.com/2018/07/16/jeff
-bezos-is-now-the-richest-man-in-modern-history.html.

206 **in 2016, 50.7 percent of US households owned no stocks at all**: Christopher Ingraham, "For Roughly Half of Americans, the Stock Market's
Record Highs Don't Help at All," *Washington Post*, December 18, 2017,
https://www.washingtonpost.com/news/wonk/wp/2017/12/18/for-roughly
-half-of-americans-the-stock-markets-record-highs-dont-help-at-all
/?utm_term=.f2498dd7e428.

210 **"Inequality is not the same thing as unfairness"**: Angus Deaton, "How
Inequality Works," *Project Syndicate*, December 21, 2017, https://www.proj
ect-syndicate.org/onpoint/anatomy-of-inequality-2017-by-angus-deaton
-2017-12?barrier=accesspaylog.

210 **"There is no evidence that people are bothered by economic inequality
itself"**: Christina Starmans, Mark Sheskin, and Paul Bloom, "Why People
Prefer Unequal Societies," *Nature Human Behaviour* 1, no. 4 (2017): article
0082, https://www.nature.com/articles/s41562-017-0082?mod=article
_inline.

Chapter 13: Stressed Be the Tie That Binds: Disconnection

211 **"The lack of a fundamental friendliness"**: Dexter Filkins, "James Mattis,
a Warrior in Washington," *New Yorker*, June 20, 2017, https://www.new
yorker.com/magazine/2017/05/29/james-mattis-a-warrior-in-washington.

212 **"connections among individuals"**: Robert D. Putnam, *Bowling Alone:*

The Collapse and Revival of American Community (New York: Simon & Schuster, 2001), 19.

212 **more than 60 percent . . . believed that "most people can be trusted":** Eric D. Gould and Alexander Hijzen, *Growing Apart, Losing Trust? The Impact of Inequality on Social Capital* (Washington, DC: International Monetary Fund, 2016).

212 **public trust in the federal government fell:** "Public Trust in Government: 1958–2017," Pew Research Center for the People and the Press, April 25, 2018, http://www.people-press.org/2017/12/14/public-trust-in-govern ment-1958-2017/.

213 **"Americans of all ages, all conditions, all minds constantly unite":** Alexis de Tocqueville, *Democracy in America*, ed. and trans. Harvey C. Mansfield and Delba Winthrop (Chicago: University of Chicago Press, 2000), 489.

213 **Anne Case and Angus Deaton uncovered a startling and dire trend:** Anne Case and Angus Deaton, "Mortality and Morbidity in the 21st Century," Brookings Institution, August 30, 2017, https://www.brookings .edu/bpea-articles/mortality-and-morbidity-in-the-21st-century/.

214 **The US suicide rate rose by 14 percent between 2009 and 2016:** "Suicide Statistics," American Foundation of Suicide Prevention, March 12, 2019, https://afsp.org/about-suicide/suicide-statistics/.

214 **in 2016, 197,000 deaths were related to suicide, alcohol, and drug abuse:** Joshua Cohen, " 'Diseases of Despair' Contribute to Declining U.S. Life Expectancy," *Forbes*, July 19, 2018, https://www.forbes.com/sites/joshua cohen/2018/07/19/diseases-of-despair-contribute-to-declining-u-s-life -expectancy/#7ca8cc96656b.

214 **44,674 people who died from HIV/AIDS at the peak of its epidemic in 1994:** Max Roser and Hannah Ritchie, "HIV/AIDS," *Our World in Data*, April 3, 2018, https://ourworldindata.org/hiv-aids.

214 **was more than 22 percent bigger than it had been at the end of the Great Recession:** "Real Gross Domestic Product," FRED, February 28, 2019, https://fred.stlouisfed.org/series/GDPC1.

215 **after assistance from the government and employer-provided benefits:** Rakesh Kochhar, "The American Middle Class Is Stable in Size, but Losing Ground Financially to Upper-Income Families," Pew Research Center, September 6, 2018, https://www.pewresearch.org/fact-tank/2018/09/06 /the-american-middle-class-is-stable-in-size-but-losing-ground-finan cially-to-upper-income-families/.

215 **"Deep child poverty was as low in 2014 as it had been since at least 1979":** Scott Winship, "Poverty after Welfare Reform," Manhattan Institute,

August 22, 2016, https://www.manhattan-institute.org/download/9172
/article.pdf.

215 **The last time the US suicide rate was as high as in 2016**: "Suicide Statistics," American Foundation of Suicide Prevention.

215 **when the annual unemployment rate peaked at almost 25 percent**:
Kimberly Amadeo, "Compare Today's Unemployment with the Past,"
The Balance, accessed March 25, 2019, https://www.thebalance.com
/unemployment-rate-by-year-3305506.

216 **"a sense of isolation" was strongly associated with suicide risk**: "Suicide,"
World Health Organization, accessed March 25, 2019, https://www.who
.int/news-room/fact-sheets/detail/suicide.

216 **"The opposite of addiction isn't sobriety, it's connection"**: Johann Hari,
" 'The Opposite of Addiction Isn't Sobriety—It's Connection,' " *Guardian*,
April 12, 2016, https://www.theguardian.com/books/2016/apr/12/johann
-hari-chasing-the-scream-war-on-drugs.

216 **Americans were "bowling alone, dying together"**: Michael J. Zoorob
and Jason L. Salemi, "Bowling Alone, Dying Together: The Role of Social
Capital in Mitigating the Drug Overdose Epidemic in the United States,"
Drug and Alcohol Dependence 173 (2017): 1–9.

217 **"The classic conditions that typically activate and aggravate authoritarians"**: Tom Jacobs, "Authoritarianism: The Terrifying Trait That Trump
Triggers," *Pacific Standard*, March 26, 2018, https://psmag.com/news
/authoritarianism-the-terrifying-trait-that-trump-triggers.

218 **Applebaum wrote in 2018 about the resulting deep disconnection**:
Anne Applebaum, "A Warning from Europe: The Worst Is Yet to Come,"
Atlantic, September 24, 2018, https://www.theatlantic.com/magazine
/archive/2018/10/poland-polarization/568324/.

218 **20 percent . . . experienced the opposite of growth**: Data supplied by
Woods and Poole Economics.

219 **"The corporation has everything needed to give the individual a setting"**:
Émile Durkheim, *Suicide: A Study in Sociology*, trans. John A. Spaulding
and George Simpson (Abingdon, UK: Routledge, 2005), 346.

219 **"Unlike in Europe, where cities and towns existed long before industrialization"**: Andrew Sullivan, "Americans Invented Modern Life. Now
We're Using Opioids to Escape It," *New York*, Intelligencer, February 20,
2018, http://nymag.com/intelligencer/2018/02/americas-opioid-epidemic
.html?gtm=bottom.

220 **"What our data show"**: Case and Deaton, "Mortality and Morbidity."

221 **gives voice to their perceptions**: Arlie Russell Hochschild, *Strangers in*

Their Own Land: Anger and Mourning on the American Right (New York: New Press, 2016), Kindle, location 139.

221 **The famous Elephant Graph, drawn by economists Branko Milanovic and Christoph Lakner**: Christoph Lakner and Branko Milanovic, *Global Income Distribution: From the Fall of the Berlin Wall to the Great Recession* (Washington, DC: World Bank, 2013), http://documents.worldbank.org /curated/en/914431468162277879/pdf/WPS6719.pdf.

222 **Increase in Real Income, 1988–2008**: Ibid.

222 **"The people who gained the least were almost entirely from the 'mature economies'"**: Branko Milanovic, "Global Income Distribution since 1988," *CEPR Policy Portal*, accessed March 25, 2019, https://voxeu.org/article /global-income-distribution-1988.

223 **They're much closer to flat lines**: Paul Krugman, "Hyperglobalization and Global Inequality," *New York Times*, November 30, 2015, https://krugman .blogs.nytimes.com/2015/11/30/hyperglobalization-and-global-inequality/.

224 **"Census data stretching back to 1790"**: Philip Bump, "By 2040, Two-Thirds of Americans Will Be Represented by 30 Percent of the Senate," *Washington Post*, November 28, 2017, https://www.washingtonpost.com /news/politics/wp/2017/11/28/by-2040-two-thirds-of-americans-will -be-represented-by-30-percent-of-the-senate/?noredirect=on&utm_term =.555e16259646.

224 **this outcome also occurred three times in the nineteenth century**: Rachael Revesz, "Five Presidential Nominees Who Won the Popular Vote but Lost the Election," *Independent*, November 16, 2016, https://www.independent .co.uk/news/world/americas/popular-vote-electoral-college-five-presi dential-nominees-hillary-clinton-al-gore-a7420971.html.

225 **politics, at least in the United States, has become more polarized**: Jeffrey B. Lewis, Keith Poole, Howard Rosenthal, Adam Boche, Aaron Rudkin, and Luke Sonnet, "Congressional Roll-Call Votes Database," *Voteview*, 2018, https://voteview.com/.

225 **fewer than 10 percent of presidential vetoes have been overturned**: "Glossary Term | Override of a Veto," US Senate, January 19, 2018, https:// www.senate.gov/reference/glossary_term/override_of_a_veto.htm.

225 **a majority of Americans consistently support tighter gun control**: Eric Levitz, "Tribalism Isn't Our Democracy's Problem. The Conservative Movement Is," *New York*, Intelligencer, October 22, 2018, http://nymag .com/intelligencer/2018/10/polarization-tribalism-the-conservative-move ment-gop-threat-to-democracy.html.

225 **"Politics is the art of the possible"**: Interview (August 11, 1867) with

Friedrich Meyer von Waldeck of the *St. Petersburgische Zeitung: Aus den Erinnerungen eines russischen Publicisten*, 2. *Ein Stündchen beim Kanzler des norddeutschen Bundes.* In *Die Gartenlaube* (1876), p. 858, de.wikisource. Reprinted in *Fürst Bismarck: Neue Tischgespräche und Interviews*, 1:248.

227 **Globally, approximately 90 percent of children are vaccinated against pertussis:** "Global and Regional Immunization Profile," World Health Organization, September 2018, https://www.who.int/immunization /monitoring_surveillance/data/gs_gloprofile.pdf?ua=1.

227 **immunization rates similar to those of Chad and South Sudan:** Hillary Lewis, "Hollywood's Vaccine Wars," *Hollywood Reporter*, September 12, 2014, https://www.hollywoodreporter.com/features/los-angeles-vaccina tion-rates/.

227 **six total deaths from the disease:** Ibid.

227 **In 2017, there were thirteen:** "2017 Final Pertussis Surveillance Report," US Centers for Disease Control, https://www.cdc.gov/pertussis/downloads /pertuss-surv-report-2017.pdf.

227 **Europe had more than eighty thousand measles cases in 2018:** Jacqui Thornton, "Measles Cases in Europe Tripled from 2017 to 2018," *The BMJ*, February 7, 2019, https://www.bmj.com/content/364/bmj.l634.

227 **"As people seek out the social settings they prefer":** Bill Bishop, *The Big Sort* (Boston: Houghton Mifflin Harcourt, 2008), 14.

Chapter 14: Looking Ahead: The World Cleanses Itself This Way

232 **"the instructions that we follow for combining raw materials":** Paul M. Romer, "Endogenous Technological Change," *Journal of Political Economy* 98, no. 5, pt. 2 (1990): S71–S102.

236 **"the largest open source community in the world":** https://github.com /open-source.

236 **world's most popular way to learn a second language:** "The United States of Languages," *Making Duolingo* (blog), October 12, 2017, http://making .duolingo.com/the-united-states-of-languages-an-analysis-of-duolingo -usage-state-by-state.

236 **nearly 15 billion Wikipedia page views during July 2018:** "Wikimedia Traffic Analysis Report—Wikipedia Page Views per Country—Overview," Stats.wikimedia, accessed March 25, 2019, https://stats.wikimedia.org /wikimedia/squids/SquidReportPageViewsPerCountryOverview.htm.

236 **half were in languages other than English:** "Wikimedia Traffic Analysis Report—Page Views per Wikipedia Language—Breakdown," Stats.

wikimedia, accessed March 25, 2019, https://stats.wikimedia.org/wiki media/squids/SquidReportPageViewsPerLanguageBreakdown.htm.

236 **"We never had a technology before that could educate"**: Sara Castellanos, "Google Chief Economist Hal Varian Argues Automation Is Essential," *Wall Street Journal*, February 8, 2018, https://blogs.wsj.com/cio/2018/02/08 /google-chief-economist-hal-varian-argues-automation-is-essential/.

240 **"We [haven't] solved the protein-folding problem, this is just a first step"**: Ian Sample, "Google's DeepMind Predicts 3D Shapes of Proteins," *Guardian*, December 2, 2018, https://www.theguardian.com/science/2018 /dec/02/google-deepminds-ai-program-alphafold-predicts-3d-shapes-of -proteins.

240 **increase the energy efficiency of data centers by as much as 30 percent**: "Safety-First AI for Autonomous Data Centre Cooling and Industrial Control," *DeepMind*, accessed March 25, 2019, https://deepmind.com/blog /safety-first-ai-autonomous-data-centre-cooling-and-industrial-control/.

240 **accounting for about 1 percent of global electricity demand**: Nicola Jones, "How to Stop Data Centres from Gobbling Up the World's Electricity," News Feature, *Nature*, September 12, 2018, https://www.nature .com/articles/d41586-018-06610-y.

246 **America generates nearly 25 percent of total global output**: Robbie Gramer, "Infographic: Here's How the Global GDP Is Divvied Up," *Foreign Policy*, February 24, 2017, https://foreignpolicy.com/2017/02/24 /infographic-heres-how-the-global-gdp-is-divvied-up/.

Chapter 15: Interventions: How to Be Good

248 **"No climate changes of the speed and scope we are currently witnessing"**: William D. Nordhaus, *The Climate Casino* (New Haven, CT: Yale University Press, 2013), Kindle, location 65.

249 **"We also are likely to encounter surprises, and some of them will be nasty"**: Ibid., 66.

249 **revenue-neutral carbon tax that went into effect in 2008**: "British Columbia's Carbon Tax," British Columbia Ministry of Environment, October 3, 2018, https://www2.gov.bc.ca/gov/content/environment/climate-change /planning-and-action/carbon-tax.

250 **signed an open letter**: "Opinion | Economists' Statement on Carbon Dividends," *Wall Street Journal*, January 16, 2019, https://www.wsj.com /articles/economists-statement-on-carbon-dividends-11547682910?mod =hp_opin_pos2.

250 **two nations responsible for approximately 45 percent of total global emissions:** "Global Greenhouse Gas Emissions Data," US EPA, April 13, 2017, https://www.epa.gov/ghgemissions/global-greenhouse-gas-emissions -data.

250 **announcing a (perhaps indefinite) delay in imposing the tax:** Matthew Dalton and Noemie Bisserbe, "Macron Blinks in Fuel-Tax Dispute with Yellow Vests," *Wall Street Journal,* December 4, 2018, https://www.wsj .com/articles/france-to-delay-fuel-tax-increase-after-violent-protests -1543925246.

250 **electricity prices for consumers have doubled since 2000:** Stanley Reed, "Germany's Shift to Green Power Stalls, Despite Huge Investments," *New York Times,* October 7, 2017, https://www.nytimes.com/2017/10/07 /business/energy-environment/german-renewable-energy.html.

250 **(after decreasing substantially for more than a decade after 1990):** "Germany's Greenhouse Gas Emissions and Climate Targets," *Clean Energy Wire,* March 21, 2019, https://www.cleanenergywire.org/factsheets /germanys-greenhouse-gas-emissions-and-climate-targets.

250 **the country has also been steadily moving away from nuclear power:** Reed, "Germany's Shift to Green Power Stalls."

251 **Nuclear power is deeply unpopular among Germans:** "Nuclear Power in Germany," World Nuclear Association, accessed March 25, 2019, http:// www.world-nuclear.org/information-library/country-profiles/countries -g-n/germany.aspx.

251 **solid majorities of citizens in twenty-four countries:** Damian Carrington, "Citizens across World Oppose Nuclear Power, Poll Finds," *Guardian,* June 23, 2011, https://www.theguardian.com/environment/damian -carrington-blog/2011/jun/23/nuclearpower-nuclear-waste.

251 **A study published in the *Lancet* in 2007:** Anil Markandya and Paul Wilkinson, "Electricity Generation and Health," *Lancet* 370, no. 9591 (September 15–21, 2007): 979–90.

251 **"Nobody died from radiation at Three Mile Island or Fukushima":** Michael Shellenberger, "If Nuclear Power Is So Safe, Why Are We So Afraid of It?," *Forbes,* June 11, 2018, https://www.forbes.com/sites/michaelshellen berger/2018/06/11/if-nuclear-power-is-so-safe-why-are-we-so-afraid-of-it /#cc9469863859.

251 **The Japanese government attributed his death to the accident:** Motoko Rich, "In a First, Japan Says Fukushima Radiation Caused Worker's Cancer Death," *New York Times,* September 6, 2018, https://www.nytimes .com/2018/09/05/world/asia/japan-fukushima-radiation-cancer-death.html.

251 **A 2016 report from the Chernobyl Forum**: D. Kinly III, ed., "Chernobyl's Legacy: Health, Environmental and Socio-Economic Impacts and Recommendations to the Governments of Belarus, the Russian Federation and Ukraine," 2nd rev. version, Chernobyl Forum 2003–5 (2006).

252 **a citizen commission in Korea recommended restarting construction**: "Blow for New South Korean President after Vote to Resume Nuclear Power Build," *Financial Times*, accessed March 25, 2019, https://www.ft .com/content/66c5c9ad-71f0-3f2a-a66d-4078e93d46e5.

252 **Taiwanese voters overturned a plan to phase out nuclear power there by 2025**: David Fickling and Tim Culpan, "Taiwan Learns to Love Nuclear, a Little," *Bloomberg*, November 28, 2018, https://www.bloomberg.com /opinion/articles/2018-11-28/taiwan-voters-give-nuclear-power-a-life line-after-election.

252 **"the quiet dismantling of the regulatory framework"**: Ellen Knickmeyer, "Trump Administration Targets Obama's Clean-Up of Mercury Pollution," PBS, December 28, 2018, https://www.pbs.org/newshour/nation /trump-administration-targets-obamas-clean-up-of-mercury-pollution.

252 **responsibilities to monitor their equipment for methane leaks**: Jennifer Ludden, "Trump Administration Eases Regulation of Methane Leaks on Public Lands," NPR, September 19, 2018, https://www.npr .org/2018/09/18/649326026/trump-administration-eases-regulation -of-methane-leaks-on-public-lands.

252 **challenges to restrictions on mercury emissions from coal plants**: Knickmeyer, "Trump Administration Targets Obama's Clean-Up."

252 **a reinterpretation of the Clean Water Act**: "Trump Administration Asks to Roll Back Rules Against Water Pollution," *The Scientist*, December 12, 2018, https://www.the-scientist.com/news-opinion/trump-administration -rolls-back-protections-against-water-pollution-65206.

253 **"The 'three strict bans' will continue to be enforced"**: "China Postpones Lifting of Ban on Trade of Tiger and Rhino Parts," *Reuters*, November 12, 2018, https://www.reuters.com/article/us-china-wildlife/china-postpones -lifting-of-ban-on-trade-of-tiger-and-rhino-parts-idUSKCN1NH0XH.

254 **"Traditionally, economists have been skeptical"**: Benjamin Austin, Edward Glaeser, and Lawrence H. Summers, "Saving the Heartland: Place-Based Policies in 21st Century America," in *Brookings Papers on Economic Activity* Conference Drafts, 2018.

255 **Glaeser is forthcoming . . . shrinking social capital**: Eduardo Porter, "The Hard Truths of Trying to 'Save' the Rural Economy," *New York Times*,

December 14, 2018, https://www.nytimes.com/interactive/2018/12/14/opinion/rural-america-trump-decline.html.

255 **"Talent is equally distributed; opportunity is not"**: Thomas Koulopoulos, "Harvard, Stanford, and MIT Researchers Study 1 Million Inventors to Find Secret to Success, and It's Not Talent," *Inc.*, August 14, 2018, https://www.inc.com/thomas-koulopoulos/a-study-of-one-million-inventors-identified-key-to-success-its-not-talent.html.

256 **receive about 75 percent of all US venture-capital funding**: Richard Feloni, "AOL Cofounder Steve Case Is Betting $150 Million That the Future of Startups Isn't in Silicon Valley or New York, but the Money Isn't What's Making His Prediction Come True," *Business Insider*, June 19, 2018, https://www.businessinsider.com/steve-case-rise-of-the-rest-revolution-startup-culture-2018-5.

256 **"By investing in underserved entrepreneurs"**: Jamie Dimon and Steve Case, "Talent Is Distributed Equally. Opportunity Is Not," *Axios*, March 21, 2018, https://www.axios.com/talent-is-distributed-equally-opportunity-is-not-1521472713-905349d9-7383-470d-8bad-653a832b4d52.html.

256 **Salesforce is buying enough carbon credits**: Akshat Rathi, "If Your Carbon Footprint Makes You Feel Guilty, There's an Easy Way Out," *Quartz*, May 3, 2017, https://qz.com/974463/buying-carbon-credits-is-the-easiest-way-to-offset-your-carbon-footprint/.

257 **Salesforce has also announced its intentions**: "Salesforce Invests in Its Largest Renewable Energy Agreement to Date, the Global Climate Action Summit, and a More Sustainable Future," Salesforce, August 30, 2018, https://www.salesforce.com/company/news-press/press-releases/2018/08/180830/.

257 **Google reached 100 percent renewable energy for all global operations**: "100% Renewable," Google Sustainability, accessed March 25, 2019, https://sustainability.google/projects/announcement-100/.

257 **United Airlines has committed**: Peter Economy, "United Airlines' Stunning New Greenhouse Gas Strategy Will Completely Change the Future of Air Travel," *Inc.*, September 14, 2018, https://www.inc.com/peter-economy/united-airlines-ceo-just-made-a-stunning-announcement-that-will-completely-change-future-of-air-travel.html.

257 **as the company dryly notes**: "Maersk Sets Net Zero CO2 Emission Target by 2050," *Maersk*, December 4, 2018, https://www.maersk.com/en/news/2018/12/04/maersk-sets-net-zero-co2-emission-target-by-2050.

258 **smelters that make aluminum . . . charge a premium**: Peter Hobson,

"Hydro-Powered Smelters Charge Premium Prices for 'Green' Aluminum," Reuters, August 2, 2017, https://www.reuters.com/article/us-aluminium -sales-environment/hydro-powered-smelters-charge-premium-prices -for-green-aluminum-idUSKBN1AI1CF.

260   **land bought by John D. Rockefeller Jr. in the 1920s:** Lisa Lednicer, "Rocke- feller and the Secret Land Deals That Created Grand Teton National Park," *Washington Post*, December 4, 2017, https://www.washingtonpost.com /news/retropolis/wp/2017/12/04/rockefeller-and-the-secret-land-deals -that-created-grand-tetons-national-park/?utm_term=.9e8d26b4bb4f.

260   **Chile expanded its total parkland by 40 percent:** Pascale Bonnefoy, "With 10 Million Acres in Patagonia, a National Park System Is Born," *New York Times*, February 19, 2018, https://www.nytimes.com/2018/02/19 /world/americas/patagonia-national-park-chile.html.

260   **was vigorously protested by the World Wildlife Fund:** Gerry Shih, "China Rolls Back Decades-Old Tiger and Rhino Parts Ban, Worry- ing Conservationists," *Washington Post*, October 29, 2018, https://www .washingtonpost.com/world/china-rolls-back-decades-old-tiger-and -rhino-parts-ban-worrying-conservationists/2018/10/29/a1ba913c-dbe7 -11e8-aa33-53bad9a881e8_story.html?utm_term=.994da09a6ff0.

261   **conserved 14 million acres in North America:** Henry Grabar, "Why Ducks' Strongest Allies Are Duck Hunters," *Slate*, May 10, 2018, https:// slate.com/business/2018/05/ducks-unlimited-which-helps-restore-wet lands-consists-mostly-of-duck-hunters.html.

263   **Swiss biotech company Syngenta was instrumental:** Jorge Mayer, "Golden Rice Licensing Arrangements," *Golden Rice Project*, accessed March 25, 2019, http://www.goldenrice.org/Content1-Who/who4_IP.php.

268   **effects of Fair Trade certification on coffee growers in Costa Rica:** Raluca Dragusanu and Nathan Nunn, *The Effects of Fair Trade Certification: Evi- dence from Coffee Producers in Costa Rica*, National Bureau of Economic Research Working Paper no. 24260, 2018.

269   **only 3 percent of Americans identified as vegan:** Maura Judkis, "You Might Think There Are More Vegetarians than Ever. You'd Be Wrong," *Washington Post*, August 3, 2018, https://www.washingtonpost.com/news /food/wp/2018/08/03/you-might-think-there-are-more-vegetarians-than -ever-youd-be-wrong/?utm_term=.d34e8f549da0.

270   **"A diet including chicken and pork, but no dairy or beef":** Linus Blomqvist, "Eat Meat. Not Too Much. Mostly Monogastrics," Break- through Institute, accessed March 25, 2019, https://thebreakthrough.org /issues/food/eat-meat-not-too-much.

Conclusion: Our Next Planet

273 **Some fossils indicate that we** *Homo sapiens* **may have left Africa as much as 180,000 years ago:** Chris Stringer and Julia Galway-Witham, "When Did Modern Humans Leave Africa?," *Science* 359, no. 6374 (2018): 389–90.

273 **By 1768, they'd killed all the sea cows:** Paul K. Anderson, "Competition, Predation, and the Evolution and Extinction of Steller's Sea Cow, *Hydrodamalis gigas*," *Marine Mammal Science* 11, no. 3 (July 1995): 391–94.

273–74 **as we spread around the planet, we wiped out the biggest animals first:** "Unprecedented Wave of Large-Mammal Extinctions Linked to Prehistoric Humans," *ScienceDaily*, April 19, 2018, https://www.sciencedaily.com/releases/2018/04/180419141536.htm.

274 **much of the land they'd inhabited turned into forest:** Ross Andersen, "Welcome to the Future Range of the Woolly Mammoth," *Atlantic*, July 10, 2017, https://www.theatlantic.com/magazine/archive/2017/04/pleistocene-park/517779/.

275 **"God blessed them, and God said unto them":** King James Bible, Genesis 1:28.

275 **"we must make Nature worthless":** Jesse Ausubel, "We Must Make Nature Worthless," *Real Clear Science*, September 19, 2015, https://www.realclearscience.com/articles/2015/09/19/we_must_make_nature_worthless_109384.html.

Index

Page numbers in *italics* refer to graphs.